ALL THINGS CENSORED

ALL THINGS CENSORED

Mumia Abu-Jamal

EDITED BY NOELLE HANRAHAN

FOREWORD BY ALICE WALKER

SEVEN STORIES PRESS

New York / Toronto / London / Sydney

A SEVEN STORIES PRESS FIRST EDITION

Seven Stories Press, 140 Watts Street, New York, NY 10013
http://www.sevenstories.com

In Canada: Hushion House, 36 Northline Road, Toronto, Ontario M4B 3E2

In the U.K.: Turnaround Publisher Services Ltd., Unit 3,
Olympia Trading Estate, Coburg Road, Wood Green, London N22 6TZ

In Australia: Tower Books, 9/19 Rodborough Road, Frenchs Forest NSW 2086

LIBRARY OF CONGRESS CATALOGING-IN-PUBLICATION DATA
Abu-Jamal, Mumia
All things censored / Mumia Abu-Jamal edited by Noelle Hanrahan
     p. cm.
    1. Abu-Jamal, Mumia. 2. Death row inmates—United States—Biography.
3. Afro-American prisoners—United States—Biography. 4. Prisoners' writings, American.
5. Criminal justice, Administration of—United States. 6. Prison—United States.
I. Hanrahan, Noelle. II. Title.

HV8699.U5 A32 2000
364.66'092—dc21
[B]   00-020285

9 8 7 6 5 4 3 2 1

College professors may order examination copies of Seven Stories Press titles for a free six-month trial period. To order, visit www.sevenstories.com/textbook, or fax on school letterhead to (212) 226-1411.

Book design by Cindy LaBreacht
Printed in the U.S.A.

IF IT WERE POSSIBLE to name all of these who have influenced, supported, or contributed to this work, the listing would itself consume perhaps half of this book. It will therefore suffice to thank those known and unknown, activists, scholars, rebels, and revolutionaries, an almost uncountable number, for their strong contribution to this book. I thank them for their part in the continuing struggle for justice and freedom, and dedicate this work to them.

The brilliant Haitian historian Michel Trouillot noted that "history is a story about power," and about "those who won."* These essays deal with the folk resisting the lure of power, and those struggling to survive against monstrous odds. In that sense, this is their book, for their struggles, their lives, are at the core of it.

By reading (or hearing) these very words, you are participating in a conspiracy of resistance. I welcome you. For the spirit of resistance is, in essence, the spirit of love.

maj

---

* Trouillot, M.-R., "Silencing the Past" (Beacon, 1995), p. 5

TABLE OF CONTENTS

SCENES

PERSPECTIVES

ESSAYS ON JUSTICE

ACKNOWLEDGMENTS

THERE IS AN OLD SAYING: "Success has many fathers; failure, only one."
Like this adage of success, this text has many parents—fathers and mothers
who brought this project to fruition: Dan Simon, the publisher; Noelle
Hanrahan, who exhibits a Taurean stubbornness that would make a bull
blush; my remarkable agent, Frances Goldin, whose love of words and language is legendary....

The nameless ones who listen are here acknowledged, for these words
were crafted with your inner ear in mind. Yet who could forget those who
dared to live remarkable lives in the midst of times of madness, thus giving
me, the writer and commentator, something worthwhile to write about?

To the remarkable Susan Barnett, a rare and courageous spirit (brought
to us by the indomitable Pam!); Ramona, who looked into the fiery face
of urban mass murder and remained "ona move"; the youthful Seeds of
Wisdom, the sons and daughters of John Africa's vision; the MOVE 9; the
revolutionary poets of the Zapatistas; the people who built movements
out of love and grit... and will. To all who resist, I thank you.

maj

NO PRISON CAN HOLD this story, and there will be no rest until Mumia is
free. It has been an honor to work with Mumia to bring his voice from the
depths of Pennsylvania's death row to the airwaves. Thank you to Dan
Simon, Tania Ketenjian, Greg Ruggiero, and Jon Gilbert at Seven Stories,
who took up the challenge of printing these banned, dangerous, and liber-
ating words. My deepest gratitude to Tanya Brannan, whose political
insights and personal comradeship literally made it possible to complete
All Things Censored; I am indebted to Jennifer Beach for her brilliant
photographs, her unwavering support, and her strategic analysis; David

Kaplowitz was an invaluable partner in the design of the book and audio engineering. Crucial support and enthusiasm came from Ted Nace, Susan Shaw and Tom Crane, Karen Rudolph and Jimmie Simmons, Assata Shakur, Inez Hedges and Victor Wallis, Hobart Spalding, Walter Turner, Colin Starger, Leslie Dibenedetto, Alice Walker, Catherine McCann, Ed Herman, Julian Holmes, Ted Gullicksen (Tenants' Union), Alli Starr (Art & Revolution), Virginia Lerner, Fireworx/Prairie Fire, Joan and Mike Hanrahan, and Terry Kupers. Thank you to Jello Biafra and Alternative Tentacles Records, who were the first to press Mumia's radio essays to compact disc. Earth First leader Judi Bari (1949–1997) was a true revolutionary who continues to inspire me every day through her legacy, which is rich with the fusing of brilliant uncompomising strategy, nonviolent direct action at the point of production, humor, and music. Alan Korn has provided crucial and stalwart support as Prison Radio's attorney. Miguel Wooding and my daughter, Miranda Judi Hanrahan-Beach, have created a hearth of resistance. Frances Goldin, Mumia's literary agent, was instrumental in making this book a reality. Chris Zimmerman, Steve Wiser, Clare Stober, and Gill Barth, from the Bruderhof Community, have been a critical lifeline to the inside of SCI Greene. Shaka Nantambu, thank you for being there for Miranda and keeping it real. Props go out to courageous journalists Amy Goodman, host of Pacifica Radio's *Democracy Now!* and Dennis Bernstein, host of *Flashpoints*/KPFA, who continue to break the ban on airing Mumia's voice. Mike Alcalay and Janice Leber conducted key field recording under harrowing conditions. Nolen Edmonston provided brilliant photography. Dolly Pomerleau and Jane Henderson of the Quixote Center and Equal Justice USA taught me how to organize on a national scale and provided me with an organizational home from which together we could dream the impossible. And a generous thank-you to the Redwood Summer Justice Project crew—Tanya Brannan, Alicia Littletree, Erica Etelson, Marvin Stender, Tony Serra, Dennis Cunningham, and Darryl Cherney—for suing the FBI for current COINTELPRO operations and daring to win!

Noelle Hanrahan
San Francisco, California
January 2000

©MAC McGILL

WE ARE IN THIS PLACE FOR A REASON

by Alice Walker

This is why we became soldiers. This is why we remain soldiers. Because we want no more death and trickery for our people, because we want no more forgetting. The mountain told us to take up arms so we would have a voice. It told us to cover our faces so we would have a face. It told us to forget our names so we could be named. It told us to protect our past so we would have a future.

This is who we are. The Zapatista Liberation Army. The voice that arms itself to be heard, the face that hides itself to be seen, the name that hides itself to be named, the red star that calls out to humanity around the world to be heard, to be seen, to be named. The tomorrow that is harvested in the past.

—GENERAL COMMAND OF THE EZLN, Aguascalientes, Oventik, Chiapas (July 27, 1996)

I WILL NOT WRITE ANY LONGER about Mumia Abu-Jamal's innocence. Millions of people around the world believe he is innocent. I will not write any longer about how he was framed: the evidence speaks for itself. I will not write any longer about the necessity of a new trial: that is obvious. The State intends to take Mumia's life for its own purpose; for all our love and work, it may succeed.

In every generation there is a case like Mumia's: a young black man is noted to be brilliant, radical, loving of his people, at war with injustice:

often while he is still in his teens, as in the case of Mumia, the "authorities" decide to keep an eye on him. Indeed, they attempt to arrest his life by framing him for crimes he did not commit, and incarcerating him in prison. There, they think of him as something conquered, a magnificent wild animal they have succeeded in capturing. They feel powerful in a way they could not feel if he were free. Imprisoning such a spirit prevents their knowing how much of the natural, instinctive, loving self they have lost, or have had stolen from them. Whether by abusive parents, horrendous schools, or grim economics. They do not know they have encaged their own masculine beauty, their own passionate soul.

This is immediately apparent when one enters the prison where Mumia is kept. The apprehensive, bored guards. And Mumia, in his orange prison uniform, alert to every spark of life on a visitor's face; seemingly interested in everything. His essays, many of them in this book, demonstrate his engaged attention to what is going on in the world; his identification with those who act against injustice and who suffer. His great love of truth and what is right. It is his integrity, in analyzing dozens of events, that makes it possible to sense he is not a murderer. Certainly not a liar. They will have to kill Mumia to silence him; he has lost his fear of death, having been threatened with it so many times; he is a free man, at last.

A man who is free, whose life has been signed away several times already, is a man I can listen to. What does such a man, unrepentant of his beliefs, have to say? And what places in the listener's soul are fed by his words? As we push off into the next thousand years, which I personally feel are going to be great, what is the fundamental voice we need to hear to start us on the journey? It is the voice of those, like the Zapatistas, like Mumia, whose love outweighs their fear.

So I will ask you to read at least one of Mumia's books, as a way to begin to feel your way into this new millennium. He has written and published books while on death row, an amazing feat, and of course he has been punished for doing so. I will encourage you to listen to his voice. Losing that voice would be like losing a color from the rainbow. I will tell you we have a reason for being here, in America, and that Mumia reminds us what it is. It is to continue to delight in who we are, because who we are is beautiful. Who we are is powerful. Who we are is strong. Mumia is us, this amazing new tribe of people that being in America has produced. With plenty consciousness, plenty beauty, plenty intelligence, and plenty hair.

We are like the Zapatistas of Southern Mexico in many ways: vastly outnumbered, many of us poor, humiliated on a daily basis by those in power, feeling ourselves unwanted, unseen, and un-named. Mumia helps us know how deeply and devoutly we are wanted; how sharply and lovingly we are seen; how honorable is our much maligned name. And like the Zapatistas, who are an indigenous people still trustful of Nature, we too can rejoice in knowing it is not too late to take direction from the Earth.

Therefore: The Ocean has told me to tell you this: As Lovers of the Life of Mumia Abu-Jamal, we must be prepared for three things: to see Mumia murdered by the state; to see him left to languish on death row indefinitely; to see him freed. What is our responsibility in the face of these things, all of them designed deliberately to cause great emotion in our hearts? Emotion that, in the past, has predictably sent us mad into the streets; our anger and frustration making us careless in our pain; set up, once more, to become victims of our grief.

If Mumia is left to languish in prison indefinitely, we must continue to try to get him out. But if he is murdered by the state or if he is set free by the state, there is something else we must do.

Ocean Says: Bring his spirit and yours to me.

Therefore: On the afternoon of his release, whether into our waiting embraces, we his global family, or whether into the infinitely vast arms of the loving Universe, let us prepare to welcome him into the place of honor his own life has created. Let us observe silence. This will be the hardest thing to do; but we can do it; and it will strengthen us. We can prepare to be silent, by making arrangements beforehand. Let us dress, if we can afford it, in white. White, because it is the color of potentiality, of emptiness, and also because, in America, it has so often been the color of our despair. Let us carry candles in all the colors of the rainbow, representing our multicolored family who have found such joy and inspiration in Mumia's life. Let us carry four stones, symbolic of Mumia's and all the ancestors' bones, and of the four directions. Let us carry sage, incense, flowers, and oranges. Let us carry, as well, a small paper photograph of Mumia and one of Judge Albert Sabo, who showed Mumia no mercy as he sentenced him to death, and another of Governor Thomas Ridge, who signed Mumia's death warrant almost the moment he took office. The fourth photograph should be of Mumia's lawyer, Leonard Weinglass, whose dedication to saving Mumia's life has been brave and unfaltering. These four men are linked for all eternity, and we should honor that. Let us, with our friends and family, and especially all the little children—each child entrusted with a flower and a single orange—make our way to the ocean. Any ocean. And if there is no ocean where you live, go to rivers, creeks, rivulets, and streams. These will eventually reach the ocean, just as you yourself will, someday.

Compose your altar there on the beach; Sabo's photograph to the left, reminding us never to forsake our hearts, and Governor Ridge's to the right, reminding us that force is not our way. Place Mumia's and Leonard's photographs in the center, to reassure us of the possibility of trust, friendship, and freedom. Use the rocks, the bones of the ancestors, to hold the photographs in place. Light your candles, place them on either side of the photographs. Light sage or incense and smudge each other. And now, in whatever way the Spirit moves, facing Ocean, speak. Mother Ocean is so immense that She touches every shore; She can accept your tears, they are of her substance, and She can hold them.

After speaking, return to silence. Burn the photographs. Sabo's first, in gratitude for having been spared his life and his fate; Governor Ridge's next, in joy that your descendants will never need to remember you as someone who wished to kill, or who actually did kill, the Beloved. Then burn Mumia's and Leonard's photographs together, reminding us that those who work for justice are seldom without allies. Bless these ashes, all of which are made holy by your love and your restraint, and send them out to sea. Ask the children to let their flowers accompany them. When your ceremony is finished, hopefully at sunset, sit on the sand, facing the ocean, and share the oranges, symbolic of the sun that those in prison rarely see; a sun so generous in its nature that men have had to build prisons to hide other men away from it. Go home, gather around a good, light meal, no part of which was tortured or enslaved. Answer every child's question thoroughly and with patience. Speak of Angelo Herndon, Hurricane Carter, Nelson Mandela, and Malcolm X. Read Mumia's censored radio commentaries aloud. Meditate together on whatever action you need to take. In remembrance of our people, in their thousands, who are imprisoned: If there is anyone in your family who is in need, abandon judgment and commit yourself to helping them.

The meaning of our life is Life itself. As mysterious and as precious as That to which we belong.

Remember to look directly into each other's eyes throughout this long day. Embrace at every opportunity. Touch often.

Alice Walker
Northern California
January 2000

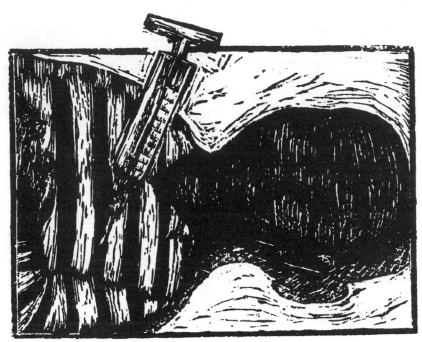

INTRODUCTION

LETHAL CENSORSHIP

The state would rather give me an Uzi than a microphone.

—MUMIA ABU-JAMAL

FOR OVER EIGHTEEN YEARS Mumia has not only been fighting to stay alive; he has been waging a constant battle for the freedom to write and speak.

Despite fierce censorship, extensive time in the "hole," and a brutal daily existence, Mumia remains a prolific journalist. His dignity and perseverance, as reflected in these recordings and in these pages, should not lull us into forgetting the conditions of his captivity in solitary confinement on death row. Life at the state-of-the-art supermaximum security control unit, State Correctional Institute at Greene, is unmitigated and unceasing torture.

Imagine your hands callused, cramped, and swollen from writing each day for hours with the cartridge of a ballpoint pen—legal briefs, letters, essays, your masters thesis—and writing everything twice because the prison might "lose" the copies you send out. Imagine having no shoes. Your feet are discolored and swollen because exercise is allowed for only one hour, five days a week in a cage. The ground of the eight-by-twelve-foot "exercise yard" is concrete and only flimsy slippers made in China, and presumably by prisoners, cover your feet.

Imagine your possessions: your books, your notes, your intellectual life, having to fit into a five-inch-deep, fourteen-inch wide box, because that is all you are allowed. Imagine before and after your weekly two-hour, completely noncontact visit having to submit to a demeaning psychosexual full-body cavity search: "Strip. Open your mouth. Stick out your tongue. Lift your balls.

Pull back your foreskin. Turn around. Spread your cheeks." During the visit your hands and feet are shackled in front and at times linked to a chain wrapped around your waist. All this because you dare to have a visitor, someone who will remain at all times separated from you by thick shatterproof glass.

Imagine solitary confinement under the constant glare of twenty-four-hour video camera surveillance.

Mumia's control unit cell has a thin mattress and a plate of steel for a bed, a shiny metal table and chair, and a combined sink and toilet. This tiny hermetically sealed room would be illegal to house a dog in. Twenty-four hours a day with no sound but your own breath, rarely glimpsing the sun or the moon in eighteen years, not being allowed to hold or touch a lover, a daughter, a father or friend. On death row at the State Correctional Institute at Greene in Waynesburg, Pennsylvania, since January 13, 1995. Before that, from 1983 to 1995, on death row at the State Correctional Institute at Huntingdon, Pennsylvania. And for six of those years, from 1985 to 1991, denied phone calls and access to TV or radio because he resisted the Pennsylvania Department of Corrections order that he cut his dreadlocks.

Mumia is entombed; not dead, but with a date to die.

Yet Mumia transcends prison. He has the rare ability to give voice to the dispossessed among us. The topics of his evocative radio essays reach far beyond his prison walls to illustrate the perspectives and the intrinsic human worth of those who exist outside the privileged upper-class world reflected in the media.

I have always wondered why the straightforward truths written and read by Mumia Abu-Jamal pose such a threat. The answer, I believe, lies in the fact that not has he only dared to survive but he has continued his uncompromising reporting. Mumia's commentaries from the depths of one of the country's most repressive prisons are dangerous; they threaten the smooth and orderly functioning of both state-sanctioned murder and modern slavery.

Once his voice hits the airwaves, Mumia's humanity cannot be ignored. The magnitude of repression hits home in our public consciousness. The anonymity of the prisoner is replaced by the reality of prisons. Mumia's voice is the sort of voice that arises at rare moments in history. Mumia's essays answer Frederick Douglass's prophetic call over a century ago in the speech "What to the American Slave Is the Fourth of July?"

The feeling of the nation must be quickened; the conscience of the nation must be roused; the propriety of the nation must be startled; the hypocrisy of the nation must be exposed. And its crimes against God and man must be proclaimed and denounced. There is not a nation on this earth guilty of practices, more shocking and bloody, than are the people of these United States, at this very hour.

The sound of Mumia's deep voice itself contains exemplary clarity, and as a writer he can convey the authentic truth of the oppressed in terms that resonate with people of every class and across every cultural divide. Indeed, this ability is precisely what makes him unique. Notes Assata Shakur,* "The first time I heard a tape of Mumia's radio broadcasts, it was the first time I fully understood why the United States government was so intent on putting him to death.... What he said was so clear, so true that I had to stop everything and concentrate on his message." Mumia's cadence, his tone, his modulation, and his writing style place him at the top of his profession. Delivered in a voice that is ideal for radio and backed by his obsessive attention to factual accuracy, his radio commentaries are unassailable by any genuine journalistic standard. It is only Mumia's allegiance to the oppressed and his refusal to censor his own reporting that has earned him the antipathy of many.

When I sat down across from Mumia at Huntingdon State Prison on July 15, 1992, he had not recorded for radio broadcast in over ten and a half years.† As I began taping his essays, I immediately realized two things. First, the potential for these essays was unlimited: Mumia has the sheer talent to be a commentator on *any* national network. Of the hundreds of individuals I had interviewed for radio, Mumia was by far the most seasoned, professional,

*Former U.S. political prisoner and Black Liberation Army member Assata Shakur was liberated from Clinton State Women's Prison in New Jersey on November 2, 1979. She was given political asylum by Cuba, where she now resides.
†Prison Radio has recorded Mumia reading seventy-two of his radio commentaries in five sessions at the State Correctional Institution at Huntingdon and the State Correctional Institution at Greene from 1992 to the present. Nineteen of these essays are featured on the enclosed compact disc. The first two sessions at Huntingdon State Prison, July 15 and October 15, 1992, were recorded on a Marantz cassette deck. Session three on August 16, 1993, at Huntingdon was digitally recorded on a Sony Pro DC-8 digital tape recorder, as was the last session allowed, October 31, 1996, at SCI Greene. The NPR session at Huntingdon on April 15, 1994, was recorded on a Nagra 1/4-inch portable, reel-to-reel tape player.

and frankly, talented person I had recorded. Second, for his voice to reach a national audience, these prison recordings had to be "air quality" and recorded as if the visiting room was a radio station sound studio. As Norman Jayo, who has dedicated his life to producing and teaching radio, once cautioned me, "Never give anyone an easy excuse to take your productions off the air. When they are going to censor you, make them come clean and make them censor the content."

The challenges of recording Mumia on death row in maximum-security prisons in noncontact visiting rooms are substantial. At both SCI Huntingdon (a hundred-year-old prison) and SCI Greene (a state-of-the-art "control unit"), the visiting rooms are small, barren, and concrete. Mumia sat on one side of a Plexiglas wall and I on the other, with only a table and a few thin inches of wire mesh through which to talk. In order to record his voice, I had to rig up a wireless headset and a directional super-cardio microphone. A guard had to "walk it around" and hand him the microphone. It was painful to watch Mumia, with handcuffs joined by just one link, put the microphone on and position it correctly. He did so to minimize the sound reverberations from the concrete and from the close proximity of the shatterproof glass. This setup required two sets of wireless gear in case of interference from prison communications equipment.

While Mumia is often able to read an essay in one take, the recording had to be stopped and the microphone adjusted if the microphone rubbed against his beard or dreadlocks or if there was excessive popping, overmodulation, or sibilance. The close proximity of the microphone to his mouth exacerbated Mumia's slight tendency toward sibilance. Though severely hampered by his handcuffs, Mumia repositioned the microphone repeatedly.

Huntingdon State Prison, in central Pennsylvania near State College, had a bustling general-population visiting room with an outdoor area and picnic tables. Off at the far end of the room were four noncontact visiting booths for Administrative Custody (AC) or "Death Cases." In the visiting booth a narrow table divided the cramped room, with barely enough space for a chair, and certainly not enough room for two people to comfortably stand or sit. Often the photographers that accompanied each recording session and I would fight about who would get to sit and who would go first. Time was precious, and each job had its own difficulties. For the photographers, the reflections of the fluorescent light off the glass barrier obscured almost every shot. From each photo session, out of hundreds of frames, only a handful have survived undistorted by glare.

We began each recording session with a quick hello, a much-practiced setup, then immediately began working. Since Mumia was not allowed to bring any paper to the interview, we corresponded by mail and typed up the essays, brought them in, and taped them to the glass, editing, and consulting as best we could. We filled the limited time with as many essays as possible. We had to record multiple takes when prison noises intruded: the squeaking of chairs, slamming of heavy doors, the clanking of keys, constant echoes, clicking of handcuffs, barked orders over loudspeakers, and the flushing toilets.

We understood that at any moment the recording could be "terminated." At each session the tape continued to roll until increasingly annoyed guards physically ushered us out. We knew that whatever we were able to put down on tape could be the last of our prison sessions, one more of the rare recordings done during these difficult years. In all, perhaps a dozen recordings and videotaped interviews of Mumia have been made during his eighteen-year incarceration.

While the most complex part of recording these essays was the technical obstacles on location at the prison, postproduction and editing presented formidable challenges as well. Once we had digital tapes in hand, I used every available technological device from digital no-noise systems to extensive analog equalization to eliminate extraneous noise. Each essay required hours of processing and over a hundred edits.

In May 1994 Mumia became a regular commentator on National Public Radio's premier newsmagazine. As I played a sample of Mumia's commentary on "Manny's Attempted Murder" for Ellen Weiss, the executive producer of *All Things Considered* at the NPR offices in Washington, D.C., she was visibly moved and stated unequivocally: "The American public needs to hear these essays. People have no idea how mass incarceration is affecting this country. This is a unique perspective that needs to be heard."

Accompanied by an NPR editor and engineer, I produced the *All Things Considered* tapes on April 15, 1994, at Huntingdon State Prison. A week later I got a call; they were going to do a national promotional campaign announcing Mumia as their new regular commentator. But the fact that NPR was about to air Mumia's essays and reach 10 million NPR listeners at over 410 stations in the United States, Canada, Mexico, South Africa, and Europe did not go unnoticed by the powerful elite.

On the eve of Mumia's first broadcast, National Public Radio fired Mumia. NPR had promoted his debut for a month, and even run clips of the essays on the air promoting the series. Then-senator Bob Dole, and the National Fraternal Order of Police's intense lobbying campaign, were directly responsible for this censorship. On May 16, the day after Mumia was pulled off the air, Dole commented from the Senate floor, "I am all for diversity on the airwaves, but those commentaries would have sent the wrong message. It is disturbing that NPR had apparently forgotten until the last minute the need to provide the balance and objectivity required in its programming. This episode raises sobering questions, not only for NPR but for the taxpayer-funded Corporation for Public Broadcasting, which has oversight authority over NPR and provides much of its funding." Senator Dole was directly threatening NPR with the loss of its funding for *even thinking* about airing Mumia's essays.

When I visited Ellen Weiss at her office again in mid-June 1994, just a month after they pulled Mumia off the air, she noted, "We did not see any red flags. I don't look to Capital Hill when I program, and I am just shocked that this was censored." Weiss then told me, "This was just an unfortunate project"; I myself was not being censored. The clear message was that if I abandoned Mumia, I could produce other programs for NPR. At that instant I knew that Mumia's career as a NPR journalist was over. And so was mine.

The ten unique and irreplaceable commentaries written and read by Mumia and recorded on April 15, 1994, by Prison Radio* remain to this day under lock and key in NPR's vaults. Despite a constitutional lawsuit and a national campaign for their release, NPR has refused to air or release these unique essays. This book and the accompanying compact disc were born in response to this censorship. We have included the text of the essays that NPR refuses to air for you to read here.

---

*Prison Radio (a project of the Redwood Justice Fund) challenges mass incarceration and racism by airing the voices of men and women in prison. Its educational materials serve as a catalyst for public activism.

Following the suppression of the "All Things Considered" tapes in August 1994, working with noted science fiction writer, Terry Bison, a close friend of Mumia, I brought a compilation of essays to Frances Goldin, Mumia's literary agent in New York who secured a contract for Mumia's first book *Live from Death Row* (Addison-Wesley, 1995).

Seemingly every time Mumia becomes publicly recognized through his recordings, books, or movies, prison officials—often at the behest of politicians—have responded by banning all interviews and subjecting Mumia to disciplinary proceedings for "conducting the business or profession of journalism." When Mumia successfully argued in court that he could not be singled out while the Pennsylvania Department of Correction allowed other prisoner interviews, they responded with the "Mumia rule," banning all interviews for all inmates in every Pennsylvania institution. In addition to repression inside the prisons, immediate and severe political and economic pressure is applied to any media outlet that dares to broadcast Mumia's voice or present a positive profile on his case.

On June 2, 1995, just minutes after Mumia was read his death warrant and transferred to a strip cell in Phase II, he called me on the phone. I pulled out my digital tape recorder, and started recording the conversation. As soon as our time was up, I called for a messenger to get that tape across town to Pacifica National News so it could air on that evening's broadcast. That twenty-minute conversation is included here.

The signing of Mumia's death warrant was timed to cripple his participation in his appeal. When his constitutionally protected legal mail was opened, authorities knew he was filing his brief in court the next business day. The governor's protocol requires that is an appeal is filed, no warrant is issued. Once on Phase II Mumia was transferred to a strip cell and lost all of his property. He was barred from having any visitors other than immediate family members, his spiritual adviser, and his lawyer. It is obscene but true that under an imminent sentence of death, Phase II prisoners are denied access to the law library. One day after his death warrant was signed, Mumia was further punished and slapped with a disciplinary action for "writing and conducting the business or profession of journalism." The timing was coldly calculated. The investigation had been going on for over a year, and Mumia freely admitted to the charge of writing. This action meant no phone calls, no commissary, and no radio or TV access. This was crafted as an attempt to guarantee that Mumia died in silence.

The harrassment and the censorship has been constant for not only Mumia but also for the journalists who have tried to tell his story. Denied access as a journalist, I began visiting Mumia as a social visitor.

In April 1996 I was banned for a year from Mumia's social visiting list for taking an "unauthorized" photo of the snow-covered razor wire and a barely discernible outline of SCI Greene. The photo was taken well beyond the gates and restricted areas. But the photo was not the issue; the fact that it later appeared next to an article entitled "Human Rights Violations at SCI Greene" was.

In the fall of 1996, after years of litigation by noted Pittsburgh attorneys Jere Krakoff and Tim O'Brien on Mumia's behalf, a small window of opportunity opened up for additional recordings. On October 31, 1996, I secured an assignment from Index on Censorship (published in England) to send a Prison Radio recording engineer and photographer to interview Mumia. The fourteen essays from this session are the only essays recorded at the State Correctional Institution at Greene. Many of these essays are included in this book and on the enclosed compact disc.

It is miraculous that this session occurred at all. Just a few weeks earlier the Pennsylvania Department of Corrections had issued a complete ban on recording, videotaping, or photographing of any inmate in Pennsylvania in Policy #DC-ADM-009-1. The policy was issued on October 11, 1996, but it went into effect one month later on November 11, just eleven days after our recording team had returned from SCI Greene with digital audiotapes in hand.

SCI Greene is so desolate and isolated that only once have I ever seen another visitor in the death row visiting area. It is located an hour north of Morgantown, West Virginia. Greene County was once a busy stop on the Underground Railroad, and today bears witness to pilgrimages to visit Mumia Abu-Jamal.

I often visited SCI Huntingdon and SCI Greene as a legal courier and a social visitor to continue the struggle to get Mumia's voice heard during the times recording sessions were not allowed. Once you arrive at the prison, there is no guarantee that you will get in for your short two-hour visit.

Rules change with each passing minute. I have had to go to town and buy different clothes, because mine were the wrong color. I've watched friends be denied entry because their state-issued ID was rejected, even though they had used the same ID to visit for years. It was painful to see a mother and her three-month-old son denied entry because they needed a postmarked form acknowledging that the mother of the child knew the prisoner's alleged crime (a surreal application of one aspect of Megan's law). This Kafkaesque scene happens on nearly every visit. Every aspect of this process is designed to break down the human connections between the prisoners, their families, and the outside world.

More recently, I was "temporarily" suspended from Mumia's visiting list for daring to bring in a single sheet of paper to my visit. After noticing that I had a piece of paper, a guard terminated our visit and in a physically intimidating way demanded the note. Immediately I ripped up the paper. With a pile of tiny scraps in front of me, I asked Mumia, "Do you think I should eat this?" He laughed and said no. Somewhat relieved, yet still unsure what to do, I stuffed the pieces in my pocket. After taking me outside the visiting booth, the guard demanded I empty my pockets. "These could be escape plans or drugs," he insisted. When I refused, he hustled off to get a "white shirt" (lieutenant). I quickly went to the open rest room and flushed the paper into the sewer. It was a small consolation to know that they would have to wade through a ton of shit to get all the pieces. Mumia and I continued our discussion until the lieutenant showed up. Eventually, after many threats, he "escorted me off the premises." What is the danger of words spoken and words written down on a single sheet of paper? (In case you were wondering, that piece of paper contained the line item budget for the work the Prison Radio and Equal Justice USA projects of the Quixote Center had been doing on Mumia's behalf, not exactly incendiary material.)

In order to counter this continuing attack on the First Amendment rights of journalists and prisoners, and the banning of new recordings by Mumia, in April 1998 I began to enlist notable artists to read new commentaries by Mumia each month and thus bring his words to life. *Democracy Now!*, Pacifica Radio's award-winning daily national newsmagazine, has committed itself to continue airing this series until the ban on recordings by Mumia is completely lifted.

In the latest victory, in August 1999, Amy Goodman, award-winning journalist and host of *Democracy Now!,* broke the ban on new broadcast commentaries by airing Mumia live via phone from the State Correctional Institution at Greene. Officials attempted to censor these calls, even ripping the phone line out of the wall in the middle of a live broadcast, but Mumia continues to exercise his rights and has succeeded in giving live commentary on the air.

State correctional departments, our national government, and the media have systematically attempted to "disappear" prisoners from the nation's consciousness. We barely hear any discussion of the culture of incarceration in the mainstream media. No prison can hold a prisoner's voice or completely suppress his or her story; but the practical obstacles to gaining access to places like SCI Greene and to getting prison stories on air, and the fact that reporting these stories requires courage and commitment, keep all but a few journalists and lawyers from venturing behind bars to report reality from inside America's prisons and jails.

One out of every 140 adults is in prison, and 5.1 million Americans are under correctional control, a percentage greater than in any other country. Texas and Florida are conducting assembly-line executions. At the current rate of increase in incarceration, half of all African-American men between the ages of eighteen and forty will be in prison by 2010. Slavery is back; in fact it was never abolished, but only institutionalized as part of the Thirteenth Amendment.

Censorship has lethal consequences, for Mumia and for thousands of others whose stories remain untold, whose rights we fail to defend, and whose oppression we fail to resist.

Whether Mumia's voice will reach the airwaves, and ultimately whether he lives or dies will be a true test of whether the freedom of the press exists. It will also depend on our independence, the depth of our courage, and our will to organize.

Toward justice and freedom.

Noelle Hanrahan
San Francisco, California
January 2000

SCENES

I. *From an Echo in Darkness, a Step into Light*

PSST!! YO, MU! Mu! You up?" asks the Italian-Cherokee tier runner, his accent betraying his South Philly roots. Stirring from the mattress, I trudge to the cell door, look down to where Mike stands, and glower at his bright face.

"What's up, man?" I grumble at sleep's interruption.

"You ready for this?" Mike asks rhetorically, his face ablaze with a smile.

"Man, what's up?" I demand, a bit peeved at the wordplay.

"Jay Smith?? He's going home!" Mike announced, and a heartfelt sense of happiness at another man's good fortune lifts my mood instantly.

"No shit, Mike?"

"Swear to God, Mu—he's packin' his gear right now. Sez he gotta order from the Supreme Court throwin' out his conviction! Ain't that somethin'?"

"Yeah, Mike. That's somethin' wonderful! Long live John Africa! That's good news, man!"

Jay Smith, a common, Anglo-Saxon, everyday American name, belonged to an old, quiet, gray-haired professional white dude who until recently was among 149 souls on Pennsylvania's death row after his conviction for three killings that sparked national attention, several books, and a television movie. Prosecutors, police, and the press painted him as an archdemon, a twisted sadist, a triple killer, and an all-around not-so-nice guy, light-years from the Lower Merion school principal and army reservist his neighbors and students knew.

Having read a news article depicting him as cold and evil, with "goat-like" gray eyes, I half expected when I met him to see him bounding around on two cloven hooves. But on appeal, it appeared as if the real animals (skunks) sent him to death row, for the Supreme Court reversed his conviction, citing prosecutorial misconduct, and his lawyer steadily uncovered lying cops, hidden evidence, and secret deals between investigators and a Hollywood novelist for inside info on the case. His prosecutor, who rose to national office on his case, fell just as swiftly when arrested and convicted on cocaine-related charges.

On Friday, September 18, 1992, at midday, the word came to Smith that his case was over; the prosecution was discharged; the defendant free to go. Having been encaged in Pennsylvania hellholes and on death row since 1979, Jay Smith packed his meager possessions, sent a few bye-byes around, shook off the ashes of twelve years, and walked away, stepping back into life. All the books, the multimillion-dollar movies of the week, and the damning news articles paled beside the reality of one man, walking from the stagnant cesspool of prison into freedom.

When one reporter asked him about his plans, he replied, "I dunno. I've been fighting for so long for this that I hadn't planned for anything beyond. I'm sixty-four—maybe in a year I can collect social security?" But what "security" exists in a system that plotted, lied, connived, and hid evidence to destroy one man's life, his possessions, his family?

II. *Requiem for Norman*

MOST MEN ON B BLOCK called him by the honorific, "old-head," but he wasn't really "old" at fifty-four-odd years, although it must be admitted that, to the majority of young men in the prison, in their early twenties, Norm must've seemed old indeed, especially with his head covered with a tight cap of apparent white wool.

Although his snowy head of hair bespoke age, his physique was that of a man half his age, well muscled and strong.

He had exercised and stretched religiously for years.

For seven years or so, Norman was held in the "hole."

Because I listened to a bit of jazz in my youth, we could converse on the gifted artists of the genre, like King Pleasure, Betty Carter, John and Alice Coltrane, etc., with a degree of ease that others, of the rap/hip-hop era, could not. He was fiercely opinionated and delighted in a good argument. Although he grew up in New York, he spent time in Philly, and as a youth, summers with family in Virginia. Although a big-city guy at heart, the southern cadences of speech, stewed into him from Virginia summers, never left him, and several times someone, hearing his "down-home" bass, would wrongly assume his point of origin was in the deep South.

He developed a habit that every time he left the cell, he would stop at the sergeant's desk for Gelusel, an antacid that he used for what seemed to be a constant upset stomach.

One day he called down. "Call the Sarge! Oh! Tell 'em I needa doctor!! My stomach! Ohh," he grunted.

Hearing the alarm in his voice, I called, and so did several others, "Dr. up! Sgt. up! 310 cellll! Dr. up!!"

It took quite a while—perhaps forty-five minutes passed before a nurse appeared at his cell—but it made little substantive difference, for she recommended Tylenol, a common painkiller that Norm promptly panned as worthless.

"Man, this stuff ain't doin' nothin' for my stomach!" he growled, the pain audible beneath the rumble of his voice.

It took days for Norm to be taken to the hospital, and when he returned, two days later, the treatment seemed to have been as worthless as the Tylenol he took days before.

"How'd it go, Norman?"

"Aw, man, they talkin' 'bout they can't find nothin'," he replied.

He continued to stop medical staff coming by to complain, and they took him out for more tests.

About a week later, some guards came by to pack up his property, and to give the latest news on his health: Cancer. Cancer of the pancreas. Malignant.

Two or three weeks after this diagnosis, Norman Whaley died in Centre County Hospital near Rockview Prison in Central Pennsylvania.

More than anything in life he longed for freedom, the company of a woman, and the sweet summer sun of Virginia (perhaps sweetened a tad more by the scat of jazz great Betty Carter). To the government that caged his flesh for the last near-decade, the newspapers that he read occasionally, and the politicians he lambasted daily as "corrupt," Norman was a non-person, a number, someone to be ignored in death, as in life.

To my knowledge, no newspaper recorded his death.

No medium marked the passing of the "old-head."

III. *Yard In*

THE LAST "YARD" of the day is finally called. "Capitals! Fourth, fifth, and sixth tier—YARD UP!" the corpulent corrections officer bellows, his rural accent alien to the urban ear.

One by one, cells are unlocked for the daily trek from cell to cage. Each man is pat-searched by guards armed with batons and then scanned by a metal detector.

Once the inmates are encaged, the midsummer sky rumbles, its dark clouds swell, pregnant with power and water. A bespectacled "white shirt" turns his pale face skyward, examining nature's quickening portent. The rumbles grow louder as drops of rain sail earthward, splattering on steel, brick, and human.

"Yard in!" the white shirt yells, sparking murmurs of resentment among the men.

"Yard in? Shit, man, we just got out here."

The guards adopt a cajoling, rather than a threatening, attitude. "C'mon, fellas—yard in, yard in. Ya know we can't leave y'uns out here when it gits ta thunderin' an' lightnin'."

"Oh, why not? Y'all 'fraid we gonna get ourself electrocuted?" a prisoner asks.

"Ain't that a bitch?" another adds. "They must be afraid that if we do get electrocuted by lightnin', they won't have no jobs and won't get paid."

A few guffaws, and the trail from cage to cell thickens.

Although usually two hours long, today's yard lasts ten minutes, for fear those condemned to death by the state may perish, instead, by fate.

For approximately twenty-eight hundred people locked in state and federal prisons, life is unlike that in any other institution. These are America's "condemned," who bear a stigma far worse than "prisoner." These are America's death row residents: men and women who walk the razor's edge between half-life and certain death.*

You will find a blacker world on death row than anywhere else. African Americans, a mere 11 percent of the national population, compose about 40 percent of the death row population. There, too, you will find this writer.

IV. *"On Tilt" by State Design*

HARRY WASHINGTON† shrieks out of an internal orgy of psychic pain: "Niggers!! Keep my family's name outcha mouf! Ya freaks! Ya filth! Ya racist garbage! All my family believe in God! Keep your twisted Satanic filth to y'allself! Keep my family's name outch'all nasty mouf!"

I have stopped the reflexive glance down in front of Harry's cell. For now, as in all the times in the past, I know no one is out near his ground-level cell—I know Harry is in a mouth-foaming rage because of the ceaseless noises echoing within the chambers of his tortured mind. For Harry and I are among the growing numbers of Pennsylvanians on death row, and

---

*As of September 1, 1999, there are 3,625 men and women on death row in thirty-nine states and jurisdictions. (Source: NAACP Legal Defense Fund, Death Row USA.)
†Not his real name, although quotes and historical facts are true.

Harry, because of mind-snapping isolation, a bitterly racist environment, and the ironies, the auguries, of fate, has begun the slide from depression through deterioration to dementia.

While we both share the deadening effects of isolation and an environment straight out of the redneck boondocks, Harry, like so many others, has slipped. Many of his tormenters here (both real and imagined) have named him "Nut" and describe him as "on tilt." Perhaps the cruel twists of fate popped his cork—who can say? A young black man, once a correctional officer, now a death row convict. Once he wore the keys, now he hears the keys, in an agonizing wait for death. The conditions of most of America's death rows create Harry Washingtons by the score.

Mix in solitary confinement, around-the-clock lock-in, no-contact visits, no prison jobs, no educational programs by which to grow, psychiatric "treatment" facilities designed only to drug you into a coma; ladle in hostile, overtly racist prison guards and staff; add the weight of the falling away of family ties, and you have all the fixings for a stressful psychic stew designed to deteriorate, to erode one's humanity—designed, that is, by the state, with full knowledge of its effects.

Nearly a century ago, a Colorado man was sentenced to death for killing his wife. On his arrival at Colorado State Penitentiary, James Medley was placed in solitary. Medley promptly brought an original writ of habeas corpus in the U.S. Supreme Court, which in 1890 consisted of six Republicans and three Democrats. In the 1890 case, *In re Medley,** the Court reached back to old English law, to the early 1700s of King George II, to conclude that solitary confinement was "an additional punishment of the most important and painful character" and, as applied to Medley, unconstitutional.

Fast-forward nearly a century to 1986, to the infamous federal court decision of *Peterkin v. Jeffes,*† where Pennsylvania death row inmates sought to have solitary confinement declared unconstitutional, and one hears a judge deny relief, saying, in the immortal words of now chief justice Rehnquist, "Nobody promised them a rose garden,"‡ That is, solitary is okay.

In re Medley, 134 U.S. 160 (1890).
†*Peterkin v. Jeffes,* 661 F. Supp. 895 (E.D.Pa. 1987) or 885 F.2d 1021 (3d Cir. 1988).
‡*Atiyeh v. Capps,* 449 U.S. 1312, 66 L.Ed.2d 785.

©NOLEN EDMONDSTON/PRISON RADIO

©NOLEN EDMONDSTON/PRISON RADIO

©JENNIFER BEACH/PRISON RADIO

©JENNIFER BEACH/PRISON RADIO

The notion that human progress is marked by "an evolving standard of decency,"* from the less civilized to the more civilized, from the more restrictive to the less restrictive, from tyranny to expanding freedom, dies a quick death on the rocks of today's Rehnquistian courts. Indeed, what other court could make the Republican-controlled Southern-Harlan-Fuller Court of the 1890s seem positively radical by comparison?

Harry continues his howlings and mindless mutterings of rage at no one in particular.

v. *Control*

IT IS FROM PENNSYLVANIA'S largest death row at the State Correctional Institute at Huntingdon, in rural south-central Pennsylvania, that I write. In the Commonwealth I am but one of 123 persons who await death.† I have lived in this barren domain of death since 1983. For several years now I have been assigned DC (disciplinary custody) status for daring to abide by my faith, the teachings of John Africa, and in particular for refusing to cut my hair. For this I have been denied family phone calls, and on occasion I have been shackled for refusing to violate my beliefs.

Life here oscillates between the banal and the bizarre.

Unlike other prisoners, death row inmates are not "doing time." Freedom does not shine at the end of the tunnel. Rather, the end of the tunnel brings extinction. Thus, for many here there is no hope.

As in any massive, quasi-military organization, reality on the row is regimented by rule and regulation. As against any regime imposed on human personality, there is resistance, but far less than one might expect. For the most part, death row prisoners are the best behaved and least disruptive of

---

*Full quotation is "evolving standards of decency that mark the progress of a maturing society." *Trop v. Dulles*, 356 U.S. S.Ct., 86 101, 78 S.Ct. 590, 598, 2. L.Ed.2d 630 (1958).
†This essay was written in 1991. Currently 223 men and women (69.95 percent people of color) await execution on Pennsylvania's death row.

all inmates. It also is true, however, that we have little opportunity to be otherwise, given that many death units operate on the "22 + 2" system: twenty-two hours locked in cell, followed by two hours of recreation out of cell. Outdoor recreation takes place in a cage, ringed with double-edged razor wire—the "dog pen."

All death rows share a central goal: human storage in an austere world, in which condemned prisoners are treated as bodies kept alive to be killed. Pennsylvania's death row regime is one of America's most restrictive, rivaling the infamous San Quentin death unit for the intensity and duration of restriction. A few states allow four, six, or even eight hours out of cell, prison employment, or even access to educational programs. Not so in the Keystone State.

Here one has little or no psychological life. Here many escape death's omnipresent specter only by way of common diversions—television, radio, or sports. TVs are allowed, but not typewriters: one's energies may be expended freely on entertainment, but a tool essential for one's liberation through the judicial process is deemed a security risk.

One inmate, more interested in his life than his entertainment, argued forcefully with prison administrators for permission to buy a nonimpact, nonmetallic, battery-operated typewriter. Predictably, permission was denied for security reasons. "Well, what do y'all consider a thirteen-inch piece of glass?" the prisoner asked, "ain't that a security risk?"

"Where do you think you'll get that from?" the prison official demanded.

"From my TV!"

Request for the typewriter denied.

TV is more than a powerful diversion from a terrible fate. It is a psychic club used to threaten those who resist the dehumanizing isolation of life on the row. To be found guilty of an institutional infraction means that one must relinquish TV.

After months or years of noncontact visits, few phone calls, and ever decreasing communication with one's family and others, many inmates use TV as an umbilical cord, a psychological connection to the world they have lost. They depend on it, in the way that lonely people turn to TV for the illusion of companionship, and they dread separation from it. For many, loss of TV is too high a price to pay for any show of resistance.

VI. *Already Out of the Game*

THE NEWEST POLITICAL FEVER sweeping the nation, the "three strikes, you're out" rage, will, barring any last-minute changes, become law in the United States, thereby opening the door to a state-by-state march to an unprecedented prison-building boom.

What most politicians know, however, is what most people do not—that "three strikes, you're out" will do next to nothing to eradicate crime, and will not create the elusive dream of public safety.

They also know that it will be years before the bills come due, but when they do, they'll be real doozies; by then, they reason, they'll be out of office, and it'll be another politician's problem. That's because the actual impact of "three strikes" will not be felt for at least ten to twenty years from now, simply because that's the range someone arrested today would face already (under the current laws), and the additional time, not to mention additional costs, will kick in then.

It seems a tad superfluous to say that already some thirty-four states have repeat offender (so called Career Criminal) laws, which call for additional penalties on the second, not the third, felony in addition to the actual crime.

As with every law, taxpayers will have to "pay the cost to be the boss." Pennsylvanians are paying over $600 million for their prisons; Californians, over $2.7 billion, topping costs for higher education. As prisons become increasingly geriatric, with populations hitting their fifties and sixties, these already atmospheric costs will balloon exponentially for expected health care costs, so that although many Americans, an estimated 37 million, don't have guaranteed health care, prisoners will, although of doubtful quality.

Frankly, its always amazing to see politicians sell their "we-gotta-get-tough-on-crime" schtick to a country that is already the world's leading incarcerator, and perhaps more amazing to see the country buy it.

One state has already trod that tough ground back in the 1970s; California "led" the nation in 1977 with their tough "determinate sentencing" law, and their prison population exploded over 500 percent; they now boast the largest prison system in the western world, 50 percent larger than the entire federal prison system. Do Californians—rushing to pass the "three strikes, you're out" ballot initiative—feel safer? A more cynical soul, viewing this prison-system-boom bill through the lens of economic interest, might suppose that elements of the correctional industry—builders, guards' unions, and the like—are fueling the boom, at least in part. Another element is the economy itself, where America enters the postindustrial age, when Japan produces the world's computer chips, Germany produces high performance autos, and America... prisons.

Prisons are where America's jobs programs, housing programs, and social control programs merge into a dark whole; and where those already outside of the game can be exploited and utilized to keep the game going.

VII. *Acting Like Life's a Ball Game*

WHEN I HEAR POLITICIANS bellow about getting tough on crime and barking out, "Three strikes, you're out," several images come to mind. I think of how quickly the tune changes when the politician is on the receiving end of some of the so-called toughness after a fall from grace. I am reminded of a powerful state appellate judge who, once caught in a bizarre web of criminal conduct, changed his long standing opinion regarding the efficacy of the insanity defense, an option he once ridiculed. It revealed in a flash how illusory and transitory power and status can be, and how we are all, after all, human.

I also think of a young man I met in prison, one of the first wave of people imprisoned back in the 1970s under new tougher youth certification statutes that allowed teenagers to be sentenced as adults. The man, whom I'll call Rabbani, was a tall, husky fifteen-year-old when he was arrested in southeastern Pennsylvania for armed robbery. The prosecutor moved that he be judicially certified as an adult, and the court agreed. Tried as an adult, Rabbani was convicted of all charges and sentenced to fifteen-to-thirty years in prison for an alleged "robbery" with a CO_2-air pistol.

His first six or seven years in this manmade hell found him constantly locked in battles with guards, and he logged more years in "the hole" than he did in general population status. He grew into manhood in shackles, and every time I saw him, he seemed bigger in size but more bitter in spirit. When we took the time to converse, I was always struck by the innate brilliance of the young man—a brilliance immersed in a bitterness so acidic that it seemed capable of dissolving iron. For almost fifteen years, this brilliance had been caged in cubes of time and steel.

For almost two of those years he tried, largely in vain, to get a judge to reconsider his case, but the one-line, two-word rejections—"appeal denied"—only served to deepen his profound cynicism. For those critical years, from age fifteen to thirty, which mark the transition from boy to man, Rabbani was entombed in a juridical, psychic, temporal box branded with the false promise "corrections." Like tens of thousands of his generation, his time in hell equipped him with no skills of value to either himself or his community.

He has been "corrected" in precisely the same way that hundreds of thousands of others have been, that is to say, warehoused in a vat that sears the very soul. He has never held a woman as a mate or lover; he has never held a newborn baby in his palm, its heart athump with new life; he hasn't seen the sun rise, nor the moon glow, in almost fifteen years. For a robbery, "armed" with a pellet gun, at fifteen years of age.

When I hear such easy, catchy, mindless slogans a "Three strikes, you're out," I think of men like Rabbani, who had one strike, if not one foul, and are for all intents and purposes already outside any game worth playing.

FOR THE SECOND TIME in as many years, the Pennsylvania Senate has passed a bill that would change the manner of executions from electrocution to lethal injections. Pennsylvania's House Judiciary Committee also passed the measure. In so doing, Pennsylvania begins the process that may add it to nineteen states that prescribe lethal injections, and takes a big step backwards. The bill's sponsor, Judiciary Committee Chair Stewart J. Greenleaf, pointed to other states as one reason for the act. Another, said Senator Greenleaf, was that it's "a more humane way." Pennsylvania's ACLU, in opposing the bill, said, "There is no humane way for the state to take a human life."

Back in 1888, New York State rejected lethal injection and hanging in favor of the more "humanitarian" method, electrocution.

A century ago, electricity was a mystery.

A popular publication of the age, *Frank Leslie's Illustrated Newspaper* (June 8, 1889), detailed the upcoming execution of William I. Kemmler by electricity with the breathless prose of a shameless ad man. Calling electricity a "more humane" method of execution, the dusty tabloid inferred Kemmler was, in a macabre sense, lucky, as he "need fear no such bungling work [as prior hangings] since he… will be executed by the Westinghouse alternating current during the week commencing June 24th."

The 1889 article, complete with a crude sketch of the new device, describes Kemmler's killing as a case of "no muss, no fuss." "At first a perceptible stiffening of the muscles is noticed, which gradually passes away; there is no struggle or outcry, and when, in fifteen seconds, the switch is opened, all signs of life are gone."

A grim experiment, using AC current, was declared a "success" on August 6, 1890, at Auburn Prison, New York, and Kemmler was killed. Such is "progress."

Today, 100 years later, a "new and improved" method of legal murder comes to the Keystone State, again touted by pols as "more humane." James Autry, were he alive, might beg to differ.

Autry, late of Texas, was put to death on March 14, 1984, and according to *Newsweek* "took at least 10 minutes to die and throughout much of that time was conscious, moving about and complaining of pain" (April 9, 1984). So much for "progress."

Legal scholars Franklin E. Zimring and Gordon Hawkins in their 1986 book *Capital Punishment and the American Agenda* (Cambridge University Press) trace the revival of the lethal injection movement to none other than then California governor Ronald Reagan, who remarked in 1973, "Being a former farmer and horse raiser, I know what it's like to try to eliminate an injured horse by shooting him. Now you call the veterinarian and the vet gives it a shot and the horse goes to sleep—that's it. I myself have wondered if maybe this isn't a part of our problem [with capital punishment], if maybe we should review and see if there aren't even more humane methods now—the simple shot or tranquilizer."

From *Death Valley Days* to Death Tally Ways, a mediocre actor, using a cowboyish analogy, strikes political pay dirt. As the island enchantress Circe of ancient Greek myth changed seamen into swine, so now does the state transform people enmeshed in the death penalty process into "wounded cattle." So lethal injection returns, after a century's hiatus. What's next for these political showmen, when this latest trick fails to properly entertain the throng?

A cup of hemlock?

From death row, this is Mumia Abu-Jamal.

*If censorship reigns there cannot be sincere flattery,
and only small men are afraid of small writings.*

—PIERRE DE BEAUMARCHAIS,
The Marriage of Figaro (1784)

ONCE AGAIN, an institution that claims homage to the "holy" First Amendment opts for silencing the dissenter rather than allowing freedom of speech. Echoing the politically motivated last-minute plug-pulling by NPR's misnamed *All Things Considered* of a series of commentaries by the writer in 1994, Temple University's Pennsylvania Radio Network (WRTI-FM and eleven affiliates across the state) cancelled its subscription to the Pacifica Radio Network's *Democracy Now!* program on the day it began airing the latest packet of commentaries, making Pennsylvania, the alleged "Cradle of Liberty," the citadel of silence and censorship.

Democracy Now!, hosted by award-winning reporter Amy Goodman, features an opposing view in this age of corporate media, and is a popular performer in the Pacifica stable. With a mission of "afflicting the comfortable and comforting the afflicted," *Democracy Now!* became one of the hottest national daily programs on the air in Pennsylvania—until now. Until, that is, it began airing the writer's opinions on America's hellish prisons. Then the powers that be, corporate and political, cut the mike.

SILENCE!

In a state that exists to service the mercenary instincts of capital, there can be no true democracy, now or ever. Indeed, any true reading of American history reveals a long train of war against democracy, and anything that smells of it, as the vast majority of people—Africans, Indians, women and poor whites—were systematically excluded from power. *Democracy Now!* seeks to challenge that hegemony, and when it dares question the prison-industrial complex, we find democracy must yield to the conjunction of politics and capital.

> Censorship reflects a society's lack of confidence in itself. It is a hallmark of an authoritarian regime.
>
> —JUSTICE POTTER STEWART
> dissenting opinion in U.S. v. Ginzburg (1965)

When NPR caved in to cop/capital pressure in 1994, it did so after then-Senator Bob Dole challenged their Corporation for Public Broadcasting government subsidies. Even democracy, it seems, has its price. The censor was once an elected official in ancient Rome whose job it was to "protect public morals." In this new empire it damns not just the speaker but the listener as well, in the name of protecting them.

Do you need to be protected from my voice?

Or do you need protection from your protectors?

From death row, this is Mumia Abu-Jamal.

ON THURSDAY, AUGUST 12, 1999, I finally got through on a call I had been trying to complete all week long: to Amy Goodman, the host of the acclaimed Pacifica news broadcast *Democracy Now!* aired over WBAI-FM in New York City, and over the network nationally. I was thrilled to get through, and as her topic was the buzz over the imminent release of sixteen Puerto Rican Independentista political prisoners, its was a perfect opportunity to express solidarity for the brave and committed Puerto Rican freedom fighters, who have suffered enormously in their long imprisonment at the hands of their cruel American colonizers. After speaking with relatives and loved ones of the Independentistas, Amy calmly announced to her listeners that she had a guest on the line (me) who might offer a few opinions on the controversy. It went something like this:

AG [Amy Goodman]: On the line now from a state correctional institution in Pennsylvania, after considerable difficulty, is our guest, Mumia Abu-Jamal, convicted in the murder of Philadelphia police officer Daniel Faulkner in 1981 in a trial that many have condemned as riddled with constitutional, and other errors.... Mumia, welcome to *Democracy Now!*

MAJ: Thank you, Amy, it is my pleasure to be with you all at *Democracy Now!*

AG: Now, Mumia, I'm sure you've heard about the controversy that we're discussing this morning; the imminent release of some sixteen

Puerto Rican political prisoners, under certain conditions... have you heard?

MAJ: Yeah, well, I did see some mention on this on the TV, and these are my thoughts on the issue: Under the constitution, one is allegedly allowed the rights of association. For these brothers and sisters, freedom ain't really freedom is it? First I wanna say: *Libertad para los presos politicos de Puertoriqueno!* Yes, "Free all Puerto Rican Political Prisoners!" Yeah! We're with that! But under the U.S. government's plan, they will be granted a kind of half-freedom; they won't be allowed to associate with each other, so their freedom of association is dead.

And I am reminded when I hear the condition about the renunciation of violence, that that is almost identical to the same condition that was put on the ANC [African National Congress] prisoners like Nelson Mandela in South Africa. And it shows that what they're being given is a form of probation in the streets, which is not freedom, because they are not free to be the political persons that they are. It is a kind of halfway acknowledgment that they are political prisoners, but it is a denial of their right to be political people in freedom, so it's a half-freedom—it is a halfway house–kind of freedom. And I agree with the past comment that was made, that it is outrageous, it should be fought because it is a kind of an allowance of their bodies to be free but a restriction on their political activities—

At this moment my phone line went dead, as a guard pulled the wire from the phone jack on the wall, disconnecting me. Another guard appeared at the cell door hollering at the top of his lungs: "This call is terminated!" When I demanded to know why, he replied, "This order came down from the very top!" I immediately called to the sergeant standing by and looking on, "Sergeant! Where did this order come from?"

He shrugged his shoulders, answering, "I dunno. We just got a phone call to cut you off."

The next day, the answer came in the form of a write-up; #A69958, where I am charged with a Class I misconduct: Unauthorized Use of the Mail or Telephone. In the write-up, the following institutional offenses are stated:

On August 12, 1999, at 0936 hours, Inmate Jamal made a telephone call to a news radio station named Pacifica Radio Network's Democracy Now. Per DC-ADM 009 News Media Relations, it states News Media requests for inmate interviews by telephone shall be approved at the discretion of the Facility Manager. Inmate Jamal did not request from the Facility Manager permission to be interviewed by the news media. In addition, inmate Jamal placed a news reporter on his IPIN list knowing full well that the person was a reporter. This is verified by the attached documentation. Also, per DC ADM 6.5.8, all communications between Capital Case inmates and the news media shall be conducted in accordance with DOC and institutional policies on visitation and telephone privileges. It should be noted inmate telephone calls are a privilege. As a result of inmate Jamal not requesting permission from the Facility Manager to be interviewed or speak with the news media, his telephone call was terminated after 11 minutes of speaking with the news media.

This write-up was signed by a lieutenant and a captain of the guards.

In order to produce this write-up, ranking staff members had to ignore their own rules; for example DC-ADM-009-1, November 11, 1996, which states:

News media are entitled to the same access to specific inmates as the general public. There shall be no special arrangements made for news media interviews with specific inmates. All communications between specific inmates and the news media shall be conducted in accordance with the DC-ADM 812 (Inmate Visiting Privileges) and the DC-ADM 818 (Inmate Telephone Calls).... [d] If an inmate wants to talk with a news media representative over the telephone, it is his responsibility to place a collect call to the reporter under guidelines set forth in DC-ADM 818—Inmate Telephone Calls.

There are rules—and there are rules, it seems, especially when the state deals with Mumia Abu-Jamal. Here, the DOC writes me up, using a rule that no longer exists! But since when have rules gotten in the way of corrupt bureaucracies which follow the foul winds of the political masters?

Clearly, we are not working with "rules": we are working with the state's exercise of its political power to censor a captive whom they, once again, have acted to silence. But, like before, it ain't working. I thank Amy and her fervent politically adept listeners at *Democracy Now!* for that great opportunity to show solidarity. You keep on listening… I'll keep on rapping!

From death row, this is Mumia Abu-Jamal.

A BRIGHT, SHINING HELL

IMAGINE.

Imagine living, eating, sleeping, relieving oneself, daydreaming, weeping—but mostly waiting, in a room about the size of your bathroom.

Now imagine doing all those things—but mostly waiting, for the rest of your life.

Imagine waiting—waiting—waiting—to die.

I don't have to imagine.

I "live" in one of those rooms, like about 3,000 other men and women in thirty-eight states across the United States.

It's called "death row."

I call it "hell."

Welcome to "hell."

Each of the states that have death rows have a different system for their "execution cases," varying from the relatively open to the severely restrictive.

Some states, like California and Texas, allow their execution cases work, education, and or religious service opportunities, for out of cell time up to eight hours daily.

Pennsylvania locks its "execution cases" down twenty-three hours a day, five days a week; twenty-four hours the other two days.

At the risk of quoting Mephistopheles, I repeat:

Welcome to hell.

A hell erected and maintained by human governments, and blessed by black-robed judges.

A hell that allows you to see your loved ones, but not to touch them.

A hell situated in America's boondocks, hundreds of miles away from most families.

A white, rural Hell, where most of the caged captives are black and urban.

It is an American way of death.

Contrary to what one might suppose, this hell is the easiest one to enter in a generally hellish criminal justice system. Why? Because, unlike any other case, those deemed potential capital cases are severely restricted during the jury selection phase, as any juror who admits opposition to the death penalty is immediately removed, leaving only those who are fervent death penalty supporters in the pool of eligible jurors.

When it was argued that to exclude those who opposed death, and to include only those who supported death, was fundamentally unfair, as the latter were more "conviction-prone," the U.S. Supreme Court, in a case titled *Lockhart v. McCree*, said such a claim was of no constitutional significance.

Once upon a time, politicians promised jobs and benefits to constituents, like "a chicken in every pot," to get elected. It was a surefire vote getter.

No longer. Today the lowest-level politico up to the president uses another surefire gimmick to guarantee victory:

Death. Promise death, and the election is yours.

Guaranteed. *Vraiment.*

A "Vote for hell" in the "Land of liberty," with its over 1 million prisoners, is the ticket to victory.

From death row, this is Mumia Abu-Jamal.

A FEDERAL CIVIL RIGHTS TRIAL in Philadelphia charging seven former Graterford Prison guards with violating the civil rights of a number of prisoners by severely beating them while they were shackled and cuffed hand and foot revealed, in glaring fashion, how in prisons there is no law, there are no rights. Despite the guilty pleas and damning testimony of five ex-guards that they and their colleagues maliciously beat, kicked, stomped, blackjacked, and tazered (that is, used a hand held electric shocking device) prisoners who committed no institutional offenses, a civil jury acquitted the seven of virtually all charges. One juror was quoted as saying, "Although it was proven that prisoners were badly beaten, no conspiracy was proven by U.S. prosecutors." One prisoner, who suffered from AIDS and thus had less internal resources with which to rebound from the horrific physical and psychological trauma he suffered in the beating, has since died.

In the month-long trial it was revealed that guards thought nineteen prisoners transferred from Camp Hill Prison, shortly after rioters and rebels nearly leveled the central Pennsylvania facility to a pile of smoldering ashes, were part of the rioting crews that had ripped the prison apart. In fact, the nineteen were nonrioters, only too glad to be leaving what came to be called "Camp Hell" and to be coming to the state's largest and blackest prison, Graterford. Instead, they were leaving the fire only to get simmered in the frying pan, so to speak. At Graterford, whose massive, haunting walls seemed to offer some relief from the raging literal and psychic infernos of Camp Hill, the nineteen men met uniform hatred and naked brutality as they were beaten, kicked, and terrorized by government officials sworn to protect the elusive peace in prisons. Guards, acting on nothing but assumptions, assaulted over a dozen men on the notion that they were "troublemakers." Some, those few who could navigate the treacherous straits and shoals of civil litigation, sued state officials for damages. Others bound up their wounds and blended into the wall, while waiting for their terms to expire, so that they could be "free" again. Several testified in the federal prosecution. One died. But all found out how fragile the system that stole their freedom was when the state committed crimes against them. All found out that words like "justice," "law," "civil rights," and yes, "crime," have different and elastic meanings depending on whose rights were violated, who committed what crimes against whom, and whether one works for the system or against it. For those people, almost a million at last count, who wear the label *prisoner* around their necks, there is no law, there is no justice, there are no rights.

From death row, this is Mumia Abu-Jamal.

A LETTER FROM PRISON[*]

I'VE BEEN TRYING to do some schoolwork, but without schoolbooks, how can it be done? The reality forced me to find the enclosed article, which I thought was in *Live from Death Row*. I don't have a copy, so I can't be sure. At any rate, I find its main points chillingly accurate, and nothing the state has done has disabused me of this notion. Take a moment, read it, you'll see it for yourself: an attack on the life of the mind.[†] It's in that regard that I address the subject of our earlier discussion re victory.

There's an old saying, I think from Mao Tse-tung, which was used to educate the guerilla army: "Tell no lies, claim no easy victories." I say that because to claim we've gained any kind of victory is to lie. We were told some things by administrators that, if applied, *would* be a step in the right direction, but it ain't hardly a victory. It's as if a man who is armed with a stick tied you up, looted your apartment of almost all your property, stole from your wallet to pay for its shipment or destroyed it, and then returned two weeks later with a shoe box of some of your stuff and said you could have it, if you paid for it.

Victory? Hardly.

---

[*]A letter written to Steve Wiser, Mumia's spiritual adviser, during a hunger strike in March 1998, in which around thirty inmates participated, demanding mainly the right of access to the legal materials of their own cases, which were removed during a March 5, 1998, shakedown. The hunger strike did get some results, but overall it was a dubious victory with respect to the seizure of the inmates' property.

[†]Pennsylvania Department of Corrections directives 801 & 802 outline a program of severe restriction in communication, visitation, a ban on all books (save the Bible of Qu'ran). See essay "Campaign of Repression: Attack on the Life the Mind."

There is something obscene about a state crowing about men capitulating to government repression. How do you capitulate to lies? There is something sinister about the government agency that calls itself "corrections" attacking the ability of men to learn, to educate themselves, and to grow in the human pursuit of knowledge. If there was any "victory," it was the government's, for they succeeded in stripping men on death row of most of their property. It was a victory for ignorance, clothed in the rags of state power, over human enlightenment. It was a victory of deadly political expedience over the forces of life.

It's for this reason that the words of Pierre Sané,* the general secretary of Amnesty International, were all but ignored by the corporate press. If he said some of these things about Cuba, China, Nigeria, or Iraq, the capitalist corporate white majoritarian press would have echoed his words from here to New Caledonia. But no, he criticized the United States, Pennsylvania, and the Greene County Gulag.

That apparently is not news fit to print.

He was right then, he's more right now.

From death row, this is Mumia Abu-Jamal.

---

*Pierre Sané had said that "death row in Pennsylvania looks and feels like a morgue. Everything is high-tech, and there is no human being in sight. From the moment that condemned prisoners arrive, the state tries to kill them slowly, mechanically and deliberately—first spiritually, and then physically.... Amnesty International has serious doubts about the fairness of Mr. Abu-Jamal's trial, which may have been contaminated by the deep-rooted racism that appears to taint the application of the death penalty in Pennsylvania.... Surely no governor, Attorney General or District Attorney, no matter how supportive of capital punishment, can publicly support a system so racially biased and unfair." Amnesty International Index; AMR 51/76/97, news release, November 25, 1997.

THE VISIT

IN THE MIDST OF DARKNESS, this little one was a light ray. Tiny, with a Minnie Mouse voice, this daughter of my spirit had finally made the long trek westward, into the bowels of this manmade hell, situated in the south-central Pennsylvania boondocks. She, like my other children, was just a baby when I was cast into hell, and because of her youth and sensitivity, she hadn't been brought along on family visits until now.

She burst into the tiny visiting room, her brown eyes aglitter with happiness; stopped, stunned, staring at the glassy barrier between us; and burst into tears at this arrogant attempt at state separation. In milliseconds, sadness and shock shifted into fury as her petite fingers curled into tight fists, which banged and pummeled the Plexiglas barrier, which shuddered and shimmied but didn't break.

"Break it! Break it!" she screamed. Her mother, recovering from her shock, bundled up Hamida in her arms, as sobs rocked them both. My eyes filled to the brim. My nose clogged.

Her unspoken words echoed in my consciousness: "Why can't I hug him? Why can't we kiss? Why can't I sit in his lap? Why can't we touch? Why not?" I turned away to recover.

I put on a silly face, turned back, called her to me, and talked silly to her. "Girl, how can you breathe with all them boogies in your nose?" Amid the rolling trail of tears, a twinkle started like dawn, and before long the shy beginnings of a smile meandered across her face as we talked silly talk.

I reminded her of how she used to hug our cat until she almost strangled the poor animal, and Hamida's denials were developing into laughter. The three of us talked silly talk, liberally mixed with serious talk, and before long our visit came to an end. Her smile restored, she uttered a parting poem that we used to say over the phone: "I love you, I miss you, when I see you, I'm gonna kiss you!" The three of us laughed and they left.

Over five years have passed since that visit, but I remember it like it was an hour ago; the slams of her tiny fists against the ugly barrier; her instinctual rage against it—the state-made blockade raised under the rubric of security, her hot tears.

They haunt me.

From death row, this is Mumia Abu-Jamal.

George Jackson was my hero. He set a standard for prisoners,
for political prisoners, for people. He showed the love, the strength,
the revolutionary fervor, that's characteristic of any soldier for the people.
He inspired prisoners whom I later encountered, to put his ideas
into practice, and so his spirit became a living thing.

—DR. HUEY P. NEWTON, PH.D.

former minister of defense of the Black Panther Party, at the
revolutionary memorial service for George Jackson in 1971

AUGUST, in both historic and contemporary African American history, is a
month of meaning. It is a month of repression.

AUGUST 1619: The first group of black laborers, called indentured
servants, landed at Jamestown, Virginia.

AUGUST 25, 1967: Classified FBI memos went out to all bureaus
nationwide with plans to "disrupt, misdirect, discredit or otherwise
neutralize" black liberation movement groups.

AUGUST 1968: The Newark, New Jersey, Black Panther Party office
was firebombed.

AUGUST 25, 1968: Los Angeles Black Panther Party members Steve
Bartholomew, Robert Lawrence, and Tommy Lewis were murdered
by the LAPD at a gas station.

AUGUST 15, 1969: Sylvester Bell, San Diego Black Panther Party
member, was murdered by the U.S. organization.

AUGUST 21, 1971: Black Panther Party field marshall George L. Jackson assassinated at San Quentin Prison, California. Three guards and two inmate turncoats were killed, three wounded.

It is also a month of radical resistance.

AUGUST 22, 1831: Nat Turner's rebellion rocked South Hampton County, Virginia, and the entire South, when slaves rose up and slew their white masters.

AUGUST 30, 1856: John Brown led an antislavery raid on a group of Missourians at Ossowatame, Kansas.

AUGUST 7, 1970: Jonathan Jackson, younger brother of Field Marshall George Jackson, raided the Marin County Courthouse in California, arming and freeing three black prisoners and taking the judge, prosecutor and several jurors hostage. All except one prisoner were killed by police fire that perforated the escape vehicle. Jon was seventeen.

And in an instance of resistance and repression,

AUGUST 8, 1978: After a fifteen-month armed police standoff with the Philadelphia-based naturalist MOVE organization,* the police raided MOVE, killing one of their own in police crossfire, and charged nine MOVE people with murder. The MOVE nine, in prisons across Pennsylvania, are serving up to 100 years, each.

August, a month of injustice and divine justice, of repression and righteous rebellion, of individual and collective effort to free the slaves and break the chains that bind us.

August saw slaves, and the grandsons of slaves, strike out for their God-given right to freedom, as well as the awesome price, the ultimate price,

---

*The MOVE organization surfaced in Philadephia during the early 1970s. Characterized by dreadlocked hair, the adopted surname "Africa," a principled unity, and an uncompromising commitment to their belief, members practice the teachings of MOVE founder John Africa.

always paid by those who would dare oppose the slave master's will. Like their spiritual grandfather, the blessed rebel Nat Turner, those who have opposed Massa in this land of unfreedom, have met murder by the state: George and Jonathan Jackson, James McLain, William Christmas, Bobby Hutton, Steve Bartholomew, Robert Lawrence, Tommy Lewis, Sylvester Bell, all suffered the fate of Nat Turner, of the slave daring to fight the slave master for his freedom.

Ruchell McGee, for the crime of surviving the Marin County Courthouse massacre, has been consigned to a life in California slave coffins, modern-day dungeons called "adjustment centers," where he has languished since August 1970. He is a political prisoner guilty of the unpardonable sin of insurrection. And though not executed by hanging like his ancestor, Nat Turner, or executed by firing squad like his co-rebels, he endures a cruel living death in the bowels of Babylon.

Their sacrifice, their despair, their determination, and their blood has painted the month black for all time. Let their revolutionary sacrifice not be forgotten nor taken in vain.

From death row, this is Mumia Abu-Jamal.

A single spark can start a prairie fire.

—MAO TSE-TUNG

PRISONS ARE REPOSITORIES OF RAGE, islands of socially acceptable hatreds where worlds collide like subatomic particles seeking the freedom of psychic release. Like Chairman Mao's proverbial spark, it takes little to start the blazes.

I thought of that spark one morning in October 1989 when I heard an eruption of violence that hit Huntingdon's B block, snatching the writer from the false escape of dreams.

A white man's rural twang spits out a rhetorical question: "Oh you like hurtin' people huh?"

Punches, grunts, thuds, and crunches echo up the steel tiers, awakening the groggy into sudden alertness.

"Get the f—— off that man, leave that man alone, you fat racist pig!!"

A quiet morning on B block is shattered, as much by the yells of fearful rage as by the blams of batons on flesh and bone.

Predictably, the beating and taunts continued until the man was thrown into a locked shower and able to call up to others, also locked in, and inform them of what happened:

"Who is that, man? What's your name, dude?"

"Tim… Tim Forest," he answers, sounding hyped, but guarded.

"What happened, Timmy?"

"They rolled on me man, for fighting that dude Weaverman."

Timmy?

The voice is familiar, as he recently worked over on B block as a tier runner for several months, lugging food trays and handling other menial block maintenance chores, working around death row and disciplinary prisoners. Thirtyish, slight of build, with an outgoing personality. I liked the guy, despite our strong political differences.

"You can't fight these people, Mu," Tim opined, adding, "You can't beat the system."

I sniffed in strong disapproval. But my arguments missed him.

So we rapped music, a common love, and I enjoyed his melodious tenor croon.

Timmy? Fightin' a guard? Fightin' a slew of guards?

By Friday, the rumor had spread on Tim's treatment on B block, and following midday Jumu'ah services,* over fifty men converged on the prison center to demand an end to the brutal beatings of cuffed men. Caught by surprise, ranking security officers assured the angry black throng that no such beatings would occur, and urged dispersal.

By nightfall, an uneasy quiet loomed over the central Pennsylvania prison.

Come Saturday morning, lockdown was launched: no movement, no jobs, no recreation, no trays served. A regimen of utter restriction. Overnight, Pennsylvania's most repressive jail becomes Pennsylvania's largest hole—the prison becomes one big hole.

The weekend passed in lockdown, and on Monday, when a mournful siren sounded, there was confusion, disbelief, and then a smattering of applause as some assumed there had been a jailbreak, in which case the siren would precede the sounding of the townshipwide alarm.

The foghorn cry fades, then cries, then fades, and then cries anew. Confusion overtook jubilation, and the applause faded to embarrassed silence. Walkie-talkies snapped to life, and the ring of keys sounded throughout the jail as all three shifts converged at dusk, en masse.

Armed, armored squads went from cell to cell, pulling, cuffing, punching, bludgeoning, kicking, brutalizing naked prisoners. Men were handcuffed, seized, dragged outside, thrown into cages, naked, beaten, and bloody.

---

*Jumu'ah: Congregational Islamic prayers performed on Fridays, beginning after the sun passes its zenith.

Huntingdon's revenge for Friday's loss of face rivaled Dixie slavocracy, with its premeditated racist raids. Naked, unarmed men awakened from deep sleep fought back against the rural mob bravely, perhaps none too wisely.

By Tuesday morning, unofficial reports put the injured at twenty-seven staff, nineteen inmates, with A Block in shambles as lockdown continued. By Wednesday, the cages were being hosed down, traces of blood washed into drains to feed the Juniata River—washed away.

For days there was lockdown. No showers, no jobs, no movement, no recreation as Huntingdon Prison became Huntingdon hole.

One participant in the bloody fracas, asked to tell what happened, answered, "It's just like Mao said, man, one spark can start a prairie fire."

Presently, prisons across the Keystone State have been smoldering in rebellion to a campaign of racist repression.

Catch the spark.

From death row, this is Mumia Abu-Jamal.

IN PHILADELPHIA, Hank Fahy's name is mud.

Convicted of the 1981 rape-slaying of a girl-child and subsequently sentenced to death, Fahy has lived in a virtual netherworld beneath the usual hell that is death row. Marked as a baby-rapist, he has had to withstand the loathing of the many who regard his crime as an act beneath contempt. Fahy's odyssey into the underworld has not been an easy one: bouts of suicide attempts have alternated with periods of an almost manic evangelical fervor, a living pendulum, swinging between visions of hell and heaven, both just beyond his grasp.

In late June 1995, while under his second death warrant, and with a date to die in July, Hank would come face-to-face with the living personification of his demons and his angel.

Even while under an active death warrant, with a date to die within two weeks, Fahy was transferred to a Philadelphia city prison, rather than the state prison at Graterford, as is customary. When he arrived, he was placed in a cell, where the words "Jamie Fahy—Rest in Peace" were scrawled across the wall: Jamie Fahy, a beautiful, troubled, love-starved young girl—beaten, murdered, and allegedly raped—was Hank Fahy's eighteen-year-old daughter.

She was barely four when he entered hell.

There is more.

From impish whisperings of those around him, he learned an astonishing fact—that the man charged with beating, killing and raping his daughter was at this prison—and not merely in the same prison—but on the very same cell block!

As if inevitable, Hank met Mark, and the hatred, kindled over years, melted into a rare compassion.

"I hated him, Jamal," Fahy confided, "but when I saw this kid, eighteen years old, I realized what a hell he was in for; and also I thought about the pain I'd be causing his mother, if I took something and stuck him."

In every prison in America, murder is no mystery. There are men on death row across the nation awaiting execution for killings committed in prison.

Hank had two weeks of life left. What did he have to lose?

"You know, Jamal, I looked at this eighteen-year-old kid, and I remembered the look on my mother's face when she was alive, when she came to visit me; the shame of seeing her son on death row; and I didn't have the heart to tell this kid, but I could see his mother lookin' at him the same way, and it hurt me, Jamal, it really did, man."

"What hurt you, Hank? Whatchu mean?"

"Well it was two things. First, this was a setup; I was 'sposed to kill this kid! Why else would they put us on the same block? Come on, man. Second, the same people that put me on death row are gonna put this kid on death row, but he don't know it yet."

"What did you tell Mark?"

"I told him, 'I forgive ya,' and I told him to let his lawyer know it, and anything I can do to help him and to keep him off death row, I'll do."

"How did you feel tellin' that boy that, Hank?"

"Ya know, Jamal, I felt good. I felt like the better man, 'cause the same system that plans to kill me, that plans to kill him, that same system that set us both up, for me to kill him and for him to get killed, can't do what I did—forgive."

"I loved my daughter, Jamal. She was my heart. But me killing that kid can't bring my Jamie back, and ya know what else, Jamal?"

"What's that, Hank?"

"I wouldn't wish death row on my *worstest* enemy."

From death row, this is Mumia Abu-Jamal.

AT FIRST GLANCE the guy looks like a black fireplug. Short, coffee-black, with a clean-shaven, glistening dome, Manny resembles a miniversion of boxing great Jack Johnson. An ex-boxer of champion status himself, Manny moves with well-muscled agility, at once at home in a ring, or out. Bigger prisoners regard him with a wary respect. Lately, though, his moves have been a little less than agile, a trifle forced.

Manny's recent history seems plucked from the pages of a Robert Ludlum mystery, but it is no tale—it is chillingly true. A lifelong epileptic, his life has revolved around the daily ingestion of the anticonvulsant Dilantin, with the sedative phenobarbital. Nonetheless, the last ten years or so had been virtually seizure-free, until coming to the hills of Huntingdon and under the "care" of its medical staff.

After an apparent setup and serious altercation with a white inmate, resulting in his assailant's hospitalization, Manny was sent to the DC (Disciplinary Custody)* max unit, a walled "prison within a prison."

There, the mystery.

There, the attempted murder.

No attack on a handcuffed inmate, the joint's usual M.O. No, tools change with the times, it seems. While in the "max," Manny experienced a series of seizures, powerful enough to leave him locked in a deep coma.

"What the f—— is goin' on?" he asked himself. He paid extra-close attention to his food. He waited. He watched. He fasted. Still, the seizures

---

*Disciplinary custody: the most restrictive housing for prisoners found guilty of a Class I misconduct.

came, in waves of increasing frequency and mind-numbing power. Why, he wondered? Why now? He noticed new medications being administered—new colors, new quantities—and asked questions: "What's this?" The answers, provided by the same persons who gave the medication, the guards, were easy, breezy, and lies: "Aw, nothin'—a new kinda Dilantin, the nurse sez—you want your medication?"

The more he took, the worse he got, the more powerful the seizures, the deeper the comas. He stopped. He filed complaints; he demanded and got outside medical care. At Altoona's hospital, Manny got his answers.

In addition to his Dilantin/phenobarbital regimen, someone had slipped in the drugs Loxitane, Artane, and Haldol (haloperidol). The mixture was like a chemical cannonball, wreaking havoc on his vision, his balance, and most ominously, his liver.

When an internist began to conduct a microbiopsy on his liver and then halted, refused to go further, and sewed him back up, Manny's instincts took over. Something was very wrong. The surgeon at Altoona told him there was a glasslike sheath over his liver, and ultrasound showed that it was swollen, distended. The Haldol, according to the authoritative *Physician's Desk Reference*, was contraindicated to use with anticonvulsants like Dilantin, as it "lowers the convulsive threshold"; in a nutshell, it causes seizures.

In dizzying internal pain, Manny continued his battles against the prison medical bureaucracy that brought him from championship form to the brink of death.

That he lives is itself a miracle.

That he fights is by power of will.

That the culprits, those who prescribed this toxic chemical cocktail, still go unnamed is an indictment against a racist system of corruption, masquerading as corrections.

Meanwhile, he waits, he fights, he strengthens himself.

From death row, this is Mumia Abu-Jamal.

THE GRAY-HAIRED TIER RUNNER brought the morning coffee, and the latest news—a shocker.

"Remember that dude Woolfolk, Mu?"

"Yeah, what about 'im?"

"He hung up last night."

"Gitta hell outta here, man! You jokin'?"

"No joke, man. He's dead. They carried him out last night."

My mind flipped to a quiet night's sleep, with no awareness of the tragedy unfolding several cells away from mine, a night of one man's anguish ended by a knotted sheet.

Craig Woolfolk, about forty-one, manic as hell—with his whining, scratchy whiskey voice, and nonstop chatter, a source of anger to many—has finally stopped.

Woolfolk—I loved the name, but didn't quite care for the man. The name Woolfolk seemed one so apt for black folk; the man was a manic chatterbox, and his voice stole many nights of rest. I thought of his unexpected, presumed suicide, and thought of many others, Pipehead just weeks ago, that have sought death's relief. It made me think of a brief written by MOVE martyr and naturalist minister Frank Africa, in the infamous case *Africa v. Commonwealth of Pennsylvania* (1981),[*] where MOVE sought its religious diet.

---

[*]*Africa v. Commonwealth of Pennsylvania,* 662 F.2d 1025 (3d Cir. 1981), The Third Circuit held that MOVE was not entitled to religious protection.

Holding, as expected, for the state and against the prisoner, the court rejected relief, but the point was made. In naturalist minister Frank's brief, he explained, with startling oratory, the contradiction between the state's denial of health and its diet of death:

Our Principle, given to us through the generosity of Our Teacher [John Africa], cuts through the bitterness of jealousy, fills in the emptiness that causes this hatred, and generates respect and trust where jealousy once was. And this is proven at the prisons where our diet is already established, for we are *widely* respected because we are *giving* direction to all those who suffer the deprivation that this system practices.... Anytime this system's prisons supply a steady diet of cigarettes that deprive folks of their health, provides a diet of junk food that deprives folks of their teeth, perpetuates a diet of perversion that deprives folks of their sex, stipulates a diet of birth control that deprives folk of their fertility, promotes a diet of drug-ridden foods and mind-torturing medications that deprive folks of their very *sanity*, and questions the relevance of *our* diet, while leaving this insanity unquestioned, this backwards analysis needs to be closely examined, for our diet is unquestionably innocent, but this disorder is as questionable as the chaotic reference it was derived from. This is why it is also foolish to deny us our diet for fear of prisoners making wine, this is a blatant insult, because it is the prisons, this system that indulges and flaunts this distortion wherever it touches, and *not* MOVE. *John Africa* has made us clean people, wise people, made us godly people.... It is ridiculous for this system's prisons to express concern about wine making, and schizophrenically pump thorazine, booze people with slow juice, phenobarbitals, make folks bodies drunk with all manner of *devastating*, emotion-wrecking chemicals, robbing their soberness with a weapon of barbiturates, intoxicating folks with up drugs and down drugs and all in between, and *leaving* them drunk and staggering with hopelessness that *drives* them to *collapse* in the clutches of suicide in attempt to escape this diabolical treachery, causing them to hang themselves in search of relief, pushing them to slit their wrists, gash their throats, crack their skulls in desperation to try and alleviate the pain that this system inflicts, forcing folks to the edge of insanity and leaving them no choice but to jump to their death.... We have seen this tragedy time and again, stretchers carting the victims of this atrocity murdered by this intruder that practices torment.

Question: Why do they still call it "corrections"?

From death row, this is Mumia Abu-Jamal.

*We are under a constitution, but the
constitution is what the judges say it is.*

—U.S. SUPREME COURT CHIEF JUSTICE
CHARLES EVANS HUGHES (1862–1948)

FOR MOST PEOPLE in the nation who wear the label of Americans, the courts of the land are like memorial sites in the heart of a city; many, perhaps most, folks know they are there, but very few people actually go to see them. In an age when the national town meeting is more apt to be experienced while sitting on one's sofa than actually going out of the house into the public, what happens in the nation's courts depends upon what the media reports happens.

Popular reporting of such events depends upon the objectives, biases, and expertise of the reporter and the interests of the publisher/editor/owner.

Every civil trial is, at base, a conflict, a contest, or a war of words. The arbiter of that conflict is also engaged in a struggle, for although we like to think judges are Olympians who rule over courts with Delphic equanimity, they are but mortals driven and sometimes riven by the same passions as other men and women.

The civil case *Abu-Jamal v. Price* began, as so many cases, with a small step. As the writer sat on Phase II, with a date to die, a guard sidled up to Cell B-4 and laid a write-up on the opened tray slot. Typed on the pressure-sensitive, yellow-tinted paper was a damning indictment: The writing of the book *Live from Death Row,* and of articles for *Scoop* newspaper, *Against the Current* journal, and other publications, was proof that inmate Jamal was guilty of operating "a business or profession" of "Journalism." Also, inmate

Jamal was a "professor of economics" for the New York–based Henry George Institute (and thus, perhaps, guilty of the profession of "teacher" of a correspondence course). The June 1995 write-up, served up on the writer's second day on Phase II, made writing (and teaching) an institutional offense, punishable by a sharp reduction in privileges. Sentenced to thirty days in the "hole," with less than sixty days to live, meant no phone calls, no visits, no TV, no radio, and no commissary privileges. It was being placed in a prison within a prison within a prison, for writing. I was sentenced to die in silence.

While waiting for the institutional "hearing," I got word to some friends, and they in turn got in touch with one of the foremost prisoner's rights lawyers, Jere Krakoff, in nearby Pittsburgh.

Krakoff wrote and offered his considerable assistance, which was accepted quickly. As a jailhouse lawyer I was aware of his work, principally the landmark *Tillery v. Owens*[*] case, where the court found, in a conditions-of-confinement case, that double-celling was an element in determining that Western State Correctional Institution at Pittsburgh was being operated in an unconstitutional manner, in violation of the "cruel and unusual" clause of the Eighth Amendment. Given the conservative bent of the judiciary, and the repressive tenor of the times, such a decision was a product of remarkable lawyering, and I realized similar skills were needed in this case.

We went to work.

THE HEARING. When one claims a violation of the First Amendment (regarding freedom of speech, of the press, of religious practice, and to petition the government for redress of grievances) in an institutional misconduct hearing, it may be more fruitful to claim a violation of the Ten Commandments, for it certainly can't go any worse.

Misconduct "hearings" are held before a prison official called a hearing examiner, who is untrained in the law. Prisoners brought before the examiner have no right to legal counsel, and may only be assisted by a willing inmate or staff. All the same, I requested the presence of Jere Krakoff, Esq., to represent me at the hearing, but this was denied out of hand.

---

[*] *Tillery v. Owens,* 907 F. 2d 41 g (3rd Cir. 1990).

Failing this, I presented my written version, arguing that any prison rule must yield to the U.S. and Pennsylvania constitutions, which both had provisions protecting freedom of speech and freedom of the press. No institutional role, I argued, could trump the first article in Pennsylvania's Declaration of Rights, nor the First Amendment to the U.S. Constitution. The hearing examiner disagreed, saying essentially that punishing someone for writing a book, or an article, had "nothing to do with first amendment Rites" (as she spelled rights—a Freudian slip?).

On June 9, 1995, she found me guilty of "engaging in the profession of journalism," writing,

> I find an abundance of evidence exists in the misconduct report that Jamal has been actively engaged in the profession of journalism. He has authored a book known as *Live from Death Row*, he currently writes columns for different newspapers including, *Scoop USA, First Day* and the *Jamal Journal*. In addition Jamal has made taped commentaries for broadcast over National Public Radio. These undisputed facts combine to establish a clear preponderance of evidence that Jamal has been engaged in both the business and profession of journalism.

And with that, on to court.

THE COURT HEARING. When one enters a U.S. court, in a civil action, the basis for action is claimed violation of the U.S. Constitution. Presumably, any prison rule must fall when it violates what has been called the supreme law of the land (the Constitution). But, as we have learned, courts engage in complex, extensive "balancing tests" when state rules and constitutional rights collide. Our case would prove no different.

In many such civil cases, the case opens with what is called a motion for a temporary restraining order or a preliminary injunction (TRO/PI). These motions, although rarely granted, place cases on a fast track, as it usually requires a prompt hearing to test the claims in a case, and to determine the likelihood of success for the side bringing the suit.

In a case where a person is being punished by the state for writing (a form of speech), the First Amendment comes into play, and a violation of the First Amendment requires what courts have called "strict scrutiny" (or closer than usual judicial attention).

The magistrate judge selected to hear the TRO/PI motion was Kenneth J. Benson, a relatively short, mustached, blue-eyed man. The hearing was held in a carpeted, highly air-conditioned courtroom that had once been assigned to former Third Circuit judge Tim Lewis, in the federal building in central, downtown Pittsburgh. Although this was only sixty-one miles from SCI Greene, the Department of Corrections (DOC) chose to bind me in chains and shackles and to temporarily transfer me to the state prison in Pittsburgh for the duration of the TRO/PI Hearings.

SCI Pittsburgh is one of the oldest prisons in the state, over a century old, situated in the city's north side, a collection of mostly black and ethnic neighborhoods, with some areas zoned for industrial use.

Assigned to a pod of nine other cells, I could easily sense the lower degree of tension on Pittsburgh's death row. Men spoke to each other easily, whether guard or inmate. A thirty-something guard with three chevrons on the shoulders of his gray uniform walked up to the door, identified himself, and gave what seemed to be his standard rap: "Here at Pittsburgh the rules are simple; you don't fuck with us—we don't fuck with you. You treat us like men—we'll treat you like a man. If you give us shit—we'll give you shit."

When I discussed this with guys on the pod, they said everybody got the same rap—and I was assured they meant it. As a rule, I was informed, they didn't harass the men, and they didn't set up and "false-ticket" prisoners (give bogus misconduct reports based on lies or concoctions). That accounted for the low level of tension sensed there. For the duration of the civil TRO/PI hearing, this would be where I slept.

Although the civil court session began at nine o'clock in the morning, court began for me shortly before 5 a.m., with a guard opening the pie slot in the door, and placing a tray therein. A quickly swallowed breakfast, a shower, and it was on to the receiving room. There, a dark suit jacket and trousers would be found, and inseams would be stapled to make the slacks stay up.

By a quarter after six, I would be chained, shackled, and seat-belted in the back of a white DOC vehicle, en route to the federal building. The armed DOC guards were a Mutt and Jeff team, one short, the other tall; one driving, the other riding shotgun. The daily escort was a state trooper, in a marked vehicle, with lights flashing through the streets of the northside.

Arriving at the federal building meant being met by at least twelve U.S. Marshals, who took custody of the prisoner. It is difficult to describe the sensation of being "escorted" to and from the courtroom by a phalanx of approximately twelve armed U.S. marshals, but it happened so often (at least four times a day) that it seems it should've become routine.

The magistrate-judge began the day's session by stating, "Good morning, all. Before we begin—and I sincerely want this not to be offensive or insulting to anyone, because no one has given me any reason to believe that there will be any misbehavior or misconduct of any kind—but it is important, I think, that I begin by informing all concerned that I will rigorously enforce… the principle that behavior in court must be appropriate at all times.…

"Consequently it is appropriate for me to say at the beginning that if there is any display of emotion, if there is any outburst, if there is any misbehavior or misconduct, then I will ask that the marshals and court security personnel remove the person who engages in that misconduct. There will be no second chance. Once someone is removed from the courtroom, they will not be allowed back in.…"

Clearly, the tone was set. The warning seemed virtually to expect some form of disruption, but where did this notion come from? Perhaps the marshals, who seemed to anticipate some form of violence, had whispered such suggestions in the judge's ear? It was unclear.

There was a barely audible grumble of resentment, but it passed quickly. Jere, who visited me briefly down in the holding cell area, accompanied by attorney Rachel Wolkenstein, confided that the magistrate had formerly been in the employ of the Department of Corrections, and as such, might not prove impartial in a case where prison officials were named as defendants. Under the Federal Rules of Civil Procedure, a motion could be brought to recuse him, Jere counseled. After some consideration, this option was rejected. He would do.

As I sat shackled in the plaintiff's seat, I looked at the man, seeking a gestalt-like impression of him. Yet he rarely, if ever, looked in my direction. As the civil TRO/PI hearings took place in the same period as the state

PCRA (postconviction) criminal hearings in Philadelphia, I was struck by the apparent differences between this federal magistrate and former common pleas judge Albert F. Sabo. Although both appeared to be relatively short men, Sabo would occasionally glare down at the defendant's bench, his hatred a palpable, tangible thing. Where Benson seemed glacial and professionally distant, Sabo seemed *invested.* His long, baleful, venomous stare, lasting for perhaps a quarter of a minute, was so nasty that I almost prayed someone else took notice of it.

Seeing no such overt expressions of malevolence, I reasoned Benson would be no better nor worse than any other jurist. The hearing began with attorney Leonard I. Weinglass taking the stand. Speaking of the initial reason the suit was filed, Weinglass spoke of learning that letters he wrote to me were seized, opened, held, and delivered in that state to me over a week later. He spoke of his paralegals being unceremoniously turned away from the prison. He spoke slowly, lawyerly, of learning that my letters to him never arrived at his office. He called this succession of events "unprecedented" and "shocking." In nearly thirty years of law practice, Weinglass said, he had never seen such interference with his and his client's legal correspondence.

It was for this very reason, he explained, that paralegals were utilized; to provide a channel of communication that was not compromised.

Under prompting by counsel, Weinglass recounted receiving a letter written by me, explaining that the "State has opened and reviewed your letters/documents… outside of my presence—there isn't even the pretense of client-lawyer confidentiality." This was confirmed when a photocopy of my letter to Weinglass, and this letter to me, turned up in the Commonwealth's file, found during the course of discovery for the case.

Krakoff continued his examination of Weinglass:

Q: When you wrote Mr. Jamal on August 16, 1994, did you send a copy of the letter to prison officials or to the Department of Corrections personnel?

A: No.

Q: Prior to writing Mr. Jamal on August 16, had you authorized prison officials or the Office of General Counsel or anyone within the Governor's Office or the Department of Corrections to read your mail?

A: No, hardly.

Q: Had you authorized any of them to photocopy your mail?

A: No.

Q: Had you authorized them to read the enclosed materials that you sent to Mr. Jamal on the 16th?

A: No.

Q: Had you authorized them to distribute your letters to anybody?

A: No.

Q: Had you authorized them to retain your letters in a file?

A: No.

Q: Did you expect that your letter would not be read by prison officials when you sent it to Mumia Abu-Jamal on the 16th of August?

A: In over twenty years of practicing law, to my knowledge no letter that I had ever written to an inmate had ever been opened or read by prison officials. And I expected the same would apply in this instance.

Informed of this breach of confidentiality, neither counsel nor client could dare write the other, for fear such correspondence would find its way into the hands of the state. Similarly, mail from another of my lawyers, Rachel Wolkenstein, was seized by the DOC, photocopied, and forwarded to various government officials. Her letter, properly marked as legal mail, contained a copy of a witness statement that was helpful to the defense. Her mail, she testified, went the same way as Len's mail: out of the prison, out of the DOC, and to various agencies of government.

Like Weinglass, Wolkenstein, an experienced criminal lawyer found this experience to be "unprecedented." Neither this witness statement, nor a lawyer's memo, were ever returned, nor acknowledged by the state.

The DOC's attorney, David Horwitz, would attempt to mitigate these actions by prison officials by arguing that the seizure of legal papers was justified by the ongoing "investigation" into whether a rule prohibiting prisoners from engaging in a business or profession was being violated.

In this testimony, Horwitz ordered further investigation even as prison officials announced they had more than sufficient evidence to prepare an institutional misconduct as noted in a memo written by Horwitz liaison and grievance officer Diane Baney:

It has recently been brought to our attention that Mumia Abu-Jamal, AM-8335, may be violating Department of Corrections policy by accepting payment for interviews, essays, etc. This information came to light when National Public Radio announced that Abu-Jamal had produced 10 three to four minute commentary radio shows which he would be compensated for in the amount of $150.00 apiece. Upon reviewing his account, it was detected that he had received payment from other publications which went unnoticed and were placed in his account. On 5-16-94, NPR issued a decision that the commentaries would not be run. However, they did indicate that Abu-Jamal would be compensated with a standard "kill fee" of $75.00 each, which is given when work is accepted but not used.

It is clear that Abu-Jamal is in violation of Department of Corrections policy....

This Baney memo, sent to Horwitz, was dated May 18, 1994. Yet the so-called investigation continued for over a year, thus allowing the state to peruse my legal mail, dealing with critical issues involving my state court appeals and conviction, with impunity!

The warden at Huntingdon Prison advised his superiors at the DOC Central Office that sufficient information had been gathered to prove a violation of DOC policy, and therefore further mail scrutiny was unnecessary. Horwitz rejected the warden's recommendation and ordered the "investigation" to continue. He admitted at the TRO/PI hearing that he ordered all legal mail intercepted, had its contents removed and photocopied, and sent copies to his office. He copied these items, and forwarded them to Brian Gottlieb, of the governor's office in Harrisburg, and to Cheryl Young, chief counsel. Horwitz testified he had no idea what these persons did with these items of privileged legal correspondence: [Questions on direct examination by the plaintiff's co-counsel, Timothy O'Brien:]

Q: Now, one thing is clear, Mr. Horwitz, with respect to Mr. Weinglass's letter—to whatever extent you read it—you came to the conclusion, did you not, that only two paragraphs in that entire correspondence could conceivably have anything to do with the investigation that you were conducting, isn't that so?

A: Yes.

Q: With respect to Mr. Jamal's letter to Mr. Weinglass, you came to the conclusion that nothing in that correspondence could be of assistance to you in your investigation; isn't that correct?

A: That's correct.

Q: So you, before you disseminated this information to anyone else, you had concluded that there was privileged material in the correspondence that had nothing whatever to do with your investigation, correct?

A: That is correct.

Q: You also came to the conclusion that there are materials in the correspondence that had to do with Mr. Jamal's defense of the death penalty case; isn't that correct?

A: That is correct.

He further stated that the invasion of the attorney-client correspondent privilege was needed to determine whether lawyers were helping me to evade the business or profession rules.

Another witness who testified for the defendants was James Hassett, the head of Greene's security staff. It was he who actually opened, read, and photocopied legal letters and documents for forwarding to David Horwitz of DOC central office, and who wrote the misconduct report of June 2, 1995, and signed the document. In the report the writer attempted to explain the delay by claiming "the justification for the timing of the misconduct is that the investigation was not completed until May 19, 1995, and that the assembly of the evidentiary materials in presentation format required additional time." In fact, Hassett's explanation fell flat when he testified at the hearing, for there he admitted that Horwitz had prepared the report, not he. And as we have seen from the Baney memo of May 18, 1994, Horwitz had more than enough "evidentiary materials" to show a violation of the business and profession rule—if that was their actual intent—fully a year before!

Thomas Fulcomer, a former warden at Huntingdon and later deputy regional commissioner of the DOC , advanced the department's justification for their punishment for my writing. The DOC, Fulcomer announced with a straight face and an impressive title, was concerned about what he termed the "big wheel syndrome," or the circumstance where a prisoner "persistently and flagrantly violates Department of Corrections policies," and by so doing becomes a countervailing authority in the prison. Folcomer's testimony was a smart one, as it was designed to tickle a judge's core fear and concern when deciding any prison case: security. It had several key problems, however: (a) Hassett, the DOC's point man during the so-called investigation, and Greene's chief of security, could point to no "big wheel" effects at Greene, and when asked about the impact of the publishing of *Live from Death Row* on the prison, admitted that guards had to field questions from prisoners about how they could put out books; and (b) Ted Alleman, a former teacher at Huntingdon, testified that the prison not only had not opposed the publishing of a book by a prisoner there, but had supported and facilitated it. Alleman set up a small publishing outfit to put out a book written by the late Aubrey "Buddy" Martin, a former death row prisoner at Huntingdon. Guess who was the warden at the time? When testimony was provided showing that the prison had actually allowed and assisted in radio interviews of Martin to promote his book, Fulcomer's "big wheel" theory sprang a major leak, for he never utilized this rationale when he was the warden at Huntingdon. Martin was never given a misconduct for this book, nor even threatened in that regard. In fact, he was praised for it.

Martin, serving several life terms stemming from the January 1970 slayings of United Mine Workers leader Joseph "Jack" Yablonsky, along with his wife and daughter, was an accomplished painter and sculptor. Huntingdon officials provided him studiolike space to do his work, and later applauded the publishing of his book, which featured photographs of many of his works of art. In direct examination by Mr. O'Brien, Alleman testified:

Q: Mr. Alleman, after you came to know Mr. Martin, did you become aware of a book that he was writing?

A: Buddy Martin was a student of mine in my class and I knew him for many years, and over a period of time we started to talk about documenting his life story, and that eventually resulted in a book.

Q: And was this book written by him while he was incarcerated at the State Correctional Institution in Huntingdon?

A: Yes.

Q: And when the book was written and while it was being written, was it understood that this book would be published for purposes of sale outside the institution?

A: Yes.

Q: And did you in fact have a publishing company at that point in time?

A: The publishing company was formed in 1985 and it was formed for the purpose of publishing this book.

Q: And was there a contract between yourself and Mr. Martin with respect to the publishing of the book?

A: Yes.

Q: And could you tell the Court whether, in accordance with the contract, if there were sales of the book in question, whether Mr. Martin was to receive any royalties?

A: The contract was that the publishing company would receive the initial revenue from the book up to the point where the costs of publication were covered, and then there was a fifty-fifty split on royalties of the book.

Q: And could you tell the Court, with respect to any of these efforts to involve the media with Mr. Martin regarding the sale of this book, if there was any involvement whatsoever with SCI Huntingdon?

A: The book was partially promoted through talk shows, and the situation was such that I was live on the air with a talk show host from my office at Tower Press, and the institution provided the capability for Buddy Martin to be in a room with a telephone and he was also live on the air and we answered questions from both the host of the show and the general public that would call in with questions....

Q: Now, aside from these particular interviews, was the institution otherwise aware of this book having been written and published?

A: Yes.

Q: Were there any reviews of the book in the local newspapers, for example?

A: Yes.

Q: What were these?

A: Well, the Huntingdon paper did a review, an extensive review of the book, and also I was on a talk show with the local host in the town of Huntingdon.

Q: Okay. And when the book was published, was there any accompanying public opposition to the book by any influential political group?

A: No, not that I know of.

Q: To your knowledge, from the date that the book was published to the date that Mr. Martin passed away, was he ever disciplined for writing the book on the basis that he had violated a rule at SCI Huntingdon prohibiting the conduct of a business or a profession?

A: No, not at all.

So much for the "big wheel" theory. The trial, like all trials, was only tangentially about truth; central to these public performances is power, and how power is defended, articulated, used, and hidden. The state, of course, is used to exercising power, but it is rarely asked to justify its use. And when forced to answer to its use of power behind prison doors, it resorted to the handiest tool in an age-old arsenal—lies. Nonsense about "big wheels" and "security" and "burdens upon staff" were administrative lies designed to obscure a naked political attack against a radical voice that they opposed.

THE MAGISTRATE RULES. Magistrate Judge Benson heard all of the principals testify at hearings in September and October 1995. Lawyers Jere Krakoff and Tim O'Brien battled in raging paper wars against Thomas Halloran of the attorney general's office.

In early June 1996 Benson issued a remarkable *Report and Recommendation** that was sixty-six pages long. Among the sources quoted or cited from were former British prime minister Winston Churchill and U.S. president Abraham Lincoln. He lauds the defendants as "conscientious" and "scrupulous" men, and goes out of his way to describe one of the defendants: "Superintendent Price appeared to this court to be an estimable man in every way" (Benson, 4). He goes on, however, to point out how they lied either on the stand or in sworn depositions, for example:

> [Finding of Fact #64] Superintendent Price's explanation that requests for interviews with plaintiff were denied due to limited staff resources are not entirely credible.... [T]he decisions to deny plaintiff media interviews were first made immediately after plaintiff's decision to publish his book was communicated to defendants

---

**Abu-Jamal v. Price*, No. 95-cv-00618, U.S. District Court, West. Dist., Pa.

[DOC deputy general counsel David] Horwitz and Price. The decisions continued, with a variety of purported justifications, for several months. These purported reasons are demonstrably false. There is no credible evidence that the conditions at the prison were such that security concerns necessitated denying the requests for interviews (Benson, 25, 56).

Despite the court's finding that prison officials put forth "demonstrably false" evidence in support of their actions, Benson found their "big wheel" defense a "reasonable" one, and a "legitimate concern of the institution" (Benson, 45). He therefore upheld the "business or profession" rule as constitutional, and upheld the state's right to open and read privileged legal mail, if that rule was being violated. To this U.S. judge at least, a prison rule was more important than the First Amendment to the U.S. Constitution. If I wrote for publication, I could be punished for doing so, and my legal mail could be rifled. The state was allowed to refuse paralegals if unlicensed, even if no such licensure is now possible. The state was enjoined from denying media interviews, and from disclosing the contents of legal mail to persons outside of the DOC.

After my years of studying civil cases, nothing in the opinion was unexpected to me. Krakoff prepared for appeals.

I resolved to continue writing, no matter what. The district court upheld the main points of the magistrate's recommendation, although expanding the legal mail provisions. We therefore had to go on.

THE COURT OF APPEALS. Although relatively little known in America (quick—name three judges on your circuit court of appeals!) the circuit courts of appeal are the final arbiters of almost every legal conflict in the nation. They are the last court before the U.S. Supreme Court, a body that hears (in the last decade or so) roughly seventy-five cases a year, and as such refuses to hear thousands of cases throughout the court term.

Pennsylvania is the largest state in both population and area in the U.S. Court of Appeals for the Third Circuit. It was to this court, one described as among the most conservative, that the case would be appealed. The panel chosen to hear the case were similarly some of the court's more conservative jurists, judges Richard L. Nygaard, Samuel A. Alito, Jr., and Donald P. Lay, a judge from the Eighth Circuit (the southern and midwestern areas of the country) sitting by designation.

Initially, the Court of Appeals noted the "formidable barrier" to a prisoner's claim that a prison regulation is unconstitutional. That "barrier" is a 1987 U.S. Supreme Court case known as the *Turner* ruling.* In *Turner*, the nation's highest court ordered deference to prison officials in many of their administrative decisions if those decisions were "reasonable." *Turner* established a four-part test as to whether a given prison regulation is reasonable: (1) there must be a valid, rational correlation between the regulation and the government objective at issue; (2) alternative means must exist to exercise the prisoner's asserted right; (3) the impact that accommodation would have on the prison environment, and prison resources generally, must be taken into account; and (4) the existence (or absence) of ready alternatives must be considered.

When the First Amendment is implicated, the regulation, to be approved, must be content-neutral. The Third Circuit panel looked at the appeal through that four-part test, and declared,

> The Superintendent of the S.C.I. Huntingdon was aware of Jamal's writings when Jamal published the Yale article in 1991. An August 16, 1992 letter to the Department noted that Jamal was approaching publishers regarding a book deal. Nevertheless, the Department did not begin to investigate him until May 6, 1994, after National Public Radio sought permission to broadcast Jamal's interviews as regular commentaries. The district court determined that "the investigation was initiated after public complaints concerning Jamal's proposed NPR commentaries were made by the Fraternal Order of Police" and concluded that any delay in the Department's enforcement of the rule was attributable to its investigatory procedures. As a result, it held that Jamal was unlikely to succeed in showing that the action was in retaliation against the content of his writings. WE DISAGREE, AND CONCLUDE THAT THE DISTRICT COURT ERRED (Third Circuit, 10).

---

* *Turner v. Safley*, 482 U.S. 78, 107 S.Ct. 2254 (1987).

Without specifically mentioning the "big wheel" theory, the court's opinion seemed to give this idea little weight, finding the prison could easily accommodate the activities of a writer, because "the record contains no evidence of such a 'ripple effect.' As explained before, Jamal was acting as a journalist from 1986, and the Department did not claim to be burdened by his actions until the Fraternal Order of Police outcry in 1994" (Third Circuit, 12).

The court found the justification for the state's rifling of attorney privileged mail to be pretextual, writing,

> The district court held that the reading and copying Jamal's legal mail was acceptable if the prison officials had "a reasonable suspicion that plaintiff was violating an institutional regulation by engaging in a business or profession in which wittingly or not one or more of his attorneys was complicit." The Department argues in support that its decision to open Jamal's legal mail was necessitated by its investigation into whether Jamal was conducting a business or profession. **THIS ARGUMENT IS NONSENSICAL.** We have difficulty seeing the need to investigate an act that Jamal openly confesses he is doing. Jamal's writing is published, and he freely admits his intent to continue. Continued investigation and enforcement of the rule invades the privacy of his legal mail and thus directly interferes with his ability to communicate with counsel (Third Circuit, 14).

We had won two of the three issues appealed to the court, and lost the third. On the state's barring of paralegals, the circuit court agreed. The court determined that a paralegal was also a social visitor (even though she actually did act as a courier for legal papers from counsel), and paralegal visits were pretexts for what were really social visits.

Thus, the court approved the application of a "rule" that had never been applied elsewhere, and was neither written nor disseminated to the general population. As such, it was as much a new "rule" (that is, one never utilized) as the "business or profession" rule, if not more so. For here was a "regulation" that required satisfaction that was impossible to meet: state licensure. SCI Greene's Superintendent Price wrote a letter to my lawyers, dated February 24, 1995, that stated:

It is not sufficient merely to designate persons as investigators and paralegals unless the identified individuals can produce documentation that they are investigators or credentialed paralegals acting under contract with or as employees of the attorney. Accordingly, please submit copies of the state licensure documents and paralegal credentials under which these individuals conduct business as investigators, or paralegals and such contract or employment documents which verify their relationship with your office as independent contractors or employees.

Krakoff assembled an impressive array of affidavits from another state prison superintendent, secretaries, and other personnel associated with several state legal services programs, which proved these conditions were unprecedented. Indeed, many working paralegals had no such formal training, nor certification, nor degrees. Indeed, at trial the DOC softened its stance, suggesting that some equivalent training would suffice in lieu of credentialing (although Horwitz never communicated this to defense counsel). In fact, in Pennsylvania, no licensure for paralegals is provided.

On this issue, however, the circuit court deferred to the state, reasoning that "visitation—whether it is legal or personal—may jeopardize the security of a facility" (Third Circuit, 15). Thus, the interests of the state prevailed.

AFTER THE COURT DECISION. No case is really over when a court issues its decision. This is especially so in prison civil rights cases, when the winner (a prisoner) goes back into the custody of the loser (the prison). While courts regard prisons as institutions to which they owe deference, prison administrators regard courts as institutions that deserve a barely concealed contempt. They are to courts what pimps are to prostitutes: useful perhaps, but hardly ever respected.

Prison administrators oppose court orders as the work of interlopers, and are sure to undermine such edicts, if not openly. After *Abu-Jamal v. Price* it would seem that if anything is safe, it would be privileged legal mail from lawyers. Several months after the circuit court ruling a letter arrived from a lawyer, with her name, her title (Esquire), her law office address, and the legend "legal mail" stamped on the front of the envelope. The envelope was ripped open and taped shut, and the words "opened by mistake" were scribbled on the envelope face.

Neat, huh?

See with what ease a court's order is made obsolete?

In a nation that claims to be run in strict accordance with the tenets of the Constitution, in which the Constitution and its amendments are termed the "supreme law of the land," what should be the fate of one who violates the "supreme law"?

What about nothing at all?

The prison warden who ordered and participated in some of the unconstitutional acts, and who lied on the stand, James Price, remained prison superintendent, working briefly at SCI Pittsburgh in that role, until his return to Greene, retiring from the post in the spring of 1999. He remains a consultant to the superintendent at Greene.

The deputy commissioner, Thomas Fulcomer, who signed off on some (if not all) of the unconstitutional actions of his subordinates at Huntingdon and Greene, who propounded the preposterous "big wheel" theory in court (while applauding the publication of one of his prisoner's books while warden at SCI Huntingdon) remains western regional deputy commissioner of the DOC.

The Greene head of security, James Hassett, who actually illegally opened, read, and copied legal correspondence from both the court and counsel (and from me to the court and to counsel) was a captain when he testified. He is now a major.

The lesson could hardly be clearer that the DOC regards violations of the so-called supreme law of the land as little more than a mere annoyance.

In such a context, what can the word unconstitutional really mean? That term, which seems to go to the core principles upon which the state rests, is instead a minor obstruction, which pales beside the state's coercive powers. It is, in fact, the civil equivalent to the slap on the wrist given to the offender. In the midst of the hearings I asked Jere to speak to the magistrate-judge about wearing the shackles for hours on end in the courtroom. After several long days in shackles, of sitting in pain, I thought it was time for the court to act. Jere did talk to the judge, who said it was out of his hands. It was a decision made by the marshals, and he had no say in the matter.

To sit in pain, for hours, for days, in a U.S. courtroom during a so-called hearing to determine if someone's civil rights were violated months before is an exercise in Kafkaesque absurdity. Is this not an admission of judicial impotence for something that happens right there in the courtroom? "Out of my hands, pally."

Indeed, how can any court that draws its authority and jurisdictional powers from the Constitution decide, in any case, that any administrative regulation, which contemplates punishment for exercise of one's constitutional rights, is superior to the Constitution?

In such a context, how can the constitution be deemed to be anything other than irrelevant? Courts are inherently conservative institutions that loathe change, and defer to the status quo. That is, they tend to perpetuate existing power relations, even though their rhetoric perpetuates the illusion of social equality. In many instances, courts barely conceal their hostility to prisoner litigants, as evinced by increasingly restrictive readings of rights raised in the courts these days.

In that sense then, *Abu-Jamal v. Price* was different from some cases, yet strikingly similar to others.

From death row, this is Mumia Abu-Jamal.

Mother Loss

RELATIVELY TALL, mountainous cheekbones, dimples like doughnuts, and skin the color of Indian corn, she left life in the South for what was then the promised land, "up Nawth." Although she lived, loved, raised a family, and worked for over half her life "up Nawth," the soft lyrical accents of her southern tongue never really left her. Words of single syllable found a new one in her mouth, often rising on the second syllable—Keith became "Ke-eeth," child became "chile," and her reedy, lengthy laughter lit up a room like a legal holiday.

She and her children lived in the PJs, the projects, and it wasn't until years later when we were grown that we understood we had lived in poverty, for our mother made sure our needs were met. She was a gentle woman who spoke well of most folk, if at all, but was like a lioness when one of her children was attacked. In the early 1960s, when her daughter got caught up in a neighborhood fracas that boiled out of control, she snapped a broomstick in two, whipped open a path down the block to where her daughter stood paralyzed by terror, grabbed her, and whipped her way back home. Only when she was safely back indoors was it found that she had been slashed while outdoors. She never noticed, so powerful was her love for her daughter.

Deep rivers of loving strength flowed through her. It is my belief that a mother's love is the foundation of every love that follows. It is the primary love relationship, the first that humans experience, and as such a profound influence on all subsequent and secondary relationships in life. It is a love relationship that surpasses all reason: perhaps that's why I thought she would live forever, that this woman who carried me, my brothers, and a sister, would never know death.

For over thirty years she smoked cigarettes, Pall Malls—which she called "pellmells"—and Marlboros, but I still thought she would live forever. When she died of emphysema while I was in prison, it was like a lightning bolt to the soul. Never during my entire existence had there been a time when she was not there. Suddenly, on a cold day in February, her breath ended, and her sweet presence, her wise counsel, was gone forever. To see one's mother die while imprisoned, to see her lifeless form while held in shackles.

From the passing of one's mother to memories of one's father, in a place infamous for its fever of fatherlessness, and, hence, its...

Father Hunger

IT HAS BEEN OVER THREE DECADES since I have looked into his face, but I find him now, sometimes hidden, in the glimpse of a mirror.

He was short of stature, shorter than I at ten years, fully, smoothly bald, with a face the color of walnuts.

He walked with a slight limp, and smoked cigars, usually Phillies.

Although short, he wasn't slight but was powerfully built, with a thickness, not a fatness, of form. His voice was deep, with the accents of the South wrapped around each word, sweet and sticky like molasses. His words often tickled his sons, and they tossed them among themselves like prizes found in the depths of Crackerjack boxes, words that were wondrous in their newness, their rarity, their difference from all others heard.

"Boys—cut out that tusslin', heah me?" And the boys would stop their rasslin', their bellies near bursting with swallowed, swollen laughter, the word vibrating, sotto voce, barely heard, in their throats—"Tusslin'?!?"

"Tusslin'—tusslin'— tusslin'—tusslin'!"

"Tusslin'!"

For days—for weeks—these silly little boys had a new toy, and with this one word could reduce the others to teary-eyed fits of fall-on-the-floor laughter.

"Tusslin'!"

He was a relatively old man when he seeded those sons, and because of his age of over half a century, he was openly affectionate in a way not usual for a man of his time. He kissed them, dressed them, and taught them, by example, that he loved them. He talked with them. And walked, and walked, and walked with them.

"Dad—I wanna ride!" I whined.

"It ain't good for you to ride so much, boy. Walkin' is good for ya. It's good exercise for ya!"

Decades later, I would hear that echo in one of my sons, and my reply would echo my father's.

His eyes were the eyes of age, so discolored by time they seemed bluish, but there was a perpetual twinkle of joy in them, of love and living.

He lived just over a decade into this son's life, and his untimely death from illness left holes in the souls of his sons.

Without a tether, I sought and found father figures, like Black Panther captain Reggie Schell, and Black Panther Party defense minister Huey P. Newton—and indeed the Black Panther Party itself, which in this period of utter void taught me, fed me, and made me part of a vast and militant family of revolutionaries. Many good men and women became my teachers, my mentors, and my examples of a revolutionary ideal—Zayd Malik Shakur, murdered by police when Assata was wounded and taken; Geronimo ji jaga (aka Pratt) who commanded the L.A. chapter of the BPP with distinction, and defended the party from deadly state attacks, himself a political prisoner who, because of the state's frame-up and judicial repression, has been separated from his family and children for a quarter of a century.*

---

*A May 29, 1997, decision by Orange County Supervisor Court judge Evert Dickey vacated Geronimo ji jaga Pratt's conviction and sentence of life imprisonment. Geronimo was released on June 10, 1997, after twenty-seven years in prison for a crime he did not commit. A federal civil rights lawsuit is now pending vs. the FBI (including special agent Richard W. Held) and the Los Angeles Police Department, which alleges civil rights violations arising out of the use of the infamous COINTELPRO program to setup and falsely imprison Geronimo.

Here, in this restrictive place of fathers without their children and men who were fatherless, one senses and sees the social costs of that loss.

Those unloved find it virtually impossible to love, and those who were fatherless find themselves alienated and at war with their own communities and families.

My own sons were babies when I was cast into this hell. Neither letters, cards, nor phone calls could heal the wounds that they and their sisters suffered during the long, lonely years of separation.

Here, in this manmade hell, I find young men bubbling with bitter hatreds and roiling resentments against absent fathers, several who have taken to the odd habit of calling this writer "Papa," certainly high irony when one notes this writer is himself an absent father (and now absent grandfather).

Perhaps conscious of this irony, I resisted the nickname, until I could no longer. I realized that I lived amid a generation of young men drunk not only with alienation but also with father hunger. I had the Black Panther Party; who did they have? Here, they have Delbert Africa, Geronimo ji jaga, Chuck Africa, Mike, Ed, and Phil Africa, Dr. Mutulu Shakur, Sundiata Acoli, and other oldheads, like myself.

I realized that I resented being "Papa" to young men I didn't know, while being denied the opportunity to be a present father to the children of my flesh and my heart, by the state's banishment.

I was also in denial.

For who was the "oldhead" they were calling? Certainly not I?

It took a trip, a trek to the shiny, steel, burnished mirror on the wall, where I found my father's face staring back at me, to recognize the real. I am he—and "they" are me.

From death row, this is Mumia Abu-Jamal.

IN EARLY JANUARY 1992 the Reverend Muhammad I. Kenyatta, hobbled by heart disease and painful diabetes, let go of life after only forty-seven years of an extraordinary spate of service, activism, and legal scholarship.

Kenyatta, who had the dexterity to be both a political opponent and a personal friend, filled his relatively short life with titles reflecting accurately a caring and brilliant spirit: ordained minister before puberty, civil rights and black economic development activist, onetime mayoral candidate of Philadelphia, law professor, and scholar.

If you asked him which one he preferred, he'd probably stifle a dimpled chuckle, and say, "None, Mu. Just say 'Grandpop.'"

In the 1960s and '70s, "Mo" Kenyatta staged demonstrations at white, wealthy inner-city churches, demanding "reparations" and neighborhood accountability, in scenes that sent shock waves through white Protestant laity and clergy, but which had their impetus more in the biblical example of Jesus flaying the moneylenders of the Temple than the zeitgeist of the militant 1960s, for Mo had a knack for making his faith merge with the moment.

In an article penned several months before his death, Mo wrote of the impact of the late Justice Thurgood Marshall, who had just retired from the U.S. Supreme Court, and what that meant to him as a black man, and a black lawyer in the United States, especially with regard to the 1954 case known as *Brown v. Board of Education* declaring racial segregation unconstitutional:

> The Negro people, personified in one Mr. Thurgood Marshall, had
> won a major victory in our quest for freedom. No, it did not change

very much very fast.... We were still poor. But the law of the land was, we now believed, on our side, at last. And we began to believe more in ourselves. Thurgood Marshall, a black lawyer, the product of a black college (Lincoln University) and a black law school (Howard University Law School) had won. Thus, we had won. Thurgood Marshall amplified our faith in ourselves and in our ability to advocate for ourselves.... Thurgood Marshall helped give us hope. Just as crucial to the civil rights movement of the 50s and 60s as our faith in ourselves was our expectation of progressive change. It has often been noted that great social revolutions are born of great expectations. Crushed under the heels of violent, systematic, legally sanctioned repression since the 1870s and the collapse of Reconstruction, we the ex-slaves seemed doomed to never be truly free. For most of us, our own solace became religion and the promise of freedom in the great Beyond.... But Marshall revived the language of the law. He joined the moral righteousness of our cause with the state-sanctioned rectitude of the law. Thirty-two times as a NAACP lawyer, he argued before the Supreme Court, the highest tribunal of the land. Twenty-nine amazing times, he walked away with victory.... Thurgood Marshall taught us hope.

I think often of Marshall when pondering what to tell my students about law and why law matters.

I remember what America was like before the revolution in law led by Marshall and his cohorts. And then I know. I must say to my students that law, real law, is first and foremost a labor of love.[*]

When the men in the death row cages told me of Marshall's passing, I thought of his staunch opposition to the death penalty, and of Mo's touching article noting Marshall's retirement.

Kenyatta was an associate law professor at the University of Buffalo, New York, where he lived with his brilliant wife, Mary, at the time of his death.

---

[*]Muhammad Kenyatta, July 22, 1991. Source unknown.

There were many who remembered him with warm affection, with his engaging manner, his audacious militance, his signal intelligence, his pervasive love, including the writer.

It is fitting that "Mo" fill this space with his reflections of the late, great Justice.

From death row, this is Mumia Abu-Jamal.

IF WALLACE WOULD DARE to run for president in Philadelphia, we four black North Philly teens would dare to protest—in his white honky face, if need be. So we did, Eddie, Alvin, Dave, and I. We began by boarding the Broad Street subway and riding to the end. Four Afros amid a sea of blonds, brunettes, and redheads, entering the citadel of urban white racist sentiment to confront the Alabaman.

We must've been insane. We strolled into the stadium, four lanky dark string beans in a pot full of white, steaming limas. The band played "Dixie." We shouted, "Black power, Ungowa, black power!" They shouted, "Wallace for president! White power!" and "Send those niggers back to Africa!" We shouted "Black power, Ungowa!" (Don't ask what Ungowa means. We didn't know. All we knew was that it had a helluva ring to it.) "Black power!" They hissed and booed. We stood up in our seats and proudly gave the black power salute. In answer, we received dubious gifts of spittle from those seated above. Patriots tore American flags from their standards and hurled the bare sticks at us. Wallace, wrapped in roars of approval, waxed eloquent. "When I become president, these dirty, unwashed radicals will have to move to the Sov-ee-yet Union! You know, all throughout this campaign these radicals have been demonstrating against George Corley Wallace. Well, I hope they have the guts to lay down in front of my car. I'll drive right over 'em!" The crowd went wild.

Helmeted cops came and told us we had to leave. We protested but were escorted out, perhaps a little relieved. Outside, Eddie, Alvin, Dave, and I saw a few other blacks from Temple University and a group of young whites, also thrown out of the rally. We gathered at the bus station to get on the "C" for North Philly. But before we could board, we were attacked by a group of white men. One of them had a lead and leather slapjack. Out-armed and outnumbered, we fought back, but four teens were no match for eight to ten grown men.

I was grabbed by two of them, one kicking my skull while the other kicked me in the balls. Then I looked up and saw the two-toned, gold-trimmed pant leg of a Philly cop. Without thinking, and reacting from years of brainwashing, I yelled, "Help, police!" The cop saw me on the ground being beaten to a pulp, marched over briskly—and kicked me in the face. I have been thankful to that faceless cop ever since, for he kicked me straight into the Black Panther Party.

From death row, this is Mumia Abu-Jamal.

*To limit the press is to insult a nation;
to prohibit reading of certain books is to declare
the inhabitants to be either fools or slaves.*

—CLAUDE-ADRIEN HELVETIUS,
FRENCH PHILOSOPHER (1715–1771)

AS MERGERS AND ACQUISITIONS reassign the power over media outlets into fewer and fewer hands, the multiple mirrors of the world coalesce into an almost singular image, creating less a mirror than a mirage, less a reflection than a refraction, a distortion that brings to mind the fun house of a carnival, where short people appear tall, and fat people seem to be painfully thin.

As a youth working as a news assistant in a major Philadelphia radio station, I had long and interesting discussions with the boss, a tall, thin, barrel-voiced Scot who was a wiry veteran of the news biz. He seemed genuinely curious about the tall, lanky Negro that he had hired, perhaps as curious as the youth himself was.

"Why do you want to be a reporter?" he asked.

"I wanna inform the people of important events in their lives," or something equally as lame.

"Do you know what reporters are?" he asked.

"Sure, reporters are people who give the news to the people," I responded, somewhat exasperated at the question.

"No—reporters are a pack of dogs fighting over who's gonna piss on a fire hydrant!"

He leaned back, clasped his hands behind the back of his head, and burst into a deep belly laugh.

I laughed too, more in dumb imitation than anything else, for the joke (if it was one) passed over my head like a Sputnik satellite.

I didn't get it.

It took years of living for me to "get it." The boss was telling me a terrible truth. Of course, I did some reporting for several years before I worked at the radio station, but I sincerely doubt whether I listed it on my résumé. I performed a variety of jobs in connection with the preparation of a newspaper called *The Black Panther*. I wrote articles, prepared articles, typed, justified, punched out headlines, did layout, and generally did anything I could to assist the editor, Judi Douglass, and the Minister of Culture, Emory Douglass, to prepare the paper for printing.

I learned the craft quite well, except for one thing: I never learned how to kowtow to state power. I wrote and reported, not from the perspective of the privileged, not from the position of the established, but from the consciousness of oppression, and from the awareness of resistance. I joined the craft from the pool of the oppressed, and worked in a community of revolutionaries fighting to, in Huey P. Newton's words, establish "revolutionary black political power." Needless to say, one does not acquire such a perspective in journalism school.

I was not stupid, and did not add this brand of on-the-job training to my job application. Yet I brought my old skills to the new job, and learned some new skills while there. From the old job, I learned perspective; from the new job, I learned phrasing, brevity, clarity, and formatting. From the old job came writing skills that captured the voice of the downtrodden, and from the new job came a knowledge of the power and potential of radio.

Those skills served me well in every job I encountered thereafter, and in some measure contributed to my departure.

Working on black radio was a dream—except for the money. The relatively meager pay was a factor in accepting a job in "white" radio. The managers of the station listened to the demo tape, and gave me the job. There was just one problem, according to my new station manager: "Mumia, we like your sound. You've got great delivery! We just think your name is… uh… uhhh… We beam our signal to South Philly, the Great Northeast, parts of Kensington, and what not, see? We kinda think your name is just a… ahh… a bit too ethnic for our audience, you understand?"

I took the job for money to help the family, not for the joy of "informing the people" (although I was committed to doing the job well), so I worked with the news director to find an air name that fit the market. I became William Wellington Cole. What my bosses did was to deradicalize and to deracialize their only African-American journalist and radio reporter in order to not disturb the delicate sensibilities of their white listeners. As this "white" (dare we call it "ethnic"?) radio station paid more for a weekend midnight-to-six skeleton shift than "black" radio's Monday-through-Friday morning block, the shift became something I could tolerate.

I used my white voice, but I kept my black soul. For several years prior to joining professional radio, I subscribed to United Nations Radio News Service, and through them had access to audio from representatives of the world's major liberation movements—the PLO (Palestine Liberation Organization), SWAPO (South West African Peoples Organization), and the like. Rarely were these voices heard on America's commercial networks, which served mostly as megaphones for American political and class elites. Rarer still would these voices be heard on a white, "ethnic" top-forty radio station. Well, William Wellington Cole, 95 PEN News, would make sure those voices of people's movements for national liberation would be heard, for wasn't this news? For many it was new information, was it not?

As in the case of international news, why not the same in local news?

Through numerous contacts in the progressive and radical movements, it was possible to cover press conferences or demonstrations from a wide range of social change communities. These voices too would enrich the usually bland "from city hall today" approach to my news coverage. This required a bottom-up, as opposed to a top-down, perspective on the news.

As one example, while working a full shift on Saturday, I took my lunch break to jump on my ten-speed, pedaled up to the site of the continuing police-MOVE confrontation, and obtained some audio from MOVE member Chuckie Africa, raging at the armed presence of hundreds of cops, arrayed for imminent attack on his home and family. As soon as I got back to the station, I cut several pieces of audio from our brief interview, and listeners to the station would hear not only the voices of then-mayor Frank Rizzo and ex-police commissioner James O'Neill, but also the angry voice of Chuck Africa, railing at the de facto occupation of his neighborhood by the armed forces of the state.

Management was not pleased.

Instead of rewarding me for my drive and initiative, I received a call from my rather irate boss, who berated me for my story selection:

"Jamal, I was listening to ya in the car yesterday—and Jeezus H. Keerist! I couldn't believe my ears.

"What wuz wrong? Mumia—Chuckie Africa?—I mean, here? Maybe that was O.K. at [W] 'HAT, but—here?"

"Well, look, Bruce—it's a continuing controversy, right? Doesn't the public deserve to hear all sides?"

"When are you gonna get it, Mumia?"

"Get what, Bruce?"

"When are you gonna get it that MOVE isn't news?"

What the mayor ate last night at a cocktail party, on the other hand, was news, it seemed. In the hothouse atmosphere of Philadelphia media, what was news was what the majority said was news. The rest was merely dismissable gossip. When the mayor called a press conference to announce some new scheme, this wasn't political grandstanding but news— real news. When people organized in staunch and principled resistance to state measures, that wasn't news. I *didn't* get it.

Wasn't news really new information, not just that which we are conditioned to seeing, hearing, and reading? Is news just that which comforts us, which reassures us, or which cutely amuses us? Or can it be that which expands us, which challenges us, or even which upsets us?

Looking at that army assembling its weapons of war against that tiny band of rebels called MOVE, I could not accept the notion that their voices, no less than the voices of Zedi Labib-Tursi of the PLO, or Theo Bin-Gurerab of SWAPO, were not newsworthy. In my news judgment, they were deeply worthy of reportage, and their perspective had to be heard. So I continued my bike-ride lunch breaks up to the MOVE house on Thirty-third and Powelton Avenue, to gather audio.

So William Wellington Cole brought listeners the voices and perspectives of resistance, through interviews with Delbert Africa, Merle Africa, Chuck Africa, the Philadelphia representative of the ANC, various UN diplomats assigned to a number of liberation movements, and the like.

It was not a total surprise, then, when I got a call for a meeting with my boss (the news director) and his boss, the station manager.

"Jamal, uh—we're gonna hafta letcha go—"

"Whoa—why, man?"

"Well, you just don't have the—uh—"

"—commitment—"

"Yeah, the commitment that we like to see at 'PEN."

"Commitment? Whachu mean, 'commitment?' I work hard; I get fresh audio; I—"

"Yeah, yeah—we know, Jamal. It's just that, uh—we don't think you—"

"—uh, fit—"

"Yeah, fit our top-forty format here."

"Yeah, Jamal—but hey, it shouldn't be hard for a guy like you to land a gig. Hell, if I had your pipes—why aren't you workin' at CBS or somethin'?"

It was the smoothest, greasiest firing I had ever experienced; being let go while your talent is praised by your firers. Utterly bizarre.

But of course I knew. I hadn't agreed with my bosses' idea of what was or wasn't "news." To challenge that concept is "to lack real commitment."

Or, put quite another way, I was committed; but not to their view of how the world should be projected, reported on, and described.

In America, censorship may often hide in the face of the fired person, whose perspective may not be in accord with those who own the enterprise, or those who influence the owners. Every journalist learns on which side his bread is buttered, and s/he either accepts this form of status quo or learns how to abide by this unwritten edict. For in a capitalist state, organized under the illusion of freedom of the press, the power to compel compliance lies not in some faceless, anonymous board of state censors (at least, not anymore) but in the power of the purse. The terror that grips the very vitals of the journalist is that wielded by the owners: the power to fire.

In a state where capital is the measure of one's worth, joblessness sends shivers down the spines of the mighty. Thus does capital discipline its wordsmiths; thus do the rulers control the scribes.

OTHER FORMS OF CONTROL. Given the wide variety of formats that exist within the radio universe in a big city, and the intense loyalty that may be engendered on the basis of station identification, each station can be a world unto itself, an omniverse, where listeners are introduced as children, grow into adolescents, mature into adults, age, and die.

Thus, when one changes employment and enters a new format, s/he enters a new world of listeners that may not have the slightest idea of one's life or work in another radio format at another station.

Moving into the news business at WUHY-FM was entering a new world, one whiter in both staff and listenership than previously experienced (with the exception of the weekend, midnight-to-six existence of William Wellington Cole). This station, one of several noncommercial stations in the city, was known for its extended periods of classical (European) music format, and its NPR network programming. As such, its listenership was quite different from those to whom I had previously been exposed. It was through that listenership that I heard an interesting offer.

A caller began the drama with a compliment: "Mr. Jamal, I've been listening to you for some time, and I really think you're quite good."

"Thank you, sir; I really appreciate the compliment."

"I didn't call merely to compliment you, I have an offer to make."

"Oh, really?"

"Mr. Jamal, have you ever given any thought to working in television?"

With such an opening, a meeting was required to explore the offer. The gentleman making the offer and I met for lunch several days later and discussed the proposal. He explained the station was interested in paying $35,000 annual starting salary, with ample increments to come. The offer, however, was conditional: I had to change my name; and I had to cut my hair. I thanked him for his offer, said I had to discuss this with my wife, and told him we would give the proposal due consideration. Once again, I was asked to deracinate myself; to present a happy, safe, false face. If my name was Jim Miklejewski, or Richard Niedermayer, it wouldn't be necessary to change it, as this isn't seen as a problem. Jamal wasn't too "ethnic," it was too black. I had talent, he was saying (in essence), but I was too black. "Whiten up!"

I declined his offer.

Censorship is a tool utilized to preserve the status quo, and to "'protect'" people from what is deemed uncomfortable social realities. Censorship, in a white supremacist state, creates an abnormal norm, and disappears that which does not conform. In such a context, blacks are sweet, happy darkies who don't discomfit white folks. They wear their blackness as a marker of shame, not a badge of pride. Good Americanized blacks are de-Africanized, and deradicalized. As ever, censorship is made real in the demands of the marketplace, and the marketplace mellows, homogenizes, and whitens its commodities (like TV performers) in order to attract audiences, to make more capital.

There is another way that censorship expresses itself in the business of media, which is less overt but perhaps more powerful in its effect. This may be seen in the role performed by editors.

Most editors would rebel at the very notion that their work is even remotely censorial. In the ideal role, editors clarify the reporter's work, cutting, honing the message that a reporter seeks to impart. There is, however, a secondary job performed by editors in the field. As management, they suggest, guide, and order the production of the final product. Thus, by indirection or by edict, they determine what is to be reported, and thus what is news.

This was seemingly the case when, as a reporter/producer at a public radio station in Philadelphia, I was assigned to the housing beat. After I had performed in that role for some time, my editor, while not formally changing my beat, assigned me to the unofficial cop beat. This meant my interviewing the police commissioner, an alleged hero cop (who reportedly achieved his position and prominence by beating handcuffed prisoners), and covering a city hall protest by several thousand cops. The police demo story made its way to the NPR network show *All Things Considered.* Perhaps the editors felt that my reporting on police needed to somehow be balanced by positive puff pieces. Perhaps he had been ordered to do it by his bosses. I don't know. Yet, as a professional I did the three pieces, even though I can't say I enjoyed doing them. They seemed to smack of a certain propaganda, and implicit within the assignment lay the assumption that I, as a reporter and as an urban African American, somehow needed teaching about the "real" nature of police.

I submit that no one knows the real nature of police better than the beleaguered inner city, for it sees their real faces. Anyone who was beaten by cops knows their true nature far better than some yuppie who has based his insights on accepted reading materials, instead of lived experience.

Yet this form of "soft censorship" occurs every day, especially when African Americans penetrate predominately white media environments. At public radio, other than the secretary and a few brothers in the mail room, I was the only black person on staff. In such a milieu, acquiescence with the status quo creates its own form of censorship: the censorship of silence. Indeed, censorship is the offspring of a power relation, for the powerful have an intrinsic interest in silencing the expressions of discontent by the powerless. At the time of my arrest, police swooped down on the station to review my tapes, in search of statements that they thought would be incriminating. They found nothing. They were undoubtedly searching for taped sentiments that could be used to justify my conviction, my sentencing, and my death, thus using my work for the ultimate form of censorship—death.

SOME THINGS CONSIDERED. When National Public Radio commissioned a series of my commentaries in the spring of 1994, it became embroiled in a firestorm of controversy. The FOP and former U.S. senator and presidential candidate Robert Dole (R-KS) raked the public network with acidic criticism, and the day before scheduled airing, the show was canceled. Dole's public threat to cut NPR's Corporation for Public Broadcasting (CPB) government funding unquestionably contributed to that decision.

It is clear that, in my case, the title *All Things Considered* did not mean "all." I confess to having felt sheer joy when the opportunity arose to return to NPR, a network where I worked as a very young reporter. I filed pieces with *All Things Considered* back then and did commentaries about life in Philadelphia, and about police-community relations in particular. But my joy at returning to NPR was short-lived and shattered when my new commentaries for *All Things Considered* were canceled in May 1994. *All Things Considered* obviously didn't include anything I had to say about the realities of life on death row and in prison.

The sort of information I would have brought to listeners once a month has not been replaced. I haven't heard any kind of commentary on NPR that reflects the awful reality of life in prison or on death row. It has been a big hole in NPR's reporting. Not only was I and Prison Radio harmed by NPR's censorship of my commentaries, but the listener was denied a perspective that remains missing from the airwaves.

It is very clear that NPR, under political and police pressure, acted as an agent of the state to extinguish my voice. This is an attempt to silence me, and we must work to defend First Amendment rights—not just my own but those of all people, of youth, of NPR listeners, and of all those who truly want to hear all things considered.

Others have written of this event at length, of *All Things Considered*'s courting this commentator, the subsequent cave-in in the midst of cop pressure, and their later quaint critique of the final product as somehow beneath their usual air quality. Indeed, nothing could be farther from the truth. Similarly, the network seemed to suggest that there was something unseemly about the airing of work done by a man under the death sentence, and appealing from that sentence. Implicit within that critique was the idea that such extraordinary coverage might contribute to sentiment that the sentence be lifted. Interestingly, NPR never questioned the propriety of hiring, and airing the work of, Louisiana lifer and prison journalist Wilbert Rideau, editor of the award-winning prison magazine *The Angolite*. Rideau, subsequent to the Abu-Jamal-NPR flap, aired several lengthy pieces recorded at "The Farm," as the ancient penitentiary named Angola is colloquially known. Rideau is on the far side of a life sentence, following a murder conviction over a quarter of a century ago for a stick-up shooting. He has been fighting unsuccessfully for a commutation for several years.

NPR's *Fresh Air* aired several of his pieces nationally in the aftermath of the Abu-Jamal controversy.

Why was it right to air Rideau's work and wrong to air Jamal's?

The difference lies in content.

Rideau's work, while expertly rendering the ennui, hopelessness, and loss engendered by a soul-killing place like Angola, concentrated on institutional and personal events at the former plantation.

My work was broader, more global, and far more a systematic critique than an institutional one. It was also overtly political in its analysis of the system.

In a word, Rideau, perceived as nonpolitical, was safer.

Rarely, if ever, does the establishment media attack systems. More often than not it assumes the viability of the existing system, utilizing the "bad apple" theory to limit, narrow, and canalize its critiques. This deep level of acceptability, this standardized assumption that state and social systems are at base OK, well functioning, and nonproblematic, contributes to a kind of willful blindness on the part of the media's portrayal of the state's organizational rules. Thus, the media functions as the ideological and propaganda support of the state, as it assumes its fundamental validity and virtually never opposes its organizational objectives, no matter how wrongheaded, stupid, or evil.

I invite any reader to review the contemporary reporting on figures like Malcolm X (Malik El-Shabazz) or even Martin Luther King, figures who launched systematic critiques of the status quo. During their lifetime most era reporting depicted both men as virtual enemies of the state (i.e., the status quo), until it was found more in the interest of the state to deploy one against the other, as in the age-old false dichotomy between the good black vs. the bad black.

Consider the reportage of police violence against so-called citizens, and you will conclude that such events are episodic rather than systemic. In any such account, the political tag line is religiously elicited that the problem is only a "few bad apples," or the equally hopeful litany that "the vast majority of men and women of this department/agency/office/unit *et al.* are good, decent, fair, conscientious," etc. While this may be so, how is this known? What data proves this conclusion?

There is no U.S. Department of Justice data base available to research this, or related questions of the degree, or rate, or severity of police violence against the citizenry.

A number of organizations have come together to publish *Stolen Lives: Killed by Law Enforcement* (2d ed., New York: Stolen Lives Project, 1999), a compilation of cases of over 2,000 citizens killed by cops, in over forty-five states and in the District of Columbia. The Stolen Lives Project, a joint undertaking of the October Twenty-second Coalition to Stop Police Brutality, Repression, and the Criminalization of a Generation; the National Lawyers Guild; and the New York–based Anthony Baez Foundation,* provides a state-by-state breakdown, over a ten-year period, of men, women, and children who were killed by officers of the state in their homes, in the

---

*The October Twenty-second Coalition National Office, P.O. Box 2627, New York, NY 10009, (212) 477-8062; National Lawyers Guild, 8124 W. 3rd St. Suite 201, Los Angeles, CA 90048, (323) 658-8627; Anthony Baez Foundation, 6 Cameron Place, Bronx, NY 10453, (718) 364-2879.

streets, and in the prisons. A vast majority of the victims are black or brown people, members of national minorities. The project draws its data from isolated press reports, lawyer's reports, and family reports. Clearly, the project lacks the database source that could cover a substantial number of other such cases. In virtually every reported case, however, the state or local prosecutor failed to prosecute the killers, no matter how egregious the killing.

What the press treats (or fails to treat) as episodic is systematic and national in scope, affecting the lives of thousands, if not tens of thousands, of citizens, whose lives and deaths are treated as unworthy of sustained media attention.

Are these "isolated" cases, a mountain in appearance but a molehill in substance? This is a fitting question for the media to resolve, but it will never be done as the media is presently constituted. For if its core function is to support the status quo the media will engage in no meaningful effort to destabilize it. Episodic, not systematic, critiques ensure a censorship of reality occasioned by institutional myopia, which microanalyzes instances while ignoring big-picture trends.

Consider the *Stolen Lives* report. What would be the national media response if these 2,000-plus stolen lives were cases involving young, white middle-class college students, or lawyers, or yuppies? An honest appraisal informs us, unequivocally, that in such an instance every front page of every major periodical would blare in headlines "National Epidemic," "Police State Approaching," "Killer Cops Get Away with Murder!" and the like. Reporting would be global, interpretive, and deep-layered.

Well, then—what, pray tell, is the difference? The answer tells us all we need to know about the institutional, race and class-based bias that pervades the media as it daily determines a life's social worth, and in a heartbeat, in a blink of an eye, clinically determines black life, Hispanic life, Samoan life, and poor "white trash" life as worthless. Thus we all are willing consumers of a product that practices censorship by class and caste while essentially disappearing the suffering and loss of the "lower classes."

THE FOURTH ESTATE. To a considerable degree, American discourse on politics, power and the state is heavily influenced by the early impact of the French Revolution on national consciousness. When we speak of left-wing or right-wing ideological perspectives, we are utilizing forms that arose in the French National Assembly during the Revolution, which referred to revolutionary, anti-royal delegates, who assembled on the left, and more conservative, monarchical elements of the assembly, who massed along the right side of the building.

Similarly, pre-revolutionary France was seen as composed of three estates: the king, the nobility and the church. At the time of the Revolution, when the wealthy bourgeoisie were vying for respect and representation commensurate with their economic influence and market power (largely as a consequence of Haitian and African slavery), they produced provocative newspapers and journals to mobilize popular antimonarchical sentiment in support of their establishment as a source of significant social power. These newspapers and journals became such powerful tools of radical organization that they were seen as a fourth estate: a part of the very process by which government functions in the new alignment. It is important to remember, however, that the press of the time was more reformist than revolutionary, and designed to meet the limited objectives of its bourgeois owners, not to topple a throne nor to spark a wide-ranging revolution. As in many cases, the Revolution outran those who sparked it, because of serious, unresolved contradictions and conflicts of the underlying social order.

That said, the essential role of the media became one that is inherently and profoundly conservative, in keeping with the class interests of its owners. It is not its job, therefore, to rock the boat, but merely to occasionally splash water.

SELF-CENSORSHIP. The form of censorship perhaps the most difficult to gauge is that which governs the self. By a form of conditioning premised upon negative response from one's editors or managers, journalists learn to stay away from certain topics, for fear they'll elicit a repeated negative response. This sensitivity is also seen as a way to protect one's job.

Peer response is equally, if not more, important, seen in the current phenomenon of pack journalism, as when hordes of reporters descend on a given personality or celebrity. That peer response was also critical to the understanding of the dog analogy advanced by the news director in informal discussion with the young news aide. Journalists in a newsroom, like B.

F. Skinner's rats in a maze of psychological testing, learn which routes lead to the "cheese." Conversely, they learn which paths are open, and which offer nasty, unpleasant, or uncomfortable lines of inquiry. To be tagged as "political" or "radical" can spell the dead end of the maze.

To avoid these ruts, self-censorship becomes rote, and a way of professional survival.

THE PRESS AS BUSINESS. At bottom, the media is a multibillion dollar industry that serves the interests of the owners, investors, and stockholders, as in every other industry. So-called public interest is, at best, purely incidental.

Profit is the objective, and the market is the arbiter. Consider the lowest-common-denominator form of programming and publishing that permeates media today.

As such, the reporter serves those interests, or (as reporter) none. As the old axiom goes, "the only free press is for those that own one."

In this context, reporters are mere products, purchased personalities packaged for the attainment merely of profit, and, as with any product, they are ultimately expendable.

It is a business, and the business of every business is capital.

That is how I came to be known as "talented," but "expendable."

From death row, this is Mumia Abu-Jamal.

THE VISAGE AND FORM of the Reverend Accelynne Williams, seventy-five, seems to exude the peace of a biblical scholar who found escape and solace in quiet study of the texts. His peaceful, elderly presence in his apartment home was shattered in late March under the boots of the Boston Police SWAT (Special Weapons and Tactics) squad, when they kicked in his door. When the gentle clergyman fled in terror to his bedroom, that door too was kicked in, and the heavily armed thirteen-member team wrestled the old man to the floor, cuffing his hands into immobility.

Rev. Williams, writhing in terror at the armed intrusion, died of a heart attack.

Boston's SWAT team attacked the Dorchester apartment after a confidential informant supplied them with information about where a large cache of cocaine, marijuana, and guns could be found. Turns out the informant gave the cops the wrong apartment.

Rev. Williams, a retired Methodist minister, was a native of Antigua, a tiny island nation located in the eastern Caribbean, who came to America with his wife Mary to be with their child, who attended college here.

What they found instead was rampant Ramboism, a jackboot against the door, all in the name of a "war" against drugs that seems to be a war on the poor and the Black. Boston's mayor and police chief, upon confirmation of Rev. William's identity and the failure of the SWATers to find the alleged cache of drugs and guns, issued an apology. Mayor Thomas Menino attended church services in a Black Baptist church and called for "healing."

For Rev. Williams, there will be no healing for "the dead know not anything, neither have they any more a reward" (Ecclesiastes 9:5). Although unintended, Rev. Williams's death, and especially its manner, point to the folly of the way the paramilitary "war on drugs" is being waged. For the question inevitably arises: what if the Rev. Williams was in possession of drugs? Are the state's methods—paramilitary strikes; humiliating arrests; draining trials; corrosive imprisonment—really designed to "help" someone? Is it more show than substance?

Every day, the liberty of thousands is stolen because they have used a substance dubbed illegal by the government. Every year, the lives of thousands are lost because they have used a substance considered "legal" by the government. There are approximately 6,000 to 7,000 deaths annually attributed to cocaine. There are approximately 400,000 deaths annually attributed to cigarettes. Guess which one is illegal? Guess which one funnels billions to government tax coffers?

The Reverend Accelynne Williams's violent and ignominious death at the hands of over a dozen armed agents of the state points to a ludicrous war on reason, not on drugs.

From death row, this is Mumia Abu-Jamal.

ON JUNE 3, 1995, one day after being served with a death warrant, I was served with a misconduct report (a "write-up") for "engaging actively in a business or profession," i.e., as a journalist.

So strongly does the state object to me writing what you are now reading that they have begun to punish me, while I'm in the most punitive section that the system allows, Phase II,* for daring to speak and write the truth.

My institutional "offense"? The book *Live from Death Row.*

It paints an uncomplimentary picture of a prison system that calls itself "Corrections," but does little more than "corrupt" human souls; a system that eats hundreds of millions of dollars a year to torture, maim, and mutilate tens of thousands of men and women; a system that teaches bitterness and hones hatred.

Clearly, what the government wants is not just death, but silence.

A "correct" inmate is a silent one

One who speaks, writes, and exposes this horror for what it is, is given a "misconduct."

Is that a "correct" system?

Is that a system of "corrections"?

In this department of state government the First Amendment is a nullity. It doesn't apply.

---

*Phase II is the stage where death row prisoners have an active death warrant and a date of exectution. They are immediately transferred to a strip cell and are severely restricted. They lose all of the possessions and the ability to visit the law library. In addition they are barred from having any visitors other than immediate family members, a spiritual advisor, and their lawyer.

No one—not a cop, nor a guard—can find a lie in *Live from Death Row*, indeed, it is precisely because of its truth that it is a target of the state and its minions—it is a truth that they don't want you to see.

Consider: Why haven't you seen, heard, or read anything like this on TV, radio, or newspapers? Newspapers, radio, and TV are increasingly the property of either multinational corporations or wealthy individuals; therefore they reflect the perspective of the rich, the established, not the poor, the powerless

In *Live from Death Row* you hear the voices of the many, the oppressed, the damned, and the bombed. I paid a high price to bring it to you, and I will pay more; but I tell you here, *I would do it a thousand times* no matter what the cost, because it is right! *Long live John Africa!*

To quote John Africa: "When you are committed to doing what is right, the Power of Righteousness will never betray you." *Long live John Africa!*

It was right to write *Live from Death Row*, and it's right for you to read it, no matter what cop, guard, prisoncrat, politician, or media mouthpiece tells you otherwise.

Every day of your life you've no doubt heard of "freedom of the press" or "freedom of speech"; but what can such "freedom" mean without the freedoms to *read* or to *hear* what you want?

As you read this, know that I am being "punished" by the government for writing *Live from Death Row* and these very words. Indeed I've been "punished" by the government for my writings since I was fifteen years of age: but I've kept right on writing.

You keep right on reading!

The printing press shall be free to every person who may undertake to examine the proceedings of the legislature or any other branch of government, and no law shall ever be made to restrain the right thereof. The free communication of thought and opinions is one of the invaluable rights of man, and *every citizen may freely speak, write and print on any subject....* No conviction shall be had in any prosecution for the publication of papers relating to the official conduct of officers or men in public capacity.—First Article, Pennsylvania Constitution (1790)

On June 9, 1995, the Commonwealth of Pennsylvania, through its Department of "Corrections," found me "guilty" of the offense of "journalism." At a crowded "misconduct" hearing held early in the day, a Department of Corrections civil service employee came to the following conclusions:

> In his written version, Jamal does not deny the charges but cites a violation of First Amendment rites [sic], the examiner finds Jamal is not being charged with a freedom of speech issue or for the content of his writings but rather he is charged for engaging in the profession of journalism which is a violation of the rules and regulations in the handbook. He has authored a book known as *Live from Death Row*, he currently writes columns for different newspapers including *Scoop U.S.A.*, *First Day* and *The Jamal Journal*. In addition Jamal has made taped commentaries for radio broadcast over National Public Radio. These undisputed facts combine to establish a clear preponderance of evidence that Jamal has been engaged in both the business and profession of journalism.

The "examiner" found me "guilty" and sentenced a man with less than seventy-five days to live to thirty days DCS, or disciplinary custody status, to start immediately.

(I've been called many things, but "convicted journalist"? That's a new one.)

Only in Pennsylvania, the birthplace of the First Amendment and of the Constitution itself, could writing, or talking, become "misconduct." Who will teach this poor "civil servant," Hearing Examiner Kerri Cross, that the documents she swore to defend and protect, the Constitutions of the United States and Pennsylvania, refer to more than "freedom of speech"?

Is a "Handbook" superior to the Constitution of the United States? Of Pennsylvania? It would seem so.

For what you, dear reader, are doing right *now* (reading my words), I face additional "misconducts" for the offense of "journalism."

At a "hearing," where my civil lawyer (J. Krakoff, Esq.) and civilian witnesses (one of my criminal lawyers, and publishers of the newspapers) were denied, this "civil servant" violated her oath to the Constitution to advance her career in the Department of Corrections. For her, the First Amendment is a "rite," a rite of passage, that she breezed by, and ignored in her haste to "get Jamal."

If my writing is now a crime, then we are now coconspirators, for you are reading it. When my right to write is denied, what of your "right" to read?

For this arrogant, silly government, death is not enough.

Silence!

Writink is Verboten. Welcome to Pennsylvania.

From death row, this is Mumia Abu-Jamal.

You remind me of my jeep,
I wanna wax ya baby,
'mind me of my bank account,
I wanna spend ya baby.

THAT'S FROM "You Remind Me of Something," by R. Kelly. The song is smooth, with a funky bottom and a sexy lead vocalist. Why does it grit my teeth every time I hear it?

Well, it's not because I'm, as one of my sons put it, an old man who just can't interpret the young whippersnappers. That said, I must admit I'm more at home with R & B, with the soft significance of an Anita Baker, or even Brownstone, singers like Sade and yes y'all, Whitney. I also enjoy much of rap for its vitality, its rawness, its irreverence, and its creativity. Rap is an authentic descendant of a people with ancient African oral traditions, from griots who sang praise songs to their kings, to bluesmen who transmuted their pain into art. For a generation born into America's chilling waters of discontent, into the 1970s and '80s, into periods of denial, cutbacks, and emergent white supremacy, one must understand how love songs sound false and discordant, out of tune with their gritty, survivalist realities.

When their mothers and fathers were teenagers, Curtis Mayfield sang "We are winners, and never let anybody say that you can't make it cause a people's mind is in your way. We're movin' on up," Earth, Wind and Fire, in exquisite harmony, "Keep your head to the sky," and Bob Marley and the Wailers thundered over a rolling bass line, "Get up, stand up, stand up for your rights."

The hip-hop generation came into consciousness on Tina Turner's "What's Love Got to Do with It," or an egocentric mix that glorified materialism, like Run DMC's "My Adidas," about a pair of sneakers, or Whodini's "Friends," how no one can be trusted. Their parents grew up in the midst of hope and Black Liberation's consciousness. The youth grew up in a milieu of dog-eat-dogism, of America's retreat from its promises, of Reaganism and white right-wing resurgence. In that sense, rap's harshness merely reflects a harsher reality of lives lived amid broken promises. How could it be otherwise? At its heart, though, rap is a multibillion dollar business, permeating America's commercial culture and influencing millions of minds.

It is that all-American corporationism that transforms rap's grittiness into the gutter of materialism: a woman—a living being—reminds a man of a thing—a car. That to me is more perverse than the much criticized "bitches and hos" comments. This is especially objectionable when one notes that in America, in the last century, in the eyes of the law, blacks were property, chattel, things, like wagons owned by whites. That a black man, some three generations later, could sing that a black woman, his God-given mate, his female self, could "remind me of my jeep," amazes me.

This isn't, nor could it be, a condemnation of rap. The late Tupac Shakur's "Dear Mama" and "Keep Your Head Up" are shining examples of artistic expressions of loving oneness with one's family and people. Creative, moving, loving, funky, angry, and real are that late young man's works, as is a fair amount of the genre. Like any art form in America, it is also a business, with the influences of the marketplace impacting upon its production. The more conscious its artists, the more conscious the art. Keep your head up.

From death row, this is Mumia Abu-Jamal.

ON A MOVE. My most heartfelt thanks to the chair, judges, and membership of PEN Oakland for this remarkable award. I accept it in the spirit in which *Live from Death Row* was written, on behalf of the damned and the oppressed. Those, to borrow Professor Derrick Bell's apt phrase, who are but "voices from the bottom of the well."

Let us not accept the soft and easy logic that these people are voiceless. No, rather it is perhaps truer that their voices are ignored by most of the white supremacist media. They are not voiceless in the hell of Huntington prison's B block; there was not silence but the cacophony of chaos—the rage of people entombed in a torture chamber, and the bellows of madness. Their voices ring to the very vaults of heaven for a distant taste of justice. Those are the voices that fill the pages of *Live from Death Row*, and it is in their name that I am honored to accept this award.

For Black Manny, who was almost killed by a prison doctor. For Solo, acquitted in a courtroom yet condemned by a kangaroo court of venal prison officials. Chuck Africa, the MOVE political prisoner, attacked, chained, and exported to out-of-state dungeons in the aftermath of the Camp Hill riots of 1989. The valiant sisters and brothers of the Black Panther Party of the past and the MOVE of the present; their voices filled my ear during my sojourn through hell and charged my pen with the ancient African spirit of resistance, that stuff seeded in us by our ancestors.

Several months after *Live's* publication, Pennsylvania officials charged me with violating rules against operating a business or profession—the profession of journalism. When I tried to explain that this was a violation of the First Amendment of the U.S. Constitution and several provisions in the Pennsylvania constitution, well, the hearing examiner rejected the argument, saying that it had nothing to do with rights. She spelled it *r-i-t-e-s*. The prison official convicted and sentenced me to thirty days in the hole, despite the fact that as I was under a death warrant I had less than ninety days to live. It took one of their courts to explain their constitutions to them, several years later. To explain what the First Amendment means.

See, for them, and indeed for most folks in America, the First Amendment is a rite; it is something locked away under glass, a relic that one dusts off every once in a while, to which we give the empty ritual of lip service. *Live from Death Row* challenged that lie, and proved that a right ain't a right if one can be punished for exercising it.

So I thank you all at PEN Oakland for this award, coming as it does from a group such as yours, a group of distinguished and accomplished writers and journalists who know the crucial difference between a *r-i-t-e* and a *r-i-g-h-t*. To paraphrase that old and wonderful slogan that began over thirty years ago in your town of Oakland, I promise to—*This call is coming from a correctional facility*—ah, write on! On a MOVE, long live John Africa's revolution. Freedom is our right and destiny.

Still live from death row, this is Mumia Abu-Jamal.

A WOMAN WORKING to feed the homeless gets involved in a confrontation with transit cops down in a major metropolitan subway. She is accosted, manhandled, thrown to the ground, and held under restraint. Another woman has her window shattered by the highway patrol when she doesn't move her car fast enough nor open her window on command. She is seized, handcuffed, and arrested.

The first woman described here, in addition to being a political leader in her own right, is the wife of a U.S. congressman. The second, a prominent professional, is the wife of a Pennsylvania state representative. Both women are African-American.

Although charges were later dropped against these women, the very fact that they were treated so crudely, despite their prominence and influence, makes one wonder about how cruelly people *without* such influence are treated by agents of the state.

The two events just described actually occurred in Philadelphia in 1993. The first involved Philadelphia city councilwoman Mrs. Jannie Blackwell, the wife of freshman U.S. Democratic representative Lucien Blackwell. The second involved a leading Philadelphia black lawyer, Mrs. Renee Hughes, past president of the prestigious Barristers Association (local affiliate of the National Bar Association) and wife of State Representative Vincent Hughes of the 170th District. That both cases were administratively "resolved" is of less importance than that the incidents occurred at all. Indeed, such incidents are but daily occurrences in the lives of black men and women in America, regardless of their station in life.

That cops can treat people so shabbily, indeed *the very people who literally pay their salaries and set their operating budgets*, gives a grim glimmer of life at the social, economic, political bottom, where people have no influence, no clout, no voice.

These cases reveal the cold contempt in which black men and women are held by white cops, even when those black men and women are in positions of state power. In truth, any control is illusory, and as totally evanescent as power itself. Police are out of control. Black politicians are out of power. When these events occur, we can only conclude that when this can happen to them, what of us?

If people can watch the massacre of MOVE people on May 13, 1985, as police firebombed MOVE headquarters, or the ATF/FBI ramming and destruction of the Koreshians of Waco, Texas, in April 1993, and still claim the police are under control, then nothing said here will convince them.

The police are agents of white, ruling-class, capitalist will—period. Neither black managers nor black politicians can change that reality. The people themselves must organize for their own defense, or it won't get done.

From death row, this is Mumia Abu-Jamal.

THE EMERGENCE OF black political and institutional leaders in America presages a crisis of confidence. Black mayors, black city executives, black legislators, and black police officials are more numerous now than at any time since the Reconstruction era.

This should be an African-American renaissance. Why then is African-American community life at such a low ebb? Why are black U.S. communities gripped in such obvious decline? Why are our people sinking in whirlpools of utter despair?

There are many reasons why the world's wealthiest African people, U.S.-born blacks, are in such a vile condition. For reasons of length, only one will be here addressed—the critical crisis of confidence in black leadership.

Initially, it must be recognized that far too many of today's black leaders are but carbon copies of the greater American political structure—in essence, politicians in blackface. They're trained by white peers to master the "art" of politics; black pols all too often mimic their trainers, rather than creatively acting to address the actual issues facing their black constituency.

In short, they do not dare do what the times demand—they do not *lead!* A look at America's big cities often shows black police officials who sit at the helm of largely white departments, with racist, murderous attacks against Africans, *by those police*, growing in intensity! The recent history of the NYPD, with the shotgunning of black grandmothers, the garroting of black youth, antiblack "intelligence" and infiltration squads, all under the "leadership" of the black police commissioner, speaks volumes on this point.

Black mayors sit in splendor over cities with inner cities in utter, naked squalor. The poor, who traditionally have spent their last hopes in voting for black mayors, are given mere promises; the wealthy, major manufacturers are given tax breaks. Something is critically, violently wrong.

What is wrong? Is it that blacks have fallen victim to the shell game of color, the three-card monte of complexion?

We must examine the *actions* of black leaders: whose interests do they serve? When a black pol sits in silence while repressive legislation is being enacted, *whose interests does he serve?* When a black police official allows racist death squads to eliminate black life with impunity, *whose interests does he serve?*

When a black mayor wins office on black votes and then ignores their economic and social needs while fawning over big-business needs, *whose interests does he serve?*

All of today's black "leaders" owe their positions to the expressions of black discontent, rage, riot, and rebellion made by the nameless black many who took to the streets in the 1960s. There would not be black mayors, black police chiefs, black salons, black journalists, unless the black angry masses had not pounded on the closed, shuttered door of opportunity. They cracked them, only so slightly, to appease the angry black throng, and quiet the ripples of discontent.

Today, those who benefited from this Age of Rage have turned their backs on those who made it possible, and embraced the class interests of their oppressors.

It's past time for blacks to expose and work to remove these traitors in blackface.

It's time for this modern-day minstrel's dance to end, and for the people to choose their true leadership.

From death row, this is Mumia Abu-Jamal.

All men have a natural and indivisible right to worship
Almighty God according to the dictates of their own consciences....
No human authority can, in any case whatever, control or interfere
with the rights of conscience, and no preference shall ever be given
by law to any religious establishments or modes of worship.

—FROM THE PENNSYLVANIA CONSTITUTION, ART. I,
SECT. 3, CALLED THE "DECLARATION OF RIGHTS."

MORE THAN ANY OTHER American state, Pennsylvania was born of the ancient longing for religious liberty by Europe's oppressed. Pennsylvania's founding citizen, William Penn, a member of the then-persecuted sect the Quakers, made specific provisions in his frame of government, the Charter of Liberties, for freedom of conscience, and freedom of religion in Article 35.

This charter dates from 1682, almost a century before the founding of the United States of America, and well over a hundred years before the First Amendment of the U.S. Constitution was ratified, in 1791.

More than any other state then, Pennsylvania should be the haven of those seeking freedom of faith.

Three centuries later, nothing could be further from the truth.

The rock upon which this illusion was shattered was (and is) the MOVE organization, which embraces the teachings of John Africa, its founder. For them, every right—the right to religious liberty, the right to self-representation, the right to freedom of association, and most important, the fundamental right to life itself—is denied.

What is liberty of conscience? The lawyer's bible, *Black's Law Dictionary*, defines it thus: "Liberty for each individual to decide for himself what is to him religious."*

For MOVE folks, this meant that John Africa's teaching, Natural Law, was for them a religion, indeed the religion that provided solace, direction, and peace in a world tossed by turbulence.

Over fifty years ago, U.S. District Judge Albert Maris provided the definition for liberty of conscience noted above, in *Gobitis v. Minersville School District* (1937), adding, "*no man*, even though he be a school director or a judge, *is empowered to censor another's religious convictions*." Maris, in 1938, was elevated to the bench of the U.S. Court of Appeals for the Third Circuit, where he remained for many years, becoming its oldest and longest-sitting appointee, and eventually a senior circuit judge, but his definition would not survive him.

By 1981, in the case *Africa v. Pennsylvania*,[†] Maris's benchmates ignored their elder jurist's teaching, and the Third Circuit ruled that the faith of MOVE members was not a religion, as MOVE's nature-based belief did not meet their tests of physical structures, religious hierarchy, and ritual. Thus in Pennsylvania, to which three centuries ago a persecuted sect fled, to establish a state based upon "liberty of conscience," the notion dies.

In the *Gobitis* case, then district judge Maris noted why such "liberty" was necessary to the nation: "To permit public officers to determine whether the views of individuals sincerely held and their acts sincerely undertaken on religious ground are in fact based on convictions religious in character *would be to sound the death knell of religious liberty*" (*Gobitis*, p. 584).[‡] To do so, Maris wrote, would be an "alien" and "pernicious" doctrine. In *Africa*, that "death knell of religious liberty" was sounded. Loudly. With its "religious tests," the court decided MOVE's religion was not a religion, but no judge admitted its opinion was "alien" or "pernicious." In fact, it was not, for there is nothing "alien" in America about the "law" being warped and twisted for political ends, and the *Africa* decision was nakedly political.

---

* *Black's Law Dictionary*, 5th ed. (St. Paul, MN: West Publ., 1979), 828.
† *Africa v. Commonwealth of Pennsylvania*, 662 F.2d 1025 (3d Cir. 1981).
‡ *Gobitis v. Minersville School District* (1937).

Black antisystematic radicals, from the ancient days of Nat Turner and Gabriel Prosser, could find nothing in the law but its lash and the noose. For black rebels like Marcus Garvey and Paul Robeson, the "law" was suspended, and repressive "Black Codes" utilized to deny and restrict.

MOVE then moves in good historic company, and is still "On the Move!"

From death row, this is Mumia Abu-Jamal.

A SPECTER HAUNTS AMERICA'S black communities. Vampirish, it sucks the souls out of black lives, leaving skeletal husks behind, mobile, animated, but emotionally and spiritually dead. This is not the result of a dark Count Drac attack, nor a spell woven by a sinister shaman. It is the direct result of global greed, governmental deception, and the eternal longing of the poor to escape, however briefly, from the crippling shackles of utter poverty.

Their quest for relief is spelled C-R-A-C-K. Crack. Rock. Call it what you will, it is in truth another word for "death" in African-American communities. Harvested in Latin America's Peruvian highlands, treated in jungle labs, "cured" in a chemical bath of ether and kerosene, carried into the U.S.A. by government-hired pilots as a way to pay the fledgling Contras' bills, cocaine comes into Chocolate City, U.S.A., and, transformed into crystalline crack, wreaks havoc on black poor life. Forgotten by the federal government, stigmatized by the state government, shunted aside, ignored, or exploited by city governments, the poor are perceived as problems or ostracized as alien others, beyond the social pale, anything but people who are not provided the basic tools of survival. It is these poor folks, locked in American Bantustans, who have fallen the hardest for crack.

Just as the "Just Say No" generation got down from the political stage, tons of a new potent poison were being peddled in poor sections of town, brought to these shores courtesy of the Iran-Contra funds diversion scheme, as masterminded by that great American hero Honest Ollie North (known as Operation Black Eagle–CIA). Why would the government (the same government that "Just Says No") dare bring cocaine into the States, if not to sell it, to turn it over into lucre, into cold cash? If their intent was to destroy it, this could have easily been done outside the U.S.A. It was not destroyed. I suspect an ulterior motive.

Recent history, back in the radical 1960s, saw a flood of pills, pot, and high-grade heroin into black neighborhoods. Radicals suspected then the malevolent hand of Big Brother opening the floodgates of drugs to drown out the black revolutionary fires of urban resistance. With a hostile U.S. Supreme Court, growing unemployment, a federal government that "kind-ly" and "gently" turned its back on the homeless, police forces marauding like Green Berets over inner cities, African-American resistance seems a likely response.

Open the floodgates, again—this time with a potent, mind-sucking, soul-ripping poison that takes utter priority over all else. The natural instinct of motherhood melts into mud next to the pangs of the crack attack.

Babies are being sold, and mothers sell themselves, in homage to the plastic vial.

Homes disintegrate into New Age caves under the spell of the 'caine. Families fall apart, as fathers are herded into newly built prisons and moth-ers haunt ho-strolls, all in an infernal lust for that sweet, deadly poison.

There is a precedent for such a diabolical scheme in U.S. history. How many Native "American" communities and tribes were devastated by the European introduction of "firewater"—that is, alcohol, rum etc.—into the tribal diet, and indeed wiped out?

This is a dire hour for Africans in the United States.

Will we survive this plague?

From death row, this is Mumia Abu-Jamal.

THERE WAS A TIME when the name of Huey P. Newton was known from coast to coast. It is a measure of changing times that for many of the young, teens and pre-teens alike, a question about him will elicit yet another question: "Huey who?"

The answer is a complex matter, for there was more than one Huey. He was a remarkable man, both at his apex, as Founder and Minister of Defense of the Black Panther Party, and at his nadir, as an alienated drug addict, caught in the crippling clutches of crack.

At his best, he was a youth of rare brilliance, who molded mass militance into a national black political movement that lit an age into radical incandescence.

At his worst, Huey's later life was a tale of a dream deferred; a bright, shining moment in African-American life, transformed with time into the bitter ashes of defeat. It came about, in large part, through a campaign of U.S. government terror that included bloody police raids on Black Panther Party offices across the country, and urban spycraft; COINTELPRO, the infamous FBI Counter Intelligence Program, wreaked sinister havoc on the lives of countless militants in America's black, brown, red, yellow, and working-class communities. To COINTELPRO, not even Huey was immune.

An early outbreak of violence between L.A.'s U.S. Organization* and the L.A. Panther chapter was spawned, COINTELPRO files now reveal, by a

---

*On January 17, 1969, COINTELPRO tactics of provoking violence between the United States and the BPP resulted in the shooting deaths of L.A. BPP leaders Alprentice "Bunchy" Carter and Jon Huggins by U.S. members George and Joseph Stiner, and Claude Hubert, in a classroom at UCLA's Campbell Hall.

government campaign of "dirty mail," forged letters from one group to the other threatening mutual violence.

The violence East Coast/West Coast party split, files now show, was whipped up by FBI–employed agents-provocateurs, whose sole function was to sow dissent in Panther ranks, leading again to internecine warfare—Panther against Panther.

On the positive side, Huey's contributions to the Black Liberation Movement were immense.

The BPP, in large part due to Huey's global influence, established in the early 1970s an Intercommunal Section Headquarters for the Party, which was, in essence, Black America's first, and only, independent embassy, on foreign (in this case, North African) soil. The BPP newspaper, which Huey called "the lifeblood of the Party," was a truly independent voice of working-class Black America, which spoke its own rich, distinctive, street language. Huey called a pig a "pig," and the paper depicted them, snout and all.

Above all, Huey, with his natural good looks, his winning heart, and that aggravatingly high, nasal, twangy Southern voice of his, was a man beloved by millions of blacks, Panther or no.

A one-time field marshal, D.C., once said of him, "Huey is the only man who could walk across America, and black folks would follow him, from coast to coast."

Once, his observation was quite true.

But in later years that would no longer be the case. The Party, beset by destructive forces, within and without, paranoid and real, lost its moorings, as the man who formed the organization lost his. In one dizzying year of indecision, he went from Defense Minister, to Supreme Commander, to Supreme Servant, to Servant, a reflection of the influences of his travel abroad, especially to North Korea.

And when the Party fell apart, burst asunder by the political and personal strains that beseiged it, he was an integral part of that process, as drugs continued to sap his brilliance and destroy his vision. It is one of the supreme ironies of life that the hand that would strike him down would be a black one, in a midnight quarrel over drug money and debts owed. His lifelong fascination with the seamier side of the streets of his youth became, in the end, a fatal attraction.

The irony is exacerbated when we learn that the man who slew Huey was a member of the Black Guerilla Family, a prison-based offshoot of the BPP; that as a youth, he ate his breakfast at one of the Bay Area Black Panther Party Community Free Breakfast Programs; and now, as a man serving a life term at the Pelican Bay SHU, has had the opportunity to read the writings of Newton, and has become inspired by the words of the man he murdered.* Perhaps it is testament to the clarity and power of Huey's revolutionary example and ideas, that such a one who took his life, has become, in his own way, a devotee.

Huey stood up, virtually alone, in that dark hour, against the armed might of the Beast and survived. In doing so he set an extraordinary example. How he died was direst tragedy; how he lived was utterly remarkable.

From death row, this is Mumia Abu-Jamal.

---

*Newton was shot and killed on August 22, 1989, in the streets of West Oakland by 22-year-old Tyrone Demetrius Robinson, a BGF foot soldier. The two reportedly argued over 14 vials of crack and $160.

"HISTORY," black militant activist Malcolm X once noted, "is best suited to reward our research."

The fiery leader's axiom leapt to mind recently when I read of the growing antiwar positions taken by Vietnam veterans.

It is a fixture in the public mind that vets from the Vietnam War were somehow "different" from veterans in other wars. For quite a few years the term "Vietnam vet" became a curse, a coded suggestion that the subject was somehow "off." According to the myth, vets of other, earlier wars were warmly embraced by society upon return.

Such a notion has fueled many a Ramboid fantasy. Like most fantasies, it is false.

Back during the Great Depression, around 1932, veterans of World War I converged on Washington, as part of a massive march and demonstration against the U.S. government policy of issuing "bonus certificates" due for cash payments, years in the future. Those at the Bonus Army March on Washington demanded Congress pay the vets off now, when money for survival was desperately needed.

They came, by the thousands, to personally petition their government, on whose behalf they had so recently fought the "Great War," for payment due them, to fight hard times.

Over twenty thousand people, men, wives and children, encamped in the area around the White House, and other federal buildings to push the demonstration for "payment now, not later." The House of Representatives passed the bill, but it was defeated in the Senate, and some vets, discouraged, left. Most, however, lived in tents, lean-tos, and cardboard boxes, and they stayed.

President Hoover issued eviction orders to the army, and as historian and present-day antiwar activist Howard Zinn details in his remarkable *People's History of the United States*:

> Four troops of cavalry, four companies of infantry, a machine gun squadron, and six tanks assembled near the White House. General Douglas MacArthur was in charge of the operation, Major Dwight Eisenhower his aide. George S. Patton was one of the officers. MacArthur led his troops down Pennsylvania Avenue, used tear gas to clear veterans out of the old buildings, and set the buildings on fire. Then the Army moved across the bridge to Anacosta. Thousands of veterans, wives, children began to run as the tear gas spread. The soldiers set fire to some of the huts, and soon the whole encampment was ablaze. When it was all over, two veterans had been shot to death, an eleven-week-old baby had died, an eight-year-old boy was partially blinded by gas, two police had fractured skulls, and a thousand veterans were injured by gas. (382)

The government's martial response to veterans who dared demand prompt payment puts the very real grievances of Vietnam's vets into a certain perspective. Rarely has history provided a better illustration of how soldiers serve government, but commanders of soldiers serve the ruling elite.

After the smoke has settled from the megabombing of Baghdad, and soldiers, their tour of duty ended, return to U.S. cities, they will find urban nightmares even worse than they left, full to the bitter brim with blight, homelessness, joblessness, and aching hopelessness.

Who will reconstruct the bombed-out neighborhoods of the South Bronx, of Brownsville, of North Philly, of Harlem?

Once more, a generation returns from war. Once more, a generation returns, after a war for empire, to emptiness.

From death row, this is Mumia Abu-Jamal.

IN THE SPRAWLING OUTSIZED metropolis that is Los Angeles, a jack-booted army of alleged "civil servants" treat the civilians they are charged with serving with ill-disguised contempt.

In the privacy of their patrol cars, city police tap out brief messages on laptop computers, unit-to-unit communications of seething hatred for many of the people they are sworn to protect.

The revelations of the Christopher Commission[*] reveal the mentality behind the badge in L.A.:

"If you encounter these Negroes, shoot first and ask questions later."

Or, "I would love to drive down Slauson [a minority street] with a flamethrower—we could have barbecue."

Or, "Capture him, beat him, and treat him like dirt. After I beat him, what do I book him for?"

Or, "Hi. Just got some Mexercise for the night."

Or, "Sounds like monkey-slapping time."

Or "Did you arrest the eighty-five-year-old lady, or just beat her up?"

"We just slapped her around a bit. She's getting MT [medical treatment] right now."

Cop-generated slurs of this ilk continue for pages. To many African Americans and Chicanos in southern California, the tone and tenor of these

---

[*]In July 1991, the Christopher Commission report was published. The commission, headed by attorney Warren Christopher, was created to conduct "a full and fair examination of the structure and operation of the LAPD," including its recruitment and training practices, internal disciplinary system, and citizen complaint system.

once-secret communications evoke a sense more of confirmation than of surprise.

The liberal clamor for Police Chief Darryl Gates's resignation is a reflection of the limits of liberalism and its dependence on symbol over substance, for the departure of Gates changes not one iota the palpable aura of hatred that radiates from the rank and file of the LAPD.

All of the Christopher Commission reforms, if implemented this very instant, would do naught to purge the pervasive taint of militaristic mania that dominates the LAPD and many similar bodies nationwide.

The big-city elites will scrub a few faces, sacrifice a few scapegoats, publish reports, memorandums, etc., ad infinitum, but in the end they will change nothing. For the function of the police is *not* to protect the people, but to protect the system and its elite. If this need be done by alienating the black, the brown, the poor, the homeless, well, them's the breaks. For none of these groups wield state power.

I suggest you carefully listen again to the cryptic remarks noted above:

"Capture him, beat him, and treat him like dirt. After I beat him, what do I book him for?"

If you listen closely enough, you may hear yourself.

From death row, this is Mumia Abu-Jamal.

RECENT PUBLISHED REPORTS have lamented the fact that Afro-American youth are remarkably resistant and virtually unresponsive to traditional, big-name public relations and big-time sports figures when the major media attempts to communicate with younger blacks. The study found deep and profound alienation among youth, and a fundamental streak of fatalism about the promise of tomorrow—a sense that "tomorrow may not come, so let's live today."

The youth, while they view large blocks of TV, perceive it from the position of outsiders, knowing that the dramas, comedies, and news programs are not designed for their consumption. Only the urbo-tech musical form known as rap touches them, for it is born of urban youth consciousness and speaks to them, in their idiom, about lives lived on the marginalia. It is this profound disassociation that forced members of the nouveau middle-class blacks to lament the youth as "the lost generation."

But are they really "lost," and, if so, to whom?

The Martinican black revolutionary Frantz Fanon[*] once opined that every generation must find its destiny, fulfill it, or betray it.

In my father's generation, southern-born of the late 1890s, their destiny was to move their families north, to lands with a promise of a better life away from our hateful homelands in Dixie. The dreams of that generation, sparked by visions of new homes, better education, new cars, and prosperity,

---

[*]West Indian psychiatrist and revolutionary writer Fratz Fanon's writings, especially *The Wretched of the Earth* (1961) had profound influence on the radical movements in the 1960s in the United States and Europe.

were in relative terms realized by some, but northbound Africans were never able to outrun the stigma of racism.

By the time the 1950s and '60s generation came of age, during the Nixon-Reagan-Bush eras, race once again defined the limits of black aspirations, and with the shifting of manufacturing jobs back down south and abroad, so went dreams of relative prosperity. The children of *this* generation—born into sobering poverty amid shimmering opulence, their minds weaned on Falcon Crestian TV excess while locked in want, watching while sinister politicians spit on their very existence—these youth are the hip-hop/rap generation.

Locked out of the legal means of material survival, looked down upon by predatory politicians and police, left with the least relevant educational opportunities, talked *at* with contempt and not talked *to* with love—is there any question why such youth are alienated? Why the surprise?

They look at the lives they live and see not "civil rights progress," but a drumbeat of civil repression by a state at war with their dreams.

Why the surprise?

This is not the lost generation. They are the children of the L.A. rebellion, the children of the MOVE bombing, the children of the Black Panthers, and the grandchildren of Malcolm; far from lost, they are probably the most aware generation since Nat Turner's; they are not so much lost as they are mislaid, discarded by this increasingly racist system that undermines their inherent worth.

They are *all* potential revolutionaries, with the historic power to transform our dull realities. If they are lost, then *find* them.

From death row, this is Mumia Abu-Jamal.

THE MUTED PUBLIC RESPONSE to the mass murder of MOVE members some eight years ago has set the stage for acceptable state violence against radicals, against blacks, and against all deemed socially unacceptable. In the 1960s and '70s the Black Panther Party defined a relationship between the police and the black community as one between an occupying army and a colony. The confrontations between MOVE and this system's armed domestic forces has given that claim credence. An article in the *Village Voice* in 1991 quoted an anonymous white cop giving his prescription for bringing law and order to Los Angeles. Consider this:

> **COP ONE:** "You wanna fix this city? I say, start out with carpet-bombing. Level some buildings, plow all these shit [beeped] under and start all over again."
> **COP TWO:** "Christ, you'd drop a bomb on a community?"
> **COP THREE:** "Yeah. There'd be some innocent people, but not that many. There's just some areas of L.A. that can't be saved."

The twisted mentalities at work here are akin to those of Nazi Germany, or perhaps more appropriately, of My Lai, of Vietnam, of Baghdad, the spirit behind the mindlessly murderous mantra that echoed out of Da Nang: "We had to destroy the village in order to save it."

As abroad, so here at home. For as the flames smothered life on Osage Avenue, police and politicians spoke of "destroying the neighborhood surrounding the MOVE house, in order to save it." Now cops patrol neighborhoods across America, armed like storm troopers, with a barely disguised urge to destroy the very area they are sworn to "serve and protect." Or perhaps we should say, "sever and dissect." As they sit and sup and smoke, what animates their minds? Are they an aid to the people, or a foreign army of occupation? May 13, 1985, should have answered that question decisively. MOVE founder John Africa wrote over a decade ago,

It is past time for all poor people to release themselves from the deceptive strangulation of society. Realize that society has failed you. For to attempt to ignore this system of deception now, is to deny you the need to protest this failure later.

This system has failed you yesterday, failed you today, and has created conditions for failure tomorrow, for society is wrong, the system is reeling, the courts of this complex are filled with imbalance. Cops are insane, the judges enslaving, the lawyers are just as the judges they confront. They are Harvard and Princeton and Cornell and Yale, and trained, as the judge, to deceive the impoverished; trained, as the judge, to protect the established; trained by the system to be as the system, to do for the system, exploit with the system, and MOVE ain't gonna close our eyes to this monster." (John Africa, *The Judges Letter.*)

It was true then, it's even truer now. This system has failed all of us. Indeed it is the problem. Organize this very day to resist it, to oppose it, to go beyond it. Demand that all imprisoned MOVE members be released and all political prisoners be freed. That is a beginning. That is a first step we can all take today. On a MOVE, long live John Africa!

It has been eight years now since the massacre. Eight years since the carnage on Osage Avenue. Eight years since an urban holocaust that stole eleven human lives. Eight years since the unjust encagement of Ramona Africa for daring to survive. Eight years since the government committed premeditated mass murder of members of the Africa family—men, women, and children. And still justice is a ghostly illusion.

To date, no judge, no jury, no judicial nor law enforcement officer, has condemned the May 13 bombing of MOVE. In fact several, including former U.S. attorney general Edward Meese and former Los Angeles police chief Darryl Gates, have applauded it.

For over seventeen years now I've written of the ongoing battles between MOVE and this system. I have seen every substantive so-called constitutional right twisted, shredded, and torn when it comes to MOVE. Since the early 1970s I've seen male and female MOVE members beaten till bloody and bones broken, locked beneath the jails, caged while pregnant, beaten into miscarriage, starved by municipal decree, sentenced to a century in prisons, homes demolished by bomb, by crane, by cannon, by fire. But I've never seen them broken.

Throughout this vicious state campaign the government, the prosecutors, the police, the courts, have had one central aim: renounce MOVE, renounce your allegiance to John Africa, and we'll leave you alone. This has been proven. In 1978 a phalanx of 500 heavily armed cops laid siege to MOVE headquarters in Powleton Village, in an alleged attempt to enforce a civil eviction order. During the shooting, a cop was killed and all adult MOVE members inside were charged with murder. Before trial, two women told investigators they would resign from the organization even though they too were arrested inside the house. All charges against the two, including murder, were dropped. At trial, nine MOVE men and women were convicted of third-degree murder, and all were sentenced to 30 to 100 years in prison.

The May 13, 1985, action was an attempt to draw attention to the earlier injustice suffered by MOVE members and demand their release.

As to their innocence, one need go no further than Judge Edwin Malmed, the trial judge of the August 8, 1978, case, who told listeners of the popular Frank Ford talk show in Philadelphia just days after their conviction that he hadn't "the faintest idea" who killed the cop, adding "they were tried as a family, so I convicted them as a family." MOVE members then were convicted of being MOVE members.

Had Ramona Africa emerged from the sea of flames wrapped in fear, had she not instead escaped with her aura of resistance intact, she would have been free long before the seven years she spent in a hellhole. Her prosecutor, describing MOVE as a cult of resistance, demanded the jury convict her of a range of charges that, if they did so, would have exposed her to over fifty years in prison. Only her naturalist faith, the teachings of John Africa, allowed her to competently defend herself, where she beat the majority of the charges. Ramona is "free" today.

From death row, this is Mumia Abu-Jamal.

FIRE-TWISTED METAL, charred brick, and dark, dry pools of soot sit behind the barbed-wire double fences of the central Pennsylvania prison known as Camp Hill.

The fires that stretched seductively and danced provocatively in the late October night have spent themselves, their hot red tongues sated from a delicious diet of destruction that left "The Hill" in ruin. Two nights of inmate outrage and prisoner rebellion earned the wages of repression, as over a reported seven hundred armed and armored guards retook the prison, in a vicious head-splitting frenzy. The riots, the raging blazes, made prime-time news; the aftermath did not, for prisoners are faceless, nameless, and voiceless.

Until now.

One of the unknown many bludgeoned, beaten bloody, and attacked by guards was a man whose name is well known: MOVE political prisoner Chuck Africa, just transferred to "The Hill" several months ago, became the prey of a phalanx of guards imported from Dallas, Pennsylvania, prison, where Chuck had just spent a harrowing five years in the infamous Dallas dungeon.

Assaulted by guards at Camp Hill, Chuck was chained and hurriedly transferred to a round of federal prisons while family, supporters, and even lawyers were give the dreaded runaround.

From Lewisburg, Pennsylvania, to the federal prison in Atlanta, Georgia, to the federal facility at Lompoc, California, Chuck Africa was dragged ragged across the United States, in a matter of days.

Throughout this marathon march across the country, prison officials have been mum on Chuck's medical condition.

This longtime follower of the revolutionary teachings of *John Africa* is no stranger to the system's adversity—as evidenced by the August 8, 1978, police assault on MOVE's headquarters in Powleton Village, West Philadelphia, where Chuck was nearly killed.

At the revealing trial of nine MOVE members, charged in the classic frame-up killing of a cop, one policeman testified how he stood looking into the basement window of the now-demolished headquarters, peering at Chuck trying to stand up amid swirling, rushing waters pumped into the house by water cannons, and opened fire, point-blank, emptying his pistol.

Chuck, and MOVE member Delbert Africa (later beaten to a pulp on national TV by cops who were afterward acquitted) were shot.

This latest assault shows this system's continuing intent to destroy, disrupt, and decimate the MOVE organization, for after a decade of unprecedented harassments and provocations, over sixty-five months straight in Dallas's dreaded dungeon, Chuck and other MOVE members, giving thanks for the teachings of John Africa, remain strong, steadfast, staunch, and committed revolutionaries, still opposed to this hypocritical infanticidal system, still embracing a doctrine in touch with nature's pulse, still in love with life! *Long live John Africa's Revolution!*

Like the brutal and retaliatory beatings of inmate rioters at Camp Hill (appropriately nicknamed "Camp Hell" by relatives), regional media, in league with government intent, provided no names of the beaten, blackjacked prisoners, as if they were invisible, and were it not for *Class-Struggle Defense Notes*, published by the Partisan Defense Committee of New York, few would know of the secretive state attack and subsequent nationwide smuggling of Chuck Africa.

The "major" media, long a mere lackey of the U.S. ruling class, is busy pumping its propaganda claims that MOVE is, in its words, a "terrorist" organization, all the while turning a blind eye to the continuing and irrefutable campaign of state terrorism that keeps innocent MOVE members caged in U.S. dungeons for over a decade, and that allows the state to drag a beaten, shackled Chuck Africa around the entire country in a blackout of media silence.

This station, this day, with this report, breaks this silence, and lifts the blackout first lifted by *Class-Struggle Defense Notes*.

With this light must come heat, and rage, enough to spark the demand: *Free Chuck Africa! Free all MOVE members! Free all political prisoners!*

From death row, this is Mumia Abu-Jamal.

SEVEN YEARS HAVE PASSED since the urban holocaust on Osage Avenue; since the Mother's Day massacre of May 13, 1985; a day that left at least eleven people dead, and Ramona Africa scarred and shackled.*

Seven years since the MOVE bombing, and on May 13, 1992, a scarred but unbowed Ramona will walk away from seven years in a cage, at Muncy Prison, Pennsylvania.

In 1986, at the conclusion of her controversial showtrial, Philadelphia Common Pleas Court judge Michael Stiles delivered his charge to the jury, telling jurors not to consider any wrongdoing done by officials because officials would be dealt with and held accountable in "other" proceedings.

In what they later told reporters was a "compromise verdict," the jury, deliberately given the false impression that city officials would be in some way penalized, and therefore Ramona should be penalized, convicted Ramona of riot and conspiracy charges.

On April 14, 1986, Ramona was sentenced to sixteen months to seven years in prison and escorted under armed guard to the Women's State Prison at Muncy, Pennsylvania. To date, she, and *only* she, has spent even a day in prison for the city's bombing, mass murder, and incineration of

---

*At the time of this commentary's writing, Ramona Africa was well into her seven-year prison term for a compromise verdict of guilty of riot stemming from the state's murderous conflagration of May 13, 1985. Ramona and several other imprisoned MOVE members were repeatedly denied parole for refusing to renounce their relationships to other MOVE people. Scarred for life from the fire, Ramona has lectured around the world on MOVE, the May 13 Massacre, and in defense of political prisoners and prisoners of war. Since her release in 1992, she has worked tirelessly in John Africa's revolution.

innocent MOVE people, and to add insult to injury, she, and other MOVE members, have been consistently denied parole at the expiration of minimum sentences, *solely* for refusing to renounce their religion—John Africa's teaching.

Alberta Africa walked out of prison after seven years in 1988; Mo Africa also did the maximum—five years *after* his conviction was reversed in 1990; after seven long years, Ramona Africa will "max out" in May 1992; Sue Africa will "max out" in 1992 after *twelve* years; Consuewella and Carlos Africa are *still* being denied parole, after being eligible for nearly five years.

The Pennsylvania Parole Board told MOVE members that parole was possible *only* if they completely disassociated themselves from the MOVE family—meaning mates, children, even parents. In essence, the price of "freedom" was renunciation of their religion, a point addressed years ago in the provocative writings of MOVE founder, John Africa:

> There ain't a example in history where a religious people didn't defend themselves when their religion was threatened, and defend themselves with *arms*, any kind of arms they could get their hands on, arms that were sometimes as lethal as the persecutors themselves were armed with, and today the defensive conduct of these religions are accepted, supported, respected, recognized by other religions, the government, society; the same damn religions, the government, society that wanna say we ain't a religion, ain't to be accepted as a valid religion, ain't to be supported as a so-called legal belief, ain't to be respected for defending our faith; if the religion of the Jew is acceptable what makes the religion of the MOVE Organization *un*acceptable, if the belief of the Catholic is respectable, what makes the religion of the MOVE Organization *dis*respectable, if the faith of the Protestant is valid what makes the faith of the MOVE Organization *in*valid, if the conduct of this government is right what makes the conduct of the governing power of MOVE wrong. . . .

On May 13, 1992, Ramona Africa walks away from a cage that held her captive for seven long, bitter years. She has not seen justice for one hour since the day she walked in.

Throughout the press in Pennsylvania, and perhaps throughout the U.S. press as well, the story of the Ramona Africa suit, or the "MOVE suit" as they often term it, has garnered banner headlines.

This civil suit, initiated by Ramona *pro se*, that is, without a lawyer, is a civil claim of a violation of her civil constitutional rights, stemming from the police bombing of MOVE headquarters in West Philly, leaving at least eleven MOVE men, women, and babies dead on May 13, 1985. The suit claims the state knowingly and intentionally used excessive and unlawful force against the occupants of 6621 Osage Avenue, and created a holocaust that night.

Among prisoners, the articles have stimulated comment, among them the ever-present comment, "She's gonna get paid." This comment never ceases to irk me. For, over and above the fact that Ramona, as with all the MOVE people, could care less about money, the fact remains that this is a civil suit, seeking civil damages, for an act that Ray Charles and Stevie Wonder both could clearly see was *criminal.*

Contrary to published opinion, as Ramona neatly points out, the May 13 bombing of MOVE by police was not *even* an accident, not a technical blooper, nor, as former Mayor Goode said, "a bad day." No! May 13, 1985, was the most premeditated police raid and destroy mission in U.S. history; a day planned and prepared for months, even years, in advance by local, state, and federal officials sworn to one unholy aim—the destruction of the MOVE organization. Their "bad day" began when one determined, scarred, smoldering black woman dodged a hellfire of police bullets to escape the plans of government to incinerate her and her family alive, and survived.

For this she was dumped into Pennsylvania's hellish prisons, sentenced to seven years in a prison madhouse of loss, pain, and alienation at Muncy's Women's Prison—for daring not to die!

Well, Mona's back, y'all.

Fueled by the generating influence of John Africa's teaching, this MOVE soldier is marching back into battle, to point out how corrupt, how thoroughly decayed, this system is, using their own so-called law. *Long live John Africa!*

Her dark, muscled arms are mottled, seared, and scarred in some places, silent testament to the flames of Osage, but her eyes are clear and calm, her fine mind sharper than the hot shards of glass that littered the backyard of Osage, sharper than the pain that stabbed at her heart when she looked back and, through the black clouds of smoke, saw her people, her brothers and sisters, the children, shot back by a rain of death, back into the inferno of Osage, forced back by a steady deadly rain of automatic police-weapons fire, forced back into eternity.

And they talkin' bouta *civil* suit for damages!

To date *no* official, not former D.A. Edward Rendell (who was himself recently declared immune from suit), not former D.A. Ronald Castille, not former U.S. attorney Edwin Dennis, nor present D.A. Lynne Abraham, has ever called *any* action by police or any other official "criminal"—not one charge. Not once. Nobody.

Just maybe, a *civil* violation, here and there, and if "proven," will only mean you, the taxpaying public, will foot the bill, and pay hard-earned bucks for political incompetence.

As I look around this dungeon on Pennsylvania's death row, I see not one soul who dared premeditate mass murder like police and political officials did on May 13, 1985, and until I do, don't tell me about a criminal justice system, 'cause there ain't no "justice" in it—it's just a criminal system.

From death row, this is Mumia Abu-Jamal.

That Justice is a Blind Goddess;
Is a thing to which we Blacks are wise:
Her bandage hides two festering sores
That once perhaps were eyes.

—FROM "JUSTICE," BY LANGSTON HUGHES

ELMER GERONIMO JI JAGA PRATT sits sweltering in a southern California prison, no doubt angry over his latest judicial mugging by the U.S. Court of Appeals for the Ninth Circuit, which refused to reconsider Pratt's appeal, solely because it was filed a day too late. Pratt, a former high-ranking Black Panther leader, has endured almost twenty long years in prison, for a crime that even an ex-FBI agent insists he did not, and indeed, could not have done.

Why is Geronimo still caged?

Because, in his youth, nearly two decades ago, he dared stand up against the white racist power structure, and attempted to lend a hand to militant efforts to defend black communities from racist cop terror. As party deputy–minister of defense, Geronimo did his job only too well, as evidenced by the fiery, genocidal police raid on the Los Angeles chapter headquarters of the Black Panther Party in 1970, an onslaught that left much of Central Avenue in smoldering ruin, but from which every L.A. Panther emerged—alive.

Geronimo's true "crime" then, was—and is—resistance, a "crime" for which Africans have historically paid the supreme penalty, and for which Pratt has paid with almost twenty years in California dungeons. In a word, the reason why Geronimo is still caged can be summed up with a sinister acronym—COINTELPRO, FBI-speak for the shadowy, malicious counterintelligence program that shadowed, harassed, silenced, and set up black activists from the Reverend Martin Luther King Jr. to Geronimo.

COINTELPRO files show Geronimo could not have committed the December 18, 1968, murder of Mrs. Kenneth Olsin, in L.A., for the simple reason that he was under FBI surveillance some four hundred miles away, in northern California, at the time of the crime.

California congressman Ron Dellums has introduced a resolution in the U.S. House of Representatives calling for Geronimo's immediate release and an investigation into the circumstances surrounding his arrest and conviction. The resolution notes in part, "Federal Bureau of Investigation wrongdoing in the case of Elmer 'Geronimo' Pratt has been established through exhaustive examinations of thousands of pages of official FBI documents obtained under the Freedom of Information Act and subsequently corroborated by the sworn testimony of a retired FBI Special Agent who has personal knowledge of the wrongdoing."

The three-judge panel of the Ninth Circuit (composed, incidentally, of Nixon and Reagan appointees) closed the courthouse door on Pratt's appeal, citing the attorney's failure to file Pratt's papers promptly.

In a move that the late black Supreme Court jurist the late Thurgood Marshall might call "exalting form over substance," the Ninth Circuit panel has apparently decided that innocence is irrelevant.

Just as surely as the U.S. Supreme Court careens rightward, so too do other federal courts, like the Ninth Circuit, move in lockstep.

That the life of a kind, decent, committed man—raised in the bayou country of Morgan County, Louisiana, and tempered in the steaming jungles of Vietnam, in youthful service to *this* government—sifts away like sand through an hourglass is of no judicial concern. One wonders at the irony of his protecting the polluted status quo that now denies him his rightful day in court.

It was a youthful, idealistic Pratt who emerged from the hells of 'Nam, only to behold the hells of Compton, California. That he chose to serve his people, as a member of the Black Panther Party, is a fact of which he can justly be proud. That he is denied the most fundamental rights, to be free of government prosecution without deception and to be heard by an impartial judge, based solely upon his BPP membership, is a fact of which Americans should be ashamed. Even 3,000 miles away, I hear his soft, yet strong, country voice saying, "Come together, fight together and rally together to see justice done!" *Free Geronimo now!**

From death row, this is Mumia Abu-Jamal.

---

*A May 29, 1997, decision by Orange County Superior Court Judge Evert Dickey vacated Geronimo ji jaga Pratt's conviction and sentence of life imprisonment. Geronimo was released on July 10, 1997, after twenty-seven years in prison for a crime he did not commit. A federal civil rights lawsuit is now pending against the FBI (including special agent Richard W. Held) and the Los Angeles Police Department, which alleges civil rights violations arising from the use of the infamous COINTELPRO program to set up and falsely imprison Geronimo.

THE NAME EDDIE HATCHER is as widely known and respected by the people as it is hated by the system.* For Hatcher, a Tuscarora/Lumbee Native American, along with his fellow Tuscarora, Tim Jacobs, brought national attention to the plight of Native and African Americans battling local governmental corruption in Robeson County, North Carolina, when they occupied offices of the *Robesonian* newspaper, demanding that the governor investigate a string of murders and suspicious deaths of Indians and African Americans there in 1988.

The occupation, an act of desperation on the two Tuscaroras' part, marked them both for government vengeance.

Hatcher, after a full acquittal of federal charges arising from the takeover, was improperly and illegally reindicted on state charges—despite his presumed double jeopardy "rights"—convicted of kidnapping, and sentenced to eighteen years in prison.

Recently, Hatcher's fight for freedom has become, in a real sense, a fight for his very life. Several years ago Hatcher, and the Robeson Defense Committee,

---

*When this text was originally written, Eddie Hatcher was seriously ill with HIV-related sickness. Thanks to the support of committed people, he made it to freedom, but remained an enemy of the state. A longtime Native American activist, Hatcher was the first person prosecuted under Ronald Reagan's 1984 antiterrorist act. He has survived two trials (one where he successfully defended himself after the North Carolina court refused to allow William Kuntsler to defend him), seven years in prison, and AIDS-related pneumonia that almost killed him. Eddie is currently in prison awaiting trial in North Carolina on capital murder charges. The state is seeking the death penalty based on Eddie's prior conviction for taking over the newsroom of the Robeson County, North Carolina, newsaper the Robesonian, to call attention to the corruption and racism prevalent in the county.

fought for the right to decent health care and justice for an African-American prisoner who suffered from AIDS, James Hall Jr. Now the bitter barrel spins, and Hatcher finds he is HIV positive.

There are few things in life that can make such undeniably bad news even worse—and one is to be HIV-positive and in prison. For people who, like Hatcher, are HIV-positive face denial of medical treatment, abominably poor medical treatment, vicious discrimination, and constant abuse, from staff and prisoners alike.

Eddie Hatcher's principled actions in occupying the offices of the *Robesonian* bespoke courage and caring, not criminality. He acted to draw the light of exposure upon a county rank with corruption, which denied the black, the red, and the poor of Robeson County the barest hint of justice. How many of us would've born the injustices in silence? Before Hatcher and Jacobs dared act, how many did?

Hatcher's federal acquittal, and subsequent state prosecution, for the same acts, shows the rabid political character of his case. Eddie Hatcher, like former prisoner Dr. Alan Berkman, Bashir Hameed of the New York Three, and Silvia Baraldini, is a political prisoner fighting for his very life!

And as they did for Dr. Berkman, the efforts of many may help Hatcher make parole, thereby extending a good life of service to others.

Every day is vital.

Help make Hatcher's dream of a long, productive life, a reality.

From death row, this is Mumia Abu-Jamal.

EDDIE HATCHER DEFENSE COMMITTEE
P.O. Box 2702, Pembroke, NC 28739
http://www.prisonactivist.org/eddie/

Eddie Hatcher, Central Prison
1300 Western Blvd., Raleigh, NC 27602

"THIRTY TO 100 YEARS no more, free MOVE now, open up the door!" A marcher's chant. To hear news accounts, their numbers weren't impressive, with less than fifty marchers participating in a May 13, 1993, march calling for the freedom of MOVE political prisoners. In this respect, local and regionally published reports were accurate, if not explanatory of the significance of the event. To be sure, it was reported that the march also marked the eighth anniversary of the police bombing and mass murder of eleven MOVE members at MOVE's home on Osage Avenue, and also the first anniversary of the day MOVE's communications minister, Ramona Africa, was released from prison after seven years as a political prisoner. So that was accurate. In their endless fascination with numbers, the media counted numbers, researched dates, took a few pictures and considered their story told. With MOVE, that is seldom if ever the case.

Who were the people marching? "We're fired up, still on the MOVE." A march chant. Their voices were light, heavy, thin, and thunderous. Theirs were the voices of MOVE men, MOVE women, and MOVE children, the young sons and daughters of revolution. Tall with lithe, lean forms or tiny bundles of baby fat, all un-cosmetic, the MOVE children marched militantly from West Philadelphia, the site of the old MOVE headquarters at Thirty-third and Powleton Avenue, site of the August 8, 1978, MOVE confrontation, to Philadelphia City Hall, which they circled twice in the rain. The children, many who were themselves, although babies, veterans from the August 8 confrontation, were a sight to behold—strong limbed, clear eyes like dark stars, teeth like shimmering pearls, radiant and beautiful.

Numbers did not disturb them, as they demonstrated for their parents, their brothers and sisters, for they were comfortable among themselves and excited about their activity.

These remarkable children, called the seeds of wisdom by John Africa, are born in revolution, in resistance, in antisystematic natural law. Their young brothers and sisters were murdered by the government on May 13, 1985. Their older brothers and sisters were also murdered by the government on May 13, and some were railroaded to nearly a century in prison. At least one child was born in prison. "Jail Rendell, set MOVE free!"—march chant.

Reporters told that a march occurred, and how many participated on that rainy day in May, but by not showing who marched, they missed the heart of the story, a story of resistance, generation by generation, and a living tale of survival.

From death row, this is Mumia Abu-Jamal

FOR HER PEOPLE, this tiny, fiery, coffee-colored woman was a legend—welfare mother, welfare activist, militant chairwoman of the Philadelphia chapter of a welfare rights organization. And then with her hard work and iron will, Roxanne Jones fought for and was elected the first black woman in Pennsylvania's three-hundred-year provincial and legislative history to be elected state senator. She wore her senatorial role, as she did any other honor and leadership role in a life rich with community activism on behalf of the poor, with ease and grace.

I knew her with loving memory from my teenage years, when she would come to my mother's house, collect me, and we, with some of her girlfriends, would "hang out" and talk about the dreams and rages poor folks talked about. To tens of thousands of North Philadelphians, she wasn't "the Senator," but not out of any lack of respect for political office; she was Roxanne, as familiar as an older sister, an aunt, a member of the family of the heart, esteemed because she was loved, and loved because she loved her people.

Who were her people? North Philadelphians, poor folks, people on welfare, people on the margins of life. I was one of her people. I hadn't seen her in years, but what does that "seeing" have to do with feeling? She fought for the poorest, and the poor loved her fiercely and returned her to office as a matter of course, from November 1984 onward. This dark, South Carolina–born beauty died on May 19, 1996, several days after her sixty-eighth birthday, reportedly of a heart attack, although those who knew her believe this strong, passionate, principled woman died from a broken heart, a heart shattered by the brutal series of bills that recently passed in her Senate chamber, which savaged the poor by cutting medical assistance to an estimated 250,000 people, signed into law by a governor, Thomas Ridge, bent on waging a war on the poor. For Roxanne, now the senator from the third legislative district from Philadelphia, the plight of the poor wasn't academic or intellectual; it was as personal as one's heart, and as she spent her young adult life as a mother on welfare, an attack on them was an attack on her. Ultimately, this committed, able, principled and caring senator was just one vote among fifty, and therefore unable to successfully parry this last and deadly blow. As they tossed the poor and ailing aside for crass political advantage, so she felt tossed and lost.

After the shock waves of her death reached across Pennsylvania and prominent politicians weighed in with words of praise, her staff issued a pointed news release: Governor Tom Ridge was not welcome at her funeral. P.S. Don't even send flowers.

Roxanne, still real.

From death row, this is Mumia Abu-Jamal

SHE SITS IN UTTER STILLNESS, her coffee-brown features as if set in obsidian; as if a mask. Barely perceptible, the tears threaten to overflow that dark, proud, maternal face, a face held still by rage.

A warm spring day in North Philadelphia saw her on her way home, after her tiring duties as a housekeeper in a West Mount Airy home. On arrival she was stopped by police, who told her she could not enter her home of twenty-three years, and that it would be torn down as part of a city program against drug dens. "My house ain't no drug den!" the fifty-nine-year-old grandmother argued. "This is my home!" The cops, strangers to this part of town, could care less.

Mrs. Helen Anthony left the scene to contact her grown children. Two hours later, she returned to an eerie scene straight out of the Twilight Zone. Her home was no more.

A pile of bricks stood amid hills of red dust and twisted debris; a lone wall standing jagged, a man's suit flapping on a hook, flapping like a flag of surrender, after a war waged by bulldozers and ambitious politicians. Mrs. Anthony received no warning before the jaws of the baleful backhoe bit into the bricks of her life, tearing asunder the gatherings and memories of a life well lived. She was served no notice that the City of Brotherly Love intended to grind her home of twenty-three years into dust because they didn't like her neighbors; they just showed up one day, armed with television cameras and political ambitions, and did it. Gone.

When reporters asked politicos about the black grandmother whose home was demolished, they responded with characteristic arrogance: "Well, the law of eminent domain gives us the right to tear down any house we wanna," they said. When coverage turned negative, out came the olive branch:

"We'll reimburse her."

"Oops, honest mistake!"

"—compensation—"

Left unquestioned is the wisdom of a policy of mass destruction planned over a brunch of brie and croissants and executed for the six o'clock news, with no regard for the lives and well-being of the people involved.

In a city with an estimated thirty thousand homeless people, why does the government embark on a blitzkrieg of bulldozing and demolishing homes, even abandoned ones? Mrs. Anthony, offered a home in compensation by red-faced city officials, is less than enthused. "The way the city treated her," opined her daughter Geraldine Johnson, "she does not want to live in Philadelphia."

Her treatment at the hands of those who call themselves "civil servants" points to the underlying indifference with which black lives, property, and aspirations are treated by the political elite. One would be hard pressed to find this degree of destructive nonchalance in a neighborhood where a white grandmother lived.

Another chapter in the tragicomedy called "the drug war."

From death row, this is Mumia Abu-Jamal.

PAM AFRICA, MINISTER and disciple of the teachings of John Africa, tells a true tale of a meeting between John Africa and a man of the cloth behind the old headquarters of the MOVE organization, in the Powelton village section of West Philadelphia.

The scene: a man, middle-aged, bearded, booted, and blue-jeaned, is called to the back door by the leader of a small group from a nearby church. Though both are black, they represent a fascinating tableau of difference. The one wears a T-shirt, sweat soaking his breast; and the other is impeccably dressed in silk, suit, and tie. The only touch missing is coattails. The one's hair is rough, gray-fringed, uncombed, and hanging like ropes to his shoulders; the other is pomaded, greased, and brushed smooth—the head of a preacher man.

The air is thick and charged with controversy for the city is threatening to remove MOVE from their property and their neighborhood after a series of highly publicized confrontations with the police that have left several MOVE men and women beaten and bloody and one MOVE baby dead.

"So, you are sayin' that all I gotta to do is pray, and everything will be alright."

"Well, that is what I am saying brother."

"If I pray the cops will stop beating up my people?"

"Yes, that is what I am saying, brotha."

"If I pray, the cops will stop killing us."

"Yes, pray in Jesus name brother, because the Bible say 'ask and it shall be given unto you.' That is it, brother."

"And if I pray, our people will truly be free?"

"Uh-huh, yes sir, brother."

"Well, c'mon, Reverend. Let's pray then. "

John Africa drops to his knees, oblivious of the soft mud already staining his jeans.

"Whoa—what you doin', brotha?"

"You said we needa pray."

"Uhh... huh—"

"Well, come on, Rev, pray with me, okay?"

"I... I... I meant pray in the church."

"Why, Reverend? Ain't God out here in the open air? Ain't God all around us. Come on? Let's kneel down here on God's earth and pray."

At this point the Reverend backs up, and John Africa says, "What is a matter? I thought that you said that we should pray. Well, come on down here and pray with me."

The Reverend continues to stand there, staring.

John Africa asks again, "What's the matter, man? That suit you got on more important than God? I thought you said that you believed in God. This dirt is God. So why don't you kneel down here and pray with me?"

"Well, uh... excuse me, brotha, but I got to be getting back to my church."

At this point the people standing around the two men began to speak.

"See, that man is down on there on his knees in the dirt. He got to be for real. That Reverend ain't nothing but a phony. He scared he is gonna dirty his suit. He talking 'bout how he believe in God, he don't believe in nothin' but that suit."

One woman comments to another, "That preacher's a hypocrite. See. That is why I don't go to no church, cuz I don't believe in the preachers, cuz they ain't nothing but liars. They ain't for real. That man there kneelin' in that dirt is for real."

John Africa goes on.

"You don't wanna to pray with me, then Rev? "

"Ah, I got to go, man.... I'm sorry."

"Why are you leaving, Rev?"

The dashing preacher beats a hasty retreat from the muddy yard. More intent, it seems, on saving silk than souls. . .

Several years later and several miles west ward, the city would torch

MOVE's home and headquarters with a helicopter-borne firebomb, incinerating John Africa and ten other longhairs, some of them women and children, in a massacre plotted to take place on Mother's Day.

The scene: smoldering remains of an entire neighborhood, only hours before the site of a blistering and bellowing inferno. Philadelphia's men of the cloth have gathered once again, though only to examine the carnage, not to weep for the fallen, nor to pray for the dead. They have come bedecked in robes and collars, the purpose of their gathering to pray in support of the mayor of the city that has bombed its own citizens, and obliterated, incarnated, and dismembered its own babies. The police commissioner, the fire chief, the mayor and his officers are almost to a man Christian—Baptists or Catholics, most of them—religious people. Yet these men who have gathered to pray are not only churchgoers; they are ministers, pastors, priests. Aside from praying, though, it seems they mean to do little. Why should they? They just winked at a full-scale war waged over mere misdemeanors, at the deaths of eleven people, blasted by a sky bomb, at the destruction of dozens of homes and the permanent scarring of a neighborhood. And so they pray and leave for home, their duties fulfilled.

Men of the cloth? Yes. But men of the spirit?

From death row, this is Mumia Abu-Jamal.

IT'S BEEN OVER A DECADE since the unprecedented boom in U.S. prison construction began, leaving this country with the highest incarceration rate in the world.

Not surprisingly, this massive transfer of public taxes to the prison economy has left state coffers nearly empty, and many public needs unmet.

In a recent report released by the National Conference of State Legislatures, the economic condition of forty-seven American states was described as in "dire fiscal straits." The reason is simple: increased government spending versus a diminished tax base, resulting in state reserves termed "nearly nonexistent" and "inadequate."

On what has the government been spending? Prisons. Increasingly, the bulk of America's tax buck goes to build or maintain America's growing penal colonies.

A recent American Bar Association (ABA) report, critical of this expensive trend, paints a powerful picture of the expensive costs of putting prison needs above social health needs. The report, the result of a three-year study by the ABA Criminal Justice Section, is sharply critical of the incarceration as dangerously ineffective and, in a sense, self-defeating. Instead of decreasing the crime rate, the report contends, the experience of incarceration may actually provoke more crime.

"It may be that the experience of being incarcerated inculcates or solidifies antisocial attitudes and behavior and/or fosters such dependency that the likelihood of criminal behavior upon release is much greater for some than if they had never been incarcerated," the report notes. Prisons, as has long been suspected, are criminogenic, meaning they generate criminal behavior.

The ABA report, in examining the social costs of prisons on those most in need of human services, finds an effect that may be termed "devastating."

The report found that it takes the combined annual income taxes of eighteen Delaware residents to pay the costs to incarcerate one person for one year, meaning those taxes could *not* be used for education, health care, environmental protection, or a myriad of other governmental services. Further, the ABA report found that the cost of construction, financing, and operating a one-thousand-cell prison in Wisconsin for one year would have paid for eleven thousand children in that state's Head Start program. Presently, some 30,000 eligible preschoolers are excluded from participation in the Wisconsin Head Start program because of lack of funding.

In Pennsylvania, libraries are being closed and university appropriations are being cut so that prisons can be built. The 1992–'93 fiscal year began with costs for state prisons at over $500 million, or half a billion dollars. California just closed out a budget for its biggest prison expansion in the United States, with a price tag of nearly two billion bucks—in one year!

Every hungry, ill-housed, uneducated, unemployed person in the United States owes his wretched condition, in some degree, to a politician who made a policy decision to let a family go homeless, or a child unschooled, so that a prison cell could be built.

It is precisely this quasi economy of legal repression that fuels the outer economy of depression.

From death row, this is Mumia Abu-Jamal.

*The courts have raised hope, spit disappointment, courted the rich
and protected their interest, it is past time for all poor people
to release themselves from the deceptive strangulation of society,
realize that society has failed you, for to attempt to ignore this system
of deception now is deny you the need to protest this failure later,
the system has failed you yesterday, failed you today and
has created the conditions for failure tomorrow.*

—FROM *The Judges Letter,* BY MOVE FOUNDER JOHN AFRICA

AMERICA'S PRESIDENTIAL RACE is history, and former president Bush is in his political retirement. The nation's media is awash in hoopla for the changing of the presidential guard, and few are the voices of dissent, of alarm. Many, perhaps tens of millions, we are told, voted not so much for Clinton as *against* Bush, or against Bush's inability to crank up America's dwindling economy. This, despite the fact that presidents have a tenuous influence on something so enormous as the national economy.

But by way of a treaty, millions of jobs may be affected—for the worse. That treaty, the so-called NAFTA pact, NAFTA for the "North American Free Trade Agreement," talks about "free trade" in everything but *labor.*

Big industries and mid-sized corporations in the United States are licking their collective lips at the prospect of traveling points south of the border, where labor is cheapest, where environmental laws are nonexistent, and where unions are mere memories. President-elect Bill Clinton, like his corporate counterpart Bush, has embraced NAFTA like the Holy Grail, and both have sworn their adherence to business whims.

It is the inherent nature of capitalism to maximize the profit margin, even if labor's return is minimized. A long history of collective bargaining, or unionism, in the United States provided workers with impressive living standards—standards, incidentally, that have been in decline for a decade. Clinton's election, given his support of NAFTA, ensures that decline will continue for millions.

Using the attractive bait of racial hatred, the Reagan-Bush camp convinced millions of whites to vote for them, and all would be well; it took a decade of union-busting, of industrial flight abroad, of economic decay for workers and expansion for management, for millions of white workers to turn away from the party of Willie Hortonist hatred—but to what?

Clinton, exploiting anti-Bush sentiment, ignored blacks and labor, spit on Sista Souljah, jettisoned Jesse Jackson, and most sinisterly, barbecued Ricky Ray Rector in an Arkansas death cell, in a not too subtle appeal to white racism for votes. Millions of whites, again like sheep, voted for him. Just as Bush-Reagan burned workers from their first days in office, Clinton's adoption of NAFTA guarantees a like result. In 1996, who will dance enough to attract white votes? Perot? Duke? Clinton? And with what? The face changes, the system doesn't.

From death row, this is Mumia Abu-Jamal.

THE BRUTAL POLICE BLUDGEONING of black Detroit father Malice Green has illustrated that the battle lines of the so-called War on Drugs could more accurately be drawn around a "War on Blacks." Published reports surfacing since the flashlight beating of the westside father of five, which left him dead of head trauma, speculated on the issue of whether Green was a user of crack cocaine, as police charged.

So what if he was?

The purported justification behind the so-called drug war is to undo or lessen the damage that drugs do. To be sure, drugs do serious harm to people by destroying their health, and taking lives as well. But was Malice Green beaten to death in his car to save him from the scourge of drugs? Were the police so concerned with saving Green from drug's ill effects that they beat his skull in with flashlights?

One is reminded of the saying that came out of the Vietnam War when U.S. troops ravaged and napalmed villagers—"We had to destroy the village, in order to save it," they said. Did the police destroy Green to save him from the sickness of drugs?

So soon after the high-tech brutality against Rodney King of L.A., and the scene is repeated this time, fatally. The "Drug War" is a cruel farce designed to obliterate those it claims to protect.

In the United States alone, over 300,000 people perish annually from that well known *legal* drug—cigarettes. In the United States alone, well over twenty thousand people die every year from the equally popular *legal* drug—alcohol. As a result of cocaine, an estimated eighteen thousand people died in 1989 and 1990. Cigarettes produce an addictive substance, nicotine, which poisons lungs, causing emphysema and death. Alcohol is literally an organic poison that destroys living tissue, such as brain tissue and livers, and is a stimulant to crime, countless traffic accidents, suicide, and death.

Will those who wield deadly (to themselves and others, through passive secondhand smoke inhalation) tobacco be beaten down in the streets? Will drinkers find Uzis pointed at their bodies when they imbibe their next alcoholic fix?

I don't think so.

So, when is a drug a "drug"?

When it destroys human life, or when it fails to return a tidy profit to U.S. industries?

Every single day, lives are shattered by police and judicial actions that crumble careers and families in the name of a "War on Drugs," while popular, financially respected drugs continue untold social, psychic, and human damage. The Malice Green case shows how the state, instead of solving a problem, creates an absurdity of "destroying a life—only to save it."

From death row, this is Mumia Abu-Jamal.

When a gang member is beaten by persons unknown in a mixed neighborhood, and the black gangs begin terrorizing WHITES, it is called racism, a bunch of cops can ride through black neighborhoods all day beatin' ass, and call it law, when a bunch of blacks beat one of these cops' ass it's called mob violence.

—JOHN AFRICA, MAY 1967

A YOUNG WOMAN, engulfed in a diabetic coma while sitting in her car, is repeatedly shot by a corps of cops who say they are threatened by her. Tyesha Miller, of Riverside, California, becomes a statistic.

A young man sitting in his car in North Philly is surrounded by a phalanx of armed cops, whose guns are pointed at him from all points. He is ordered to raise his hands. When he does so, he is shot to death by one of the cops, who insists he thought he saw a gun. The eighteen-year-old is unarmed. Dontae Dawson becomes a statistic.

An emigrant from the West African nation of Senegal comes to America, taking an apartment in New York's Bronx Borough. When four NYPD cops approach his door, reportedly looking for a rapist (he was not a suspect), he is shot at forty-one times. Nineteen shots hit him. Amadou Diallo was unarmed, and will never return alive to West Africa.

In case after case after case, in city after city, from coast to coast, such things happen with alarming regularity, worsened by the realization that in most cases cops who have committed these acts, which if committed by others would constitute high crimes, will face no serious prosecution, if any prosecution at all.

They are, the corporate media assures us, "just doing their jobs," "under an awful lot of pressure," or "in fear," and therefore justified in what they do. In the language of the media, the very media that make their millions off the punishment industry calling for the vilest sentences known to man, turn in the twinkling of an eye into paragons of mercy, who lament that the "fine young men" who "served their community" are in "trouble," or have "suffered enough."

The suffering of the slain, because they are young and black, is all but forgotten in this unholy algebra that devalues black life, while heightening the worth of the assailants because they work for the state.

The worst lie that is often trotted out in such cases is when politicians and media people sing the praises of such people, who are called, by virtue of their jobs, "public servants." Since when have servants (of any kind) acted in the vile, arrogant, monstrous manner that many of these cops do in black, hispanic, and poor communities? Since when have such servants been in the position to slaughter, shoot, humiliate, and imprison the very public they are sworn to serve?

They are servants, if at all, of the public structures of which they are a part, not of the people. They are servants, if at all, of the state. They serve the interests of capital, of the wealthy, of those who run this system from their bank vaults and corporate offices.

They do not serve the poor, the powerless, nor the uninfluential.

They never have.

They are an armed force organized to protect the interests of the established, and those who own capital. The history of labor in this country is splattered by the blood of trade unionists who were beaten, shot, and crushed to the earth for striking against the trusts, combinations, and mega-corporations of capital. Who did the beating? The shooting? The crushing? The cops, who served the interests of a state that declared, as did the Supreme Court, that unions were "criminal conspiracies," and that the Constitution was "based upon the concept that the fundamental private rights of property are... morally beyond the reach of popular majorities."[*]

Capital's voice (the media) and their agents (the politicians) unite in a

---

[*]Frances Fox Piven and Richard A. Cloward, *The New Class War: Reagan's Attack on the Welfare State and Its Consequences,* revised, expanded ed. (New York: Pantheon, 1982), citing Charles A. Beard, *An Economic Interpretation of the Constitution of the United States* (New York: Free Press, 1965).

chorus of support for their legalized killers, who bomb babies with impunity (remember May 13, 1985, in Philadelphia?), who shoot unarmed kids in their cars and unarmed African emigrants, whose only capital crime is being black in modern-day America.

This daily legalized violence proves that violence is not a problem to the system—when it is their's against the people.

This awful crime must cease.

From death row, this is Mumia Abu-Jamal.

Should smoking, drinking alcohol,
exposing oneself to contaminants in the
workplace, or staying on one's feet too long
also be subject to criminal penalty?

—PENNSYLVANIA REPRESENTATIVE
LOUISE BISHOP, JUNE 1990

ALL ABOUT US CAN BE SEEN the ravages and ruin that results from the
"drug war" of the late twentieth century. Shattered lives, freedom enshack-
led, governments corrupted, and economies disrupted, all casualties in this
politicized "war."

It is estimated that 70 percent of the nation's enormous prison population (over 1.2 million men and women) is based upon, or related to, drugs.
Not only does this enormous public expenditure drain resources away from
educational and other social concerns, but the human cost bespeaks a gen-
erational tragedy. How many mothers, fathers, sons and daughters have
been caged because the ruling political order has condemned a certain
chemical substance? How many men and women have had their lives
destroyed by drugs that are legal? Why is one drug deemed legal and another illegal? Why does the government damn one drug, while openly supporting another?

Aren't *all* drugs bad for you?

Illegal drugs like cocaine and meth, when used to excess, cost an estimated 10,000 lives (or deaths) a year. Legal drugs like alcohol and tobacco
(nicotine) cost over 500,000 deaths per year. The *Wall Street Journal*
(December 8, 1995) reported the existence of a fifteen-page draft report
from the smoking giant Philip Morris that found nicotine, an active ingre-

dient in tobacco, to be a "similar, organic chemical" to cocaine, morphine, quinine, and atropine. "While each of these substances can be used to affect the human physiology," the report stated, "nicotine has a particularly broad range of influence."

Nicotine, a chemical cousin of cocaine, like its relative, affects the brain. Furthermore, nicotine and other pollutants in tobacco contribute to pulmonary emphysema, a deadly lung disease.

Who can question the poisonous impact of alcohol in crime, drunk driving, domestic violence, and liver disease?

If nicotine is "chemically similar" to cocaine, why does the government pay subsidies to farmers to grow tobacco? Why does the government allow its sale through cigars, cigarettes, snuff, and dip to millions every day? Why are American tobacco companies exporting tons of this poison to Asia, Africa, and much of the Third World?

Of course, the answer is dough, bucks, baksheesh—money.

The megamillion-dollar tobacco companies ply their politicians with the funds for their campaigns; the politicians who write laws ignore the millions who die bitter, choking, emphysemic deaths, and turn a blind eye on this poison.

This column is not suggesting that smoking or drinking be made statutory crimes. (The Eighteenth Amendment, which prohibited import, sale, transport and manufacture of alcohol, proved the error of that method, and was later repealed.)

It is to show the hypocrisy of a government that okays the drugs it can tax, and fights the drugs it can't tax.

From death row, this is Mumia Abu-Jamal.

*Never before have diseased ruminants
(animals that chew their cud) been fed
to other ruminants. We are in a
mass experiment which is killing us.*

—PROFESSOR TIM LAING,
DEPARTMENT OF FOOD POLICY,
THAMES VALLEY UNIVERSITY, U.K.

A GROWING PANIC IS BREWING in the so-called civilized world, over the
"mad cow disease" recently uncovered in England, where the disease passed
over to humans by their eating of tainted meat.

Hundreds of millions of meat eaters are forced to do something that the
multibillion dollar meat industry has tried to do their level best to prevent—
to think of the Big Mac, the "Fatburger," the "everything-on-it" beef burger,
as the flesh of a sentient, once-living being, or to put it more nakedly, as a
dead cow.

Modern-day packaging conspires to have us ignore much of what we eat,
for as the old advertising axiom informs us ("sell the sizzle, not the steak"),
we are driven by the familiar, the comfortable, deadly habits that stifle our
thinking and silence the human faculty of questioning. We go to massive
food factories ("supermarkets") and literally pay for our poisons, mega-
chemical-laden dead foods, juices that have never wet the insides of fruit,
eggs that have never been inside chickens, and meats that come from four-
legged, dazed dope addicts fed on awful offal. With the hypnotic magic of a
sexy jingle in our heads ("Things go better with—"; "Have it your way!") or
our eyes dazed by a hip label, we put our down payment on our deaths.

Meanwhile, the same "authorities" assure us that we face "minimal risk." MOVE political prisoner and revolutionary naturalist Mike Africa dashes that old claim:

> That's of course, what they say about *everything* they produce cuz ain't *none* of that stuff safe. But now people are lookin' at that 'minimal risk' them people are talkin' bout, and it makes them look at *who's* tellin 'em that. All them years the cigarette industry been tellin' people that cigarettes didn't cause cancer in the face of cancer-ridden millions who smoke. Nuclear plants parked next to residential districts—tellin' them people it posed 'minimal risk' while the town is full of legless children, babies born with hearts *outside* their chest, and industry sayin' the cause is somethin' *else*.

MOVE founder John Africa unequivocally condemns the entire system that feeds the people death for profit:

> This system has misled people to believe that they can't live comfortably *with the single principle of God* and can't live comfortably with*out* the multiple problems of industry, for the system has created a policy of sickness, tricked folks into believing that they can't do without industry.... It is insane not to resist something that gives nothin' but *sickness* to *you, your mothers, your fathers, your babies, your family.*

With every bite of beef henceforth must be mingled the fear that accompanies the knowledge that the beast off which you feed may have fed on another diseased beast, or on shredded newspaper, or on offal.

Will you trust the merchant?

Will you trust yourself?

From death row, this is Mumia Abu-Jamal.

MUMIA ABU-JAMAL speaking at the Church of the Advocate in Philadelphia, at a memorial for Fred Hampton, the 21-year-old Black Panther Party Illinois State Chairman who was assassinated by the FBI and the Chicago Police Department on December 4, 1969. COURTESY OF MUMIA ABU-JAMAL

FBI SURVEILLANCE OF Mumia Abu-Jamal began during the late '60s, when he and his friends at Benjamin Franklin High School were organizing to change the name of the school to Malcolm X High School. COURTESY OF MUMIA ABU-JAMAL

A FRONT-PAGE PHOTO in the *Philadelphia Inquirer* of Mumia Abu-Jamal at sixteen (1969), as lieutenant minister of information for the Philadelphia Black Panther Party. © JAMES/PHILADELPHIA INQUIRER

MUMIA ABU-JAMAL, a reporter for Channel 12, WHYY-TV, interviews basketball star Julius Erving as the 76ers battle for the NBA Championship, 1980. COURTESY OF MUMIA ABU-JAMAL

MUMIA ABU-JAMAL, news director of Philadelphia radio station WHAT. COURTESY OF MUMIA ABU-JAMAL

a special dimension to radio reporting.

MUMIA ABU-JAMAL, as a news reporter for NPR's premier Philadelphia radio
station WUHY (now WHYY), was featured as a rising star by *Philadelphia* magazine
in a 1981 article.

MUMIA AND his son Mazi, circa 1981. COURTESY OF MUMIA ABU-JAMAL

MUMIA ABU-JAMAL in the crowd of reporters at a press conference featuring Philadelphia mayor and former police chief Frank Rizzo, August 8, 1978.
COURTESY OF MUMIA ABU-JAMAL

HUNTINGTON STATE PRISON, October 1992. © HEIKE KLEFFNER

STATE CORRECTIONAL INSTITUTE at Greene in Waynesburg, PA.
Aerial photograph. Highlighted area shows where Mumia is being held.

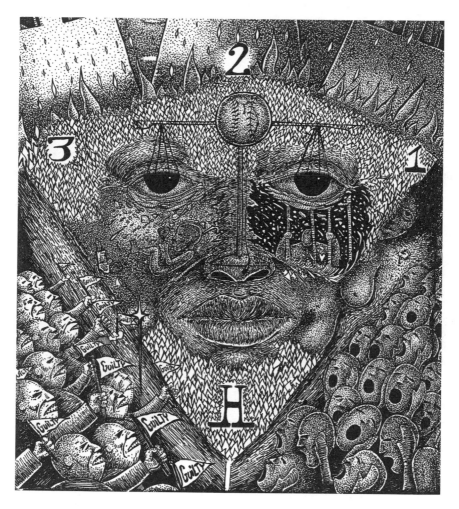

One is amazed and even astonished to consider those millions who today claim spiritual lineage from a being called Christ, for if one were from outer space and able to view life on this planet for a century or so, one might observe this:

> Christians are the wealthiest humans on the third planet. They seem to be the most violent humanoids, having brought about two world wars, tens of thousands of murders, and millions of rapes, assaults, and lynchings. They're the only group to have dropped an atomic bomb on other, non-Christian people, to have colonized and enslaved whole races of other humans—Africans, indeed the bulk of the non-Christian world—and to have committed genocide on an unsurpassed scale—American Indians, Jews, for example. One of their nations, where vast numbers of Christians have settled, called America, cages and imprisons more of its people per capita than any other nation-state. They destroy and fail to replenish enormous expanses of land to secure quantities of paper called "money." Their cities have vast numbers of people who live in the streets, whom they call "homeless."

This alien perspective seems facetious, of course, but it allows us to ask questions that challenge that body of humankind that claims spiritual descent from the Jewish carpenter of Nazareth. Isn't it odd that in this nation, the majority of the population, Christian adherents, claim to pray to and adore a being who was a prisoner of Roman power, an inmate on the empire's death row, that the one they consider the personification of the creator of the universe was tortured, humiliated, beaten, and crucified on a barren scrap of land, on the imperial periphery at Golgotha, the place of the skull? That the majority of its inhabitants called adherents of the crucified god strenuously support the state's execution of thousands of its imprisoned citizens, that the overwhelming majority of its judges, prosecutors, and lawyers, those who condemn, prosecute, and sell out the condemned, claim to be followers of the fettered, spat upon, naked god? Who are we speaking of, Baal of Babylon, Jupiter of Rome, or Christ of Christendom?

After the passage of two millennia, how can one even envision a future where life is safe to live, where the seas, the air, the very sun, don't threaten extinction? How far the ideal from the real. How many of us whose god is Mammon have sold out the worth of this wondrous earth for a shiny token? In how many of us can the voice of God be heard amid the tinkle of coins and the rustle of paper?

I speak from Pennsylvania's death row, a bright, shining, highly mechanized hell. In this place, a dark temple to fear, an altar of political ambition, death is a campaign poster, a stepping stone to public office. In this space and time, in this dark hour, how many of us are not on death row?

From death row, this is Mumia Abu-Jamal.

FIVE HUNDRED YEARS:
CELEBRATIONS OR DEMONSTRATIONS?

AS THE YEAR 1992 comes roaring out of time, minds turn to the upcoming marking of five hundred years since the Spanish conquest and European "discovery" of what came to be called the New World.

Depending on one's perspective, October 1992 is either cause for celebration or condemnation in belated response to the confused arrival of Admiral Christopher Columbus, or as the Spanish prefer, Cristobal Colon.

His colossal error in navigation resulted in naming the red-skinned inhabitants "Indians," a mistake based upon his firm reckoning that he had landed in India. Initial logs of his landing spoke admirably of a warm and friendly meeting with the dark inhabitants, who received the Europeans with, in Columbus's words, "Great amity towards us." They were "a loving people without covetousness," who "were greatly pleased and became so entirely our friends that it was a wonder to see."

Sadly, the same could not be said for the Christians, who coveted not only the tiny islands but the lion's share of the mainland. After they instituted slavery and caused widespread suffering and death, they stole land they so coveted.

There are no descendants of the "Indians," actually the Arawaks, who met Columbus.* The tribe was exterminated in the space of a generation under pressure of European slavery, genocide, and disease.

Not content with stealing land from the native people, the colonists stole people from another land, launching a black holocaust that sent millions of

---

*See Ward Churchill, *A Little Matter of Genocide: Holocaust and Denial in the Americas, 1492 to the Present* (San Francisco: City Lights Books, 1999), 86–88 ; Paul G. Legassé, ed., *The Concise Columbia Encyclopedia*, 3rd ed. (New York: Columbia University Press, 1994), 217, 718–719; Gary B. Nash, *Red, White and Black: The Peoples of Early North America* (New Jersey: Prentice Hall, 1974), 35–39; among others.

Africans into a nightmare of dehumanization, deculturization, slavery, and death via the dreaded Middle Passage. Central to this epoch of historic criminality was the use and global manifestation of racism to justify this carnage. One early British apologist for European theft of Red lands, pamphleteer Robert Gray wrote (1609):

> "Although the Lord hath given the earth to children of men, the greater part of it [is] possessed and wrongfully usurped by wild beasts, and unreasonable creatures, or by brutish savages, which by reason of their Godless ignorance, and blasphemous idolatrie, are worse than those beasts which are of most wilde and savage nature."

Today, five centuries after Columbian contact, a bare 750,000 Indians live in some twenty-seven U.S. states, scattered over roughly three hundred reservations, where once well over ten million Indians lived free. The vaunted "progress" boasted of has hardly touched Indian communities, where alcoholism is endemic and rates of unemployment range from 14 percent to 67 percent with a national average unemployment rate of over 43 percent.

It would seem that the most directly impacted and affected of peoples touched by the landing of Europeans at Hispanola in 1492 have the least reason to celebrate the subsequent five hundred years.

They, misnamed "Indians," became the New World's first slaves, the most deprived, the most exploited, the most neglected, in an intentional pattern of conquest and mass liquidation in the face of white thirst for *Lebensraum*, or living room.

Even when they renounced their traditional faith and folkways, as did the Cherokee of New Echota, Georgia, who converted to Christianity, built housing and buildings and government in the European manner, and even kept black slaves, it did not save them from massive land theft, a corrupt government stealing of their property, and the gunpoint march to reservations that left thousands dead, black and red, on the Trail of Tears.

Many will mark five hundred years with tears and bitterness.

From death row, this is Mumia Abu-Jamal.

DEMOCRACY, the dictionary informs us, means "government by the people." Generations have been weaned on the premise that the United States is a "democracy" and this is "government by the people," but a brief foray into history reveals otherwise.

The history of Africans, of course, shows government as an aider and abettor of the vilest oppressions on these shores, from the U.S. Constitution's Article 1, Section 3, which held Africans as "three-fifths of all other persons," to *Dred Scott v. Sanford* (1857),[*] where the U.S. Supreme Court determined that the phrase, "We, the People" in the Constitution's preamble did not refer to Africans, *whether slave or free*, and therefore Africans were not beneficiaries of constitutional "guarantees," *nor were their descendants* "should they become free."

Certainly, as regards Africans in America, the notion of "government by the people" did not include them in this democracy. Native Americans, misnamed "Indians," fared little better. The same constitutional provision that made Africans three-fifths of a person excluded Indians altogether from representation, and its companion document, the Declaration of Independence, called them "merciless Indian savages." Their share of "democracy" was genocide on a scale that would make a Nazi blanch.

In this, their sacred ancestral lands, the U.S. Supreme Court recently ruled that their religious practice must give way to the needs of business, and might be bulldozed and "developed" by business interests without violating the Constitution.

---

[*]*Dred Scott v. Sanford,* 19 U.S. (How.) 393, 407, 15 L.Ed 691 (1857).

Asians were initially specifically excluded from the United States from the earliest days; the U.S. Immigration Act of 1790 allowed citizenship only for "free white persons." Many U.S. states, especially California, made it illegal for a Chinese person to testify in court: for example, a California statute of 1863, c. 70, stated that "no Indian, or person having one-half or more of Indian blood, or Mongolian or Chinese, shall be permitted to give evidence in favor of, or against, any white person" (section 14). In February 1884 the California legislature promulgated a "new" constitution, and in Article 12, section 2, prohibited the employment of Chinese or Mongolian—*even native-born*—in any corporation, public or private.

Many of these laws stood until 1940s federal decisions reversed them. The World War II confiscations and mass internments of Japanese property and persons are still within living memory—this, while Italo- and German-Americans, even as Fascist and Bund parties blossomed here, were never subject to mass concentration camps.

It's important to note that Japanese internment happened with the blessings of the U.S. Supreme Court. To these millions of black, red, and yellow souls, then, government for *centuries* meant denial, exclusion, refusal, and sanction. To them, "democracy" was but a synonym for white tyranny, often under the cloak of "law."

And why refer to women under the misleading rubric of "minority," when women constitute 52 percent of the nation's population and thus, *the majority*? To the extent they have been denied representation, it only accents the obvious illusion of a "democracy" that has historically frustrated and oppressed the majority of its people at the minority's whim.

For, if women are 52 percent, Blacks 12.5 percent, Hispanics 9.5 percent, and Asians/Native American/others 3.8 percent, then Americans have been systematically excluded from democracy's empty promises.

Only in America can a "democracy" oppress the majority.

From death row, this is Mumia Abu-Jamal.

"PRESIDENTS REAGAN AND BUSH have ensured that the federal courts will not be representative. Instead, they are a bastion of White America. They stand as a symbol of White Power." Can you guess who said these words?

I'd wager most folks missed the identity of the speaker. Stephen Reinhardt, justice of the Ninth Circuit Court of Appeals, made those remarks during commencement for law school graduates at Golden Gate University in San Francisco, spring 1992. Reinhardt told the throng of potential attorneys, "What the African-American community perceived from the Supreme Court decisions was that the federal judiciary is no longer interested in protecting the rights of minorities, that federal judges are far more concerned with... protecting the interests of white males."

To support his argument, Reinhardt pointed to the recent *McCleskey* decision,[*] where the U.S. Supreme Court rejected overwhelming evidence of a racial disparity in death sentences; the dismissal of a civil suit filed by a black man injured by the infamous Los Angeles police chokehold; and a host of rulings narrowing civil and voting rights laws.

And that ain't all.

Across the United States, an astonishing number of people in the "land of the free" are caged up in pens. In fact, the U.S. now imprisons over a million people, with over four million under "correctional control." The number of incarcerated blacks, especially black males, is striking. Over 3,109

---

[*]*McCleskey vs. Kemp*, 481 U.S. 279 (1987).

persons per 100,000 are locked up in the United States; in South Africa, the number is 729 black males, per 100,000 population, meaning the Pretoria regime imprisons less than one-fourth of the black male population the U.S. does.

Look at it this way: the number of people imprisoned in the United States is more than the number of people who live in thirteen states; the number of people in American jails and prisons would constitute the eleventh largest city in the nation; and the number of all people under "correctional" control (meaning prison, jail, probation, or parole) is one and a half times greater than the population of Chicago or Nicaragua.

While Judge Reinhardt speaks solely of the federal system, surely the same or worse can be said of state court systems, where politics is more overt as an influence on who goes to jail and who doesn't. This system of encagement is accompanied by a severe and reactionary reign of constitutional and statutory repression, from America's highest court, the Supreme Court, to the local justice of the peace.

The Fourth Amendment, said to "guarantee" freedom from search and seizures, has been scuttled by the state. The First Amendment is an afterthought violated daily by the state, where dissidents are imprisoned for refusing to renounce their faith (as in MOVE), and Indian sacred lands are violated for the All-American god of business.

As evidenced by the recent instances of martial law in San Francisco and Los Angeles,* not to mention the mass deportation of Spanish-speaking Americans back to Mexico without notice or hearing, the Constitution is possessed of all the power and relevance of toilet paper.

This is America 1992—the largest, blackest prison population on earth; a judiciary of white, male, biased millionaires; a land smoldering in racial, class, sexual, and ecological conflict; a nation in chains.

From death row, this is Mumia Abu-Jamal.

---

*Martial law was invoked in San Francisco and Los Angeles during the rebellion resulting from the Rodney King verdict.

DON'T TELL ME about the valley of the shadow of death. I live there. In south-central Pennsylvania's Huntingdon County, a hundred-year-old prison stands,* its gothic towers projecting an air of foreboding, evoking a gloomy mood of the dark ages. I, and some forty-five other men, spend about twenty-two hours a day in six-by-ten-foot cells. The additional two hours may be spent outdoors in a chain-link-fenced box, ringed by concertina razor wire, under the gaze of gun turrets.

Welcome to Pennsylvania's death row.

I'm a bit stunned. Several days ago, Pennsylvania's Supreme Court affirmed my conviction and sentence of death by a vote of four justices, three did not participate.

As a black journalist who was a Panther way back in my young teens, I've often studied America's long history of legal lynchings of Africans. I remember a front page of the Black Panther newspaper bearing the quote, "A black man has no rights that a white man is bound to respect," attributed to U.S. Supreme Court chief justice Robert Taney of the infamous *Dred Scott* case, where America's highest court held that "neither Africans, nor their free descendants, are entitled to the rights of the Constitution."†

Deep, huh?

---

*The Pennsylvania Department of Corrections death row unit at Huntingdon State Prison, described here by Jamal in the 1980s. On January 13, 1995, Jamal was transferred to the State Correctional Institute at Greene, a new supermaximum security control unit that now houses the vast majority of Pennsylvania's death row inmates, and has significantly worse conditions.
†*Dred Scott v. Sanford*, 19 U.S. (How.) 393, 407, 15 L.Ed 691 (1857).

Perhaps I'm naive, or maybe I'm just stupid, but I really thought the law would be followed in my case, and the conviction reversed. Really.

Even in the face of the brutal Philadelphia MOVE massacre on May 13, Ramona Africa's frame-up, Eleanor Bumpers, Michael Stewart, Clement Lloyd, Allan Blanchard, in countless police slaughters of blacks from New York to Miami, with impunity, my *faith* remained. *Even* in the face of this relentless wave of antiblack state terror, I thought my appeals would be successful.

Even with all I knew, I still harbored a belief in U.S. law, and the realization that my appeal has been denied is a shocker.

Now, I could intellectually understand that American courts are reservoirs of racist sentiment and have been historically hostile to black defendants, but a lifetime of propaganda about American "justice" is hard to shrug off.

I need but look across the nation, where as of October 1986 blacks constituted some 40 percent of men on death row, or across Pennsylvania, where as of August 1988, 61 out of 113 men—some 50 percent—are black,[*] to see the truth, a truth hidden under black robes and promises of equal rights.

Blacks are just 9 percent of Pennsylvania's population, just under 11 percent of America's.[†] As I said, it's hard to shrug off, but maybe we can try this together. How? Try out this quote I saw in a 1982 law book by a prominent Philadelphia lawyer named David Kairys: "Law is simply politics by other means."[‡]

Such a line goes far to explain how courts really function, whether today, or 130 years ago in the Scott case. It ain't about law, it's about politics by other means.

Now ain't that the truth.

---

[*]As of September 1, 1999, there are 3,625 men and women on death row in thirty-nine states and jurisdictions; 43 percent are black. In Pennsylvania, of the 223 men and women on death row, 62.7 percent are black. Source: Death Penalty Information Center and NAACP Legal Defense and Education Fund.

[†]Census Profile Race and Hispanic Origin, Profile No. 2, June 1991, U.S. Census Bureau, U.S. Department of Commerce, Washington, D.C.

[‡]David Kairys, *Legal Reasoning in Politics of Law*, (1982) 24: 16–17. Citing M. A. Foley, "Critical Legal Studies," *Dickinson Law Review* 91 (Winter 1986): 473.

As time passes, I intend to share with you some truths in this column. I continue to fight against this unjust sentence and conviction. Perhaps we can shrug off and shred some of the dangerous myths laid on our minds like a second skin, such as the "right" to a fair and impartial jury of our peers, the "right" to represent oneself, the "right" to a fair trial even.

They're not rights.

They're privileges of the powerful and the rich. For the powerless and the poor, they are chimeras that vanish once one reaches out to claim them as something real or substantial. Don't expect the big networks or megachains of "Big Mac" media to tell you. Because of the incestuousness between the media and government, and big business—which they both serve—they can't.

I can.

Even if I must do so from the valley of the shadow of death, I will.

From death row, this is Mumia Abu-Jamal.

IN EVERY PHASE AND FACET of national life, there is a war being waged on America's poor. In social policy poor mothers are targeted for criminal sanctions for acts that, if committed by mothers of higher economic class, would merit treatment at the Betty Ford Center. In youth policy, governments hasten to close schools while building boot camps and prisons as their "graduate schools." Xenophobic politicians hoist campaigns to the dark star of imprisonment for street beggars, further fattening the fortress economy. The only apparent solution to the scourge of homelessness is to build more and more prisons.

In America's 1990s, to be poor is not so a much socioeconomic status as it is a serious character flaw, a defect of the spirit. Federal statistics tell a tale of loss and want so dreadful that Dickens, of *A Tale of Two Cities* fame, would cringe.

Consider: seven million people homeless, with less than two hundred dollars in monthly income. Thirty seven million people, 14.5 percent of the nation's population, living below poverty levels. Of that number 29 percent are African Americans, meaning that over 10.6 million blacks live in poverty.

Both wings of the ruling "Republicrat" Party try to outdo themselves in announcing new, ever more draconian measures to restrict, repress, restrain, and eliminate the poor. One is reminded of the wry observation of French writer Anatole France: "The Law, in its majestic equality, forbids the rich as well as the poor to sleep under bridges, to beg in the streets and to steal bread."

Already U.S. manufacturers have fled to NAFTA-friendly Mexico, and only the Zapatista insurgency in Chiapas has slowed an emerging flood of Western capital. Outgunned in the industrial wars by Japan and Germany, the United States has embarked on a low-technology, low-skill, high-employment scheme that exploits the poor, the stupid, and the slow via a boom in prison construction, America's sole growth industry. Increasingly, more and more Americans are guarding more and more American prisoners for more and more years. And this amid the lowest crime rate in decades. No major political party has an answer to this social dilemma, short of cages and graves for the poor.

The time is ripe for a new, brighter, life-affirming vision that liberates, not represses, the poor, who after all are the vast majority of this Earth's people. Neither serpentine politics, nor sterile economic theory that treats them—people—as mere economic units offers much hope. For the very politicians they vote for spit in their faces, while economists write them off as "nonpersons."

It must come from the poor, a rebellion of the spirit that reaffirms their intrinsic human worth, based upon who they are rather than what they possess.

From death row, this is Mumia Abu-Jamal.

The Rich rob the poor and the poor rob each other.

—SOJOURNER TRUTH

IF ONE EXAMINES SOCIAL, political, and economic policy in the 1990s, an unmistakable picture emerges of the poor as people who are despised for their very poverty, and punished for their lack of wealth. The state and its cultural elite project this picture until it permeates political and popular culture, and is reflected in public policy.

Why did the government launch its attack on the welfare system? What was behind its rhetoric?

If you analyze it closely, you'll find the push for this policy came from American business. Here's why: the "business cycle" is crucial to capitalist economies. (This is also known as the recurrent tendency of economic "boom and bust" periods). Back in 1958, an economist noted that when unemployment rises, wages fall. This is so because when most workers are employed, business is pressed to react to wage demands. However, when there is significant unemployment, business knows it can find labor at lower wages. Thus, unemployment drives down wages for all workers, as it decreases job security.

What does this have to do with welfare?

Well, welfare is a form of income maintenance, and as such it has served as a buffer between the employed and the unemployed. Therefore, workers were not desperate for any job that they could find. When workers are not desperate, when they have security, they demand higher wages from capital. Who would've thought that the poorest among us, those on welfare, strengthened and stabilized the wages of workers?

It's for this reason that capital launched its attack on income maintenance programs through its political agents (Republicans and Democrats), using the sleight-of-hand label "welfare reform." Both parties of big business joined hands in the battle against the poorest, egged on by big-business media conglomerates, who are but subsidiaries of even bigger businesses. This interest can be summed up in one word: capital.

Why do you think every time news comes out about low unemployment, Wall Street panics and stocks tumble?

When masses of people are unemployed, that's called "good for business"! How can what's bad for people be good for business? So what is to be done?

The French unemployed took to the streets nationally, rocking the neoliberal establishment with a wave of militant demonstrations. This remarkable mobilization showed the power of a movement of unemployed, which beat back the state's attempts to cut back on French income maintenance programs. That movement leaped across the border to Germany, where marches sprung up in over 200 cities.

We can learn from the French, who did not hesitate to organize and mobilize the poor and unemployed.

The slogan of the French may not translate well to us here, but it bears repeating: "Who sows misery reaps rage."

The politicians ain't the solution—the people are.

Let us organize.

From death row, this is Mumia Abu-Jamal.

In all criminal prosecutions, the accused
shall enjoy the right to a speedy and public trial,
by an impartial jury of the state and district
wherein the crime shall have been committed.

—SIXTH AMENDMENT, U.S. CONSTITUTION

MUCH OF THE PROPAGANDA beamed around the world proclaims the glories of U.S. democracy—"free" elections, representative government, and trial by jury. The following is assuredly not broadcast.

William Henry Hance was convicted of killing a Georgia prostitute back in 1978 and sentenced to death.[*] His trial, and even his subsequent retrial, took place before predominantly white juries. One of those jurors, the only black juror, filed a sworn affidavit that she never agreed to the death sentence, a claim seconded by another, white juror. The second juror paints a picture of a trial that was more a lynching than a legal proceeding.

This juror, Pamela Lemay, swore in a notarized affidavit that she heard another white juror, a woman, state, "The nigger admitted he did it, he should fry." At several instances, at the hotel and during deliberations out of the black juror's presence, Ms. Lemay swore she heard other white jurors refer to Hance as "a typical nigger" and "just one more sorry nigger that no one would miss." During deliberations as to whether Hance should be executed or sentenced to life, a juror remarked that execution would be best because that way, "There'd be one less nigger to breed."

---

[*]*Hance v. Zant,* 114 S.Ct. 1392 (1994).

This, in America, is the true meaning of a "jury of peers."

Did any of this bother either the Georgia superior court, the Georgia Supreme Court, the U.S. Supreme Court, or the Georgia Board of Pardons and Paroles?

Absolutely not.

On April 31, 1994, at 10 P.M., William Henry Hance, a man both retarded and mentally ill, was executed, that is, "legally lynched," by the government of Georgia—by electrocution.

Georgia's state motto is "Wisdom, Justice, and Moderation." In the case of William Henry Hance, these three elements seem sorely lacking.

In an emergency appeal to the U.S. Supreme Court hours before Hance's electrocution, Justice Harry A. Blackmun, in a dissenting opinion in Hance's case, wrote that even if he hadn't "reached the conclusion that the death penalty cannot be imposed fairly within the constraints of our constitution… I could not support its imposition in this case." Quoth Blackmun: "There is substantial evidence that William Henry Hance is mentally retarded as well as mentally ill. There is reason to believe that his trial and sentencing proceedings were infected with racial prejudice. One of his sentencers has come forward to say that she did not vote for the death penalty because of his mental impairments."

A majority of the Supreme Court rejected this reasoning. And in the last analysis, the courts and agencies of both Georgia and the United States agreed with the anonymous juror at his trial who believed that Hance would be better off dead, that his death would mean "one less nigger to breed."

U.S. Supreme Court associate justice Harry A. Blackmun, the Court's senior justice, recently announced his retirement, after he finally held as a matter of constitutional law that the death penalty as currently administered is unconstitutional. Blackmun, in *Callins v. Collins,** announced his position in a lengthy dissent that severely criticized the Court majority for "having virtually conceded that both fairness and rationality cannot be achieved" in death penalty cases, adding that "the Court has chosen to deregulate the entire enterprise, replacing—it would seem—substantive

---

Callins v. Collins, 114 S.Ct. 1127 (1994); quotes verbatim.

Constitutional requirements with mere aesthetics." In what appeared to be judicial bitterness, Blackmun further announced, "From this day forwards, I no longer shall tinker with the machinery of death."

Blackmun's dissent, recounting Supreme Court precedents from its "Death Docket" is a grim telling of judicial restrictions—cases ranging from the 1976 case *Gregg v. Georgia,*[*] which reinstated the death penalty, to more recent cases like *Herrera v. Collins,*[†] where the Court denied a hearing to a man trying to prove innocence.

But if Blackmun's denunciation of his benchmates seemed bitter, the response from some on death row seemed equally acerbic. "Why now?" asked one. "What it mean?" said another. The eighty-five-year-old jurist's long trek from *Gregg v. Georgia,* when the death penalty was reinstated, to *Callins v. Collins,* where he condemns capital punishment process to unconstitutionality in a singular dissent, comes almost a quarter of a century too late for many in the shadow of the death house.

Blackmun's critical fifth vote with the *Gregg* majority made the death penalty possible, and formed the foundation for the plethora of cases that he now condemns in *Callins,* like *McCleskey, Herrera, Sawyer,*[‡] and others, for without *Gregg* the others would not be. Further, Blackmun's dissent, though remarkable in passioned discourse, is of negligible legal force, and will save not one life, not even defendant Callins. Blackmun, in his death penalty jurisprudence at least, assumes the late Justice Marshall's mantle of "the lone dissenter," a Jeremiah preaching out in a dry, searing judicial wilderness, where few will hear and none will heed his lamentations.

Had he joined Marshall (while he lived) and Brennan (while he adjudicated), a life block might have emerged with enough light and enough strength to fashion a bare majority by attracting two stragglers. But this never occurred, and in his dissent in *Callins,* Blackmun suggests that it may never occur. As he wrote, "Perhaps one day this court will develop procedural rules and verbal formulas that actually will provide consistency, fairness and reliability in a capital sentencing scheme. I am not optimistic that such a day will come. I am more optimistic though that this court

---

[*] *Gregg v. Georgia,* 96 S.Ct. 128, 428 U.S. 153, 49 L.Ed.2d 859 (1976).
[†] *Herrera v. Collins,* 113 S.Ct. 853 (1993).
[‡] *Sawyer v. Whitley,* 112 S.Ct. 2514 (1994).

eventually will conclude that the effort to eliminate arbitrariness while preserving fairness in the infliction of death is so plainly doomed to failure that it, and the death penalty, must be abandoned all together. I may not live to see that day, but I have faith that eventually it will arrive."

To which, some on death row opine, no time soon.

From death row, this is Mumia Abu-Jamal.

EVERY DAY IN AMERICA the trek continues, a black march to death row.

In Pennsylvania, where Afro-Americans constitute 9 percent of the population, well over 60 percent of its death row inhabitants are black. Across the nation, although the numbers are less stark, the trend is unmistakable. In October 1991 the Bureau of Justice Statistics released its national update, which revealed that 40 percent of America's death row population is black—this, out of a population that is a mere 12 percent of the national populace. The five states with the largest death rows have larger percentages of African Americans on death row than in their statewide populations.[*]

Statistics are often flexible in interpretation and, like scripture, can be cited for any purpose. Does this mean that African Americans are somehow innocents, subjected to a setup by state officials? Not especially. What it *does* suggest is that the state's actions, at all stages of the criminal justice system, from booking at the police station to arraignment at the judicial office, pretrial, trial, and sentencing stage before a court, treats African American defendants with a special vengeance that white defendants are not exposed to.

This is the dictionary definition of "discrimination." In the 1987 case *McCleskey v. Kemp*,[†] the famed Baldus study revealed facts that unequivocally

---

[*]As of September 1, 1999, there are 3,625 men and women on death row in thirty-nine states and jurisdictions; 43 percent are black. In Pennsylvania, of the 223 men and women on death row, 62.7 percent are black. Source: Death Penalty Information Center and NAACP Legal Defense and Education Fund.
[†]*McCleskey v. Kemp*, 481 U.S. 279 (1987); quoted verbatim.

proved that (1) defendants charged with killing white victims in Georgia are 4.3 times as likely to be sentenced to death as defendants charged with killing blacks; (2) six of every eleven defendants convicted of killing a white person would not have received the death sentence if their victim had been black; and (3) cases involving black defendants and white victims are more likely to result in a death sentence than cases featuring any other racial combination of defendant and victim.

Although the U.S. Supreme Court, by a razor-thin 5–4 vote, rejected McCleskey's claim, it could hardly reject the facts underlying them. Retired justice Powell said, in essence, "differences don't amount to discrimination."

The bedrock reason why McCleskey was denied relief was the fear, again expressed by Powell, that "McCleskey's claim, taken to its logical conclusion, throws into serious question the principles that underlie our entire criminal justice system." How true. McCleskey can't be correct, or else the whole system is incorrect.

Now that couldn't be the case, could it?

From death row, this is Mumia Abu-Jamal.

*It is about time the Court faced the fact that the white
people in the South don't like the colored people.*

—WILLIAM H. REHNQUIST, LAW CLERK, 1953,
*in Renata Adler, "The Bork-Rehnquist Poison,"
the New Republic (September 14–21, 1987): 45.*

A LIGHT SKINNED NATIVE of Lanape lineage sidles up to a fellow prisoner
in a nearby steel cage for a bit of small talk. "Damn man," the Indian youth
exclaims in his northeastern Pennsylvania nasal twang, "I been here too
damn long."

"Why you say dat runnin' Bear?"

"Well cuz I caught myself sayin 'poh-leece' insteada 'puh-leese' [police],
and 'fo' instead of 'four.'"

The two men yak it up. Gallows humor.

Bear, for the first time in his life, lives in a predominantly black community, albeit an artificial warped one, for it is bereft of the laughter of women
or the bawling of babes. Only men "live" here. Mostly young black men.

Welcome to Huntingdon's death row, one of three in Pennsylvania. If
the denizens of death row are as black as molasses, the staff, the guards, the
ranking officers, the *civilian* staff, are white-bread.

Long-termers on the row, those here since '84, recall a small but seemingly significant event that took place back then. Maintenance and construction staff, forced by a state court order and state statute to provide men
with a minimum of two hours' daily outside exercise, rather than the customary fifteen minutes every other day, erected a number of steel, cyclone-
fence boxes, which strikingly resemble dog runs or pet pens. Although staff
assured inmates that the pens would be used only for disciplinary cases, the

construction ended and the assurances were put to the test. The first day after completion of the cages, death cases, all free of any disciplinary infractions, were marched out to the pens for daily exercise outdoors. Only when the cages were full did full recognition dawn that the only men caged were African.

Where were the white cons of death row?

A few moments of silent observation proved the obvious. The death row block offered direct access to two yards: one composed of cages, the other "free" space—water fountains, full-court basketball spaces and hoops, and an area for running. The cages were for the blacks on the row. The open yards were for the whites on death row. All of the men condemned to death, the blacks, due to racist insensitivity and sheer hatred, condemned to awaiting death in indignity. The event provided an excellent view, in microcosm, of the mentality of the criminal system of injustice, suffused by the toxin of racism.

The notes of a youthful law clerk of 1953 are the ruling opinions of America's highest court of today. The clerk of yesteryear is today's chief justice, and the word *South* can be applied to North, West, East, or Court equally well. A people who once looked to the Court for enlightened protection now face only benighted hostility. Nowhere is that clearer than in capital cases before the Court, for in America, let it be clear beyond cavil, at the heart of this country's death penalty scheme is the crucible of race.

Who would dare argue otherwise after examining the pivotal case *McCleskey v. Kemp** (1987), where the Court took a delicate moonwalk backward, away from a mountain of awesome evidence that demonstrated incontrovertibly the gross disparity between how black and white capital defendants were treated, depending principally upon the victim's race. McCleskey's claims, wrote the Court's centrist, Justice Powell, cannot prevail, because "taken to its logical conclusion, McCleskey throws into serious question the principles that underlie our entire criminal justice system."

Put quite another way, the Court denied McCleskey relief while accepting as valid his essential facts, not because his studies or their conclusions were untrue but because of the impact such findings would have on other cases. Welcome to the great march backward.

---

*McCleskey v. Kemp, 481 U.S. 279 (1987).

McCleskey, of course, was not alone. At base, *McCleskey* revealed a system of demonstrable, documented imbalance, where race of victim and race of a defendant determined whether one would live or die. This, the Court said, was perfectly constitutional.

Robert A. Burt, a Yale law scholar, has examined the implications of *McCleskey* in light of the 1986 case *Lockhart v. McCree*,[*] where the court similarly rejected the argument that a death-qualified,[†] proprosecution, pro-capital punishment jury offends the fundamental constitutional command for a fair, impartial jury. Professor Burt wrote,

> When we add this finding [i.e. that capital-case juries tend to be white and male because blacks and women are generally anti-death-penalty and are thus excluded] to the evidence gathered in *McCleskey*, that capital juries impose the death penalty with disproportionate frequency on blacks who murder whites and infrequently in response to any murders of blacks, a grim portrait of the American criminal justice system emerges. This portrait shows that law enforcement in the most serious and publicly visible cases is entrusted predominantly to groups of white men who value white lives more than blacks; and thus they take special vengeance on blacks who murder whites and are much less concerned about the murder of blacks. Indeed, its low valuation of blacks coupled with its special arousal when blacks murder whites suggests a law enforcement regime that acts as if our society were gripped by fears about, and prepared to take preemptive strikes against, an explosion of race warfare.[‡]

From daybreak to dusk, black voices resound in exchanges of daily dramas that mark time in the dead zone; the latest on a lawyer; the latest on a lover;

---

[*]*Lockhart v. McCree*, U.S. Ark., 106 S.Ct. 1758, 90 L.Ed. 137.
[†]Definition of death-qualified jury: in order to be seated a jury must be able to impose penalties prescribed by the law, such as the death penalty, therefore any person not able to vote for the death penalty cannot sit on a jury in a capital case. Hence, these juries are pro-prosecution, proconviction, and pro–death penalty.
[‡]Robert A. Burt, "Disorder in the Court: The Death Penalty and the Constitution," Michigan Law Review 85 (August 1987):1798. A Yale law scholar examined the implications of *McCleskey* in light of the 1986 case *Lockhart v. McCree*.

tidbits of thought bouncing off bars of steel and walls of stone, relentlessly, in a wait for death.

There are echoes of *Dred Scott* in today's *McCleskey* opinion, again noting the paucity of rights held by Africans in the land of the free, who "had for more than a century before been regarded as beings of an inferior order, and altogether unfit to associate with the white race, either in social political relations; and so far inferior, that they had no rights that the white man was bound to respect."*

Chief Justice Taney sits again, reincarnate, on the Rehnquist Court of the modern age. Taney's Court, in *Scott*, left intact the power of the slaver by denying constitutional rights to Africans, even if born in the United States. Rehnquist's Court, in *McCleskey*, leaves intact the power of the state to further cheapen black life.

One hundred and thirty years after Scott, and still unequal in life, as in death.

From death row, this is Mumia Abu-Jamal.

Dred Scott V. Sanford, 19 U.S. (How.) 393, 407, 15 L.Ed. 691 (1857); quoted verbatim.

The Date: December 4, 1969
The Time: 4:45 a.m.
The Place: 2337–2339 West Monroe Street
The City: Chicago, Illinois—"the Windy City"

THE ABOVE CLUES offers little hint to the uninitiated. The date, time, place, city given ring few bells, and rare is the published report that marks the passing of this date into the hoary mist of history. Some, however, *do* remember. The date evokes anguish, anger, bittersweet memories of one of this system's episodes of infamy—the police murder of Fred Hampton, deputy chairman of the Illinois chapter of the Black Panther Party.

Yes, his good name is remembered, but why is it not *known?* Why have not those who claim to "inform" black folk dared tell his vitally important story? Why do black kids, overdosing on the name Martin Luther King Jr., not know the name of Fred Hampton?

Chairman Fred was a committed and charismatic black revolutionary who, in his short twenty-one years, did not only touch the lives of those on Chicago's West Side; his infectiously rebellious style swept the United States, electrifying and organizing blacks, whites, and Hispanics with his radical spirit.

It was precisely his uncommon empathy and radiant charisma that placed him on the government's hit list, that drew FBI and regional state assassins to West Monroe on a mission of murder and mayhem, and that ended an extraordinary life. In a raid planned months in advance, police, using an FBI informant, William O'Neal, smuggled a paralyzing drug into Chairman Fred's coffee.*

Doped by police, Hampton never fully awoke the night of the raid, as forty-two shots rang out, converging on his bed. His mate, Panther Deborah Johnson, although pregnant, was both beaten and wounded. One other Panther, Mark Clark, twenty-two, was killed by cop fire, his body found behind the door.

To date, twenty-two years later (as in the MOVE murders), *no one has ever been charged*, let alone convicted, of this murder.

Hours after the police executions, astute Panther officials opened up the scene of carnage to the people of the neighborhood. This writer, as well as thousands of others, toured this deadly scene, witnessing the lines of automatic weapons fire that ripped through the clapboard walls, most eloquent evidence of the shoot-*in*, not the shoot-out, at 2337. The FBI and State Investigation Bureau claims of first Panther fire made by Illinois state attorney Edward Hanrahan rang hollow.

This system wants Fred Hampton's tale to remain untold, his militant memory to fade, his life of service to black folks and the black revolutionary struggle to pass unknown. The media has covered up this recent history, but some remember; perhaps now you will too.

Remember those who have gone before.

Remember those whom the system wants you to forget.

Remember those who fought against this system.

Remember Chairman Fred Hampton, and his assassins!

From death row, this is Mumia Abu-Jamal.

---

*COINTELPRO (Counter Intelligence Program) of the F.B.I. was designed to destroy the black liberation movement by illegal and violent means. After the assasination of Martin Luther King Jr. and Malcolm X, this program focused virtually entirely on the Black Panther Party.

William O'Neal the informant who worked for the COINTELPRO agent Roy Mitchell (FBI) got a floor plan which showed where Fred Hampton slept. The information on Hampton being drugged prior to the raid derives from a thin-layer chromatography examination performed on a sample of Fred Hampton's blood by Cook County Chief toxicologist Eleanor Berman.

THERE IS A LEGAL CONCEPT called "stare decisis" with which all lawyers and law students are familiar, meaning to abide by, or adhere to, decided cases. Such a concept allows people to know what the law is, and frowns against changes from case to case, from year to year. It is a concept fast fading from modern-day law, as demonstrated by the starkly rightward tilt of the U.S. Supreme Court.

Recently another court has joined the wave of reaction. Dhoruba Bin-Wahad, several decades ago a member of the famed Black Panther 21, spent nineteen years in New York State gulags after a dubious trial peppered with official lies, rigged witnesses, and officially sanctioned innuendos, on attempted murder charges. In March 1990 a State Supreme Court justice freed Bin-Wahad, based in part upon undeniable violations of long-standing law uncovered after years of painstaking review of FBI FOIA (Freedom of Information Act) files, records from the infamous COINTELPRO (counterintelligence program) documents, and data on government dirty tricks against prime black activists from the 1970s, such as Bin-Wahad.

Once free, the energetic, principled, loquacious rebel hit the ground running, speaking at radical student venues from Brooklyn to Berlin on behalf of the plight of black political prisoners and the youthful resurgence of black nationalism.

As can be assumed, this did not sit well with the state. It appealed, and in December 1991 the state's highest court of appeals issued an extraordinary ruling.

The court, voting 4–3, announced that the case underlying Bin-Wahad's reversal, *People v. Rosario* (1961), was to be "narrowed," and that the state's hiding of evidence favorable to the accused was no longer the basis for per se reversal of convictions. In so doing, the appeals court overruled the lower court's order freeing Bin-Wahad, and sent the case back for rehearing in the Supreme (trial-level) Court. For exactly thirty years, *People v. Rosario* had been the law of New York State, but when Bin-Wahad proved it had been violated, the state's highest court reacted by changing the law.

Judge Vito Titone, one of the three dissenters, wrote tellingly of the effect of the court's ruling in *People v. Bin-Wahad*: "After reading the majority's opinion, one is left with the impression that rules of law are merely matters of policy preference to be invoked, modified or simply ignored when their consequences are… inconvenient or undesirable."

Much the same could be said of courts around the country, who utilize so-called laws as tools for political ends.

For Bin-Wahad, the wretched ex post facto revision of long-settled law is no philosophical issue, but the continued expression of the same "law" that consigned his forefathers to centuries of unpaid toil, and stole almost twenty years from a life rich with promise, by consigning his flesh to New York's most infamous hellholes on a bogus conviction that was as unlawful then as it is now.

The cruel pounding of the judicial gavel in *People v. Bin-Wahad* sounds suspiciously like the soul-crushing clang of a cell door slamming shut.

From death row, this is Mumia Abu-Jamal.

TWO BLACKS, TWO GEORGIANS

A YEAR AGO, OCTOBER 1991 featured two very different stories, from two vastly different black Georgians. One was Clarence Thomas, the conservative jurist who, in striving to attain his coveted seat on the Supreme Court, opined he had no philosophical difference with capital punishment; the other was Warren McCleskey, the well-known death row prisoner who boldly challenged the Georgia capital punishment scheme as inherently biased.

In October 1991, one went to a position of supreme judicial power; the other went to an ignoble death in Georgia's electric chair; one ascended the Seat of Power; the other expired upon the Seat of Penalty.

Both made their own marks upon that mystery called history. Thomas—the second African American nominated to the United States Supreme Court, on a platform that seemed inimical to black social and economic interests, ascended the bench over an outcry of black opinion, as inflamed as it was unprecedented. McCleskey—whose challenges to Georgia's death penalty practices proved clearly biased infliction of death sentences based upon race of victim—lost his court fight, and ultimately his life, in one of the most controversial Supreme Court opinions of recent history.[*]

Thomas's mark was subservience; McCleskey's mark was resistance. Thomas did the bidding of his powerful white, conservative benefactors and was rewarded with appointments of increasing prominence; McCleskey, against enormous odds, battled the historically biased practices

---

[*] *McCleskey v. Kemp*, 481 U.S. 279 (1987).

of the government in Fulton County, Georgia, all the way to the U.S. Supreme Court, and his reward was a tortured death by the state.

McCleskey's 1987 case, which presented undeniable data of the discriminatory nature of the American death penalty process, has become a historic case as much as *Dred Scott*. The famous Baldus study, which supported McCleskey's claims, was rejected by the Court as a sociological study that revealed "differences" that weren't necessarily "discriminatory."

Retired Justice Brennan denounced the conservative Court's opinion as a "fear of too much justice." One wonders if Thomas, an unabashedly unorthodox born-again conservative, would've seen the facts arising like the red dust of his native Georgia, and condemned the process as de facto unconstitutionally discriminatory, or a mere "difference" unworthy of correction or condemnation?

It would be "cute," perhaps, to add that old standby of indecision— "time will tell"—but for Warren McCleskey, time tells nothing, for time ran out.

There are battles ahead over the most fundamental issues, i.e., life and death, simmering and percolating at the "Court of Last Resort" this term.

How Thomas decides them will determine lives or deaths well into the next century, and whether McCleskey's "high-tech legal lynching" constituted an opportunity or an omen.

From death row, this is Mumia Abu-Jamal.

"I HAVE A RIGHT TO NOTHING which another has a right to take away." So said Thomas Jefferson, America's third president, who as a slaveowner knew a great deal about "rights taken away," and the nation he helped found knows a great deal about it too. Americans are taught, and the world is told, of the First Amendment to the Constitution, which supposedly "guarantees" fundamental rights to free exercise of religion, freedom of speech, and freedom of association. So state history books numbering into the millions. In truth, such rights are illusory. The recent controversy involving this writer is an excellent case in point.

Hired by the prestigious *All Things Considered* program aired on the NPR network to produce brief commentaries, this writer, who reported for NPR prior to his imprisonment, remarked to one supporter that he felt like he was returning home. NPR, stung by an FOP (Fraternal Order of Police) campaign—in which the FOP branded the writer a "monster" and heaped abuse on the network—mumbled something about "misgivings" and, without informing the writer, canceled the airing of the commentaries.

It is perhaps poetic justice that the FOP campaign began on May 13, 1994, several days before the scheduled air date, for it marked nine years to the day after the Mother's Day MOVE massacre of at least eleven MOVE babies, women and men in West Philadelphia by the aerial bombing of MOVE's home in 1985. Philadelphia police shot and killed fleeing MOVE women and children, forced others back into a burning building, and stood by while several blocks of West Philadelphia homes were consumed by flames.

Who are the real monsters?

The same FOP that incinerated, decapitated, and dismembered people with judicial impunity call me a "monster"! Are they then angels?

What rights of "free speech" exist when it can be denied because the state objects to the speaker?

The same system that denied me the alleged "right" to self-representation, that intentionally denied me my "right" to an impartial jury of my peers, that steered me to "trial" before a judge who was a life member of the FOP and known as a "prosecutor's dream"; that denied me the right to examine and/or cross-examine witnesses; and that went back over a decade to introduce evidence of my Black Panther Party membership and statements (said to be "protected" under the First Amendment's "guarantee" of "free" association and "free" speech) and used these to argue for a death sentence—these are the selfsame forces that successfully censored me from the genteel listeners of NPR's *All Things* [that the police will allow] *Considered.*

They have demonstrated how the media is mastered by police power and how the First Amendment once again is but a dead letter.

They have made my point—and I hope yours.

From death row, this is Mumia Abu-Jamal.

THE FEDERAL TRIAL of four Los Angeles cops, forced by the public orgy of rebellion and rage that rocked the city a year before in response to acquittals stemming from the brutal Rodney King beating, ended in a jury compromise—two guilty, two acquitted. While observers may be dispirited by the fact that two cops who brutalized, traumatized, and pummeled King were acquitted, the trial itself raises some serious and disturbing questions. While no one would call the writer a cop lover, it is my firm opinion that the federal retrial of the four L.A. cops involved in King's legalized brutality constituted a clear violation of the Fifth Amendment of the United States Constitution, which forbids double jeopardy. The Fifth Amendment provides, in part, "nor shall any person be subject for the same offense to be twice put in jeopardy of life or limb."

Like millions of Africans in America, Chicanos, and a host of Americans, the acquittals of the L.A.-cop four in the Simi Valley state assault trial was an outrage that solidified the conviction that there can be no justice in the courts of this system for black people. Although not a *reason* for the L.A. rebellion, it certainly was a psychic straw that broke the camel's back.

The Simi Valley "trial," like the King beating itself, was both obscene and commonplace, for neither all-white pro-police juries nor state-sanctioned brutality are rarities to those who live in U.S. tombs as opposed to reading about them. The point is, the federal LAPD/King civil rights trial was a *political* prosecution, spurred by international embarrassment stemming from the raging flames of L.A., without which no prosecution would have occurred.

It also reveals how the system, under the pressure of an outraged people, will betray the trusts of their own agents, so one need not ask how they would treat, and do treat, one not their own, especially under public pressure.

The same system that denied the four L.A. cops their alleged constitutional rights denies the rights of the poor and politically powerless daily with impunity, and will further utilize the Stacey Koon case to continue to do so. To be silent while the state violates its own alleged constitutional law to prosecute someone we hate is but to invite silence when the state violates its own laws to prosecute the state's enemies and opponents.

This we cannot do.

We must deny the state that power. The national ACLU is also of the opinion that the second, federal prosecution violated the Fifth Amendment to the U.S. Constitution. I believe it is upon that basis that the convictions will later be reversed by an appellate court.

It is ironic that many of those who did not oppose the federal civil prosecutions feel it inappropriate for the federal system to review state convictions under habeas corpus statutes. The only thing this second, federal civil rights violation case has done is provide the system with camouflage, to give the appearance of justice.

The illusion is never the real.

From death row, this is Mumia Abu-Jamal.

AMERICAN MASS MEDIA is a marvel of technology. It is whiz-bang, sparkle, glitter, and satellite wizardry. It is a master plan of methods to communicate, and a pauper's worth of substance. With such technology, how are people so woefully misinformed? The average American neither knows nor cares about the vast world beyond the nation's border. The average American student knows little math, no history, and very little geography, and nor does he or she want to know. Americans have computers in school, dozens of TV stations, and the most aggressive news media on earth. Does that mean they're better informed?

Hardly.

On November 2, 1995, the United Nations General Assembly voted overwhelmingly—117 to 3—to condemn the United States for its continuing blockade of Cuba.* The international community called the United States blockade "a flagrant act of aggression" and "a blatant violation of international law." That the UN vote was reported at all in American media is amazing, for such news is more often than not passed over entirely by the American press; but where was information about the blockade itself, the effects suffered by the Cuban people, in-depth comments from United Nations delegates and leaders around the world? For a more substantive report, one had to listen to the BBC World News Service, for the rest of the world takes note of events the U.S. prefers to ignore.

American media is a business, and it has a mission; not to inform Americans, but to entertain them. Every media enterprise in America

---

*United Nations General Assembly Plenary, 1a-19, *Press Release GA/8983*, 48th Meeting (AM), November 2, 1995.

reports the drivel that Marcia Clarke and Chris Darden are "secret" love birds, but the vote of a global assembly condemning U.S. actions received only scant coverage at best.

Why?

The media is a source of titillation more than information. The mission of the media is to please, to comfort, and primarily to sell. When TV was developed, it was promised that every American would learn about the world in his living room. When computers were developed, wasn't it said that they would be invaluable learning tools and that children would learn more, faster? National scholastic tests show otherwise, as kids master computers as toys, and learn splendid hand to eye coordination, but little else.

The media paints false pictures of the nation and the world, pictures designed to serve corporate masters and to make America look good. This feel-good media approach serves the American delusion of white supremacy but it does not inform. When the *New York Times* echoes *Star* magazine, what can the word *media* mean?

How could millions be surprised at Minister Farrakhan's enormous influence among blacks unless the media wasn't doing its job? How could they look at a million and count less than half that number?

The major media, like its racist projections, is to be rejected, not consumed. For your very patronage gives it life.

From death row, this is Mumia Abu-Jamal.

A LIFETIME MAY PASS without an individual having been personally addressed by government. For millions, government is a remote venture, conducted by quasi representatives in their name, with their silence ofttimes taken as acquiescence.

Never is an individual as personally involved with government as when faced by the power of a court, when his or her freedom and very life is at stake, at the tender mercies of the state. And rarely has a case been clearer than when a black man actually sued a United States court for his freedom from slavery. The case? *Dred Scott v. Sanford,* 1857. Perhaps you've heard of the case, but have you ever read it? It is an eye opening piece of African and American history, running over a hundred pages. In his opinion, Chief Justice Roger Brooke Taney—a bony, stooped slave owner from Maryland—wrote:

> The question is simply this, can a Negro, whose ancestors were imported to this country and sold as slaves, become a member of the political community formed and brought into existence by the Constitution of the United States, and as such become entitled to all the rights and privileges and immunities guaranteed by that instrument to the citizen. The plea applies to that class of persons only whose ancestors were Negroes of the African race, and imported into this country and sold and held as slaves. We think they are not, and that they are not included and were not intended to be included under the word "citizens" in the Constitution and can therefore claim none of the rights and privileges which that instrument provides for, and

secures to, citizens of the United States. On the contrary, they were at that time considered as a subordinate and inferior class of beings, who had been subjugated by the dominant race, and whether emancipated or not, yet remained subject to their authority and had no rights or privileges but such as those who held the power in the government might choose to grant them. They had for more than a century before been regarded as beings of an inferior order, and altogether unfit to associate with the white race, either in social or political relations, and so far inferior that they had no rights which the white man was bound to respect and that the Negro might justly and lawfully be reduced to slavery for his benefit.

In these words, uttered by one of America's most brilliant jurists, the face of U.S. racist oppression was made plain. The plaintiff, the slave Dred Scott, who sued for his freedom, and that of his wife Harriet and his daughters Eliza and Lizzy, fourteen and seven respectively, in U.S. courts, found a court of law but not of justice, which rejected his claim, saying since he wasn't a citizen, the rights guaranteed in the Constitution, including the right to sue, didn't apply. One hundred and thirty six years after Scott, and still we find courts of law but not of justice.

From death row, this is Mumia Abu-Jamal.

IN A CASE KNOWN AS *Strickland v. Washington,* the U.S. Supreme Court drastically narrowed the range of challenges to the effectiveness and compe- tence of counsel at criminal trials. The Sixth Amendment to the U.S. Con- stitution provides a right in all criminal cases to "assistance of counsel." The Sixth Amendment notwithstanding, are people facing imprisonment and severe punishment actually receiving effective and competent assistance of counsel?

You decide.

If your lawyer actually went to sleep during your trial, would you think he or she was effective? This is what an appeals court ruled in a case called *People v. Tippins,* 1991. "Although Defense Counsel slept during portions of the trial," the opinion read, "counsel provided defendant meaningful rep- resentations."

What about if your lawyer was high on drugs during the trial? When an appellate court was faced with just such an instance, in the case known as *People v. Bedilla,* 1990, this was their learned analysis: "Proof of a defense counsel's use of narcotics during a trial does not amount to a per se violation of the Constitutional right to effective counsel." Note that in this case, counsel admitted using heroin and cocaine throughout the trial.

And in the case *Commonwealth v. Africa,* specifically involving MOVE political prisoner Mike Africa, the trial lawyer later admitted to daily cocaine and marijuana use, but that issue wasn't raised on appeal.

It would seem that a fairly competent lawyer, having researched the evi- dence, would pay some attention to how his client was dressed at trial. Not so, said a court of appeals in a case known as *People v. Murphy*, 1983: "Counsel's seeming indifference to defendant's attire, though defendant was wearing the same sweatshirt and footwear in court that he wore on the day of the crime, did not constitute ineffective assistance."

In all of these real cases, the attorneys involved were deemed competent in their representations, and their clients' convictions were upheld. Under these cases counsel means little more than presence by a lawyer at trial, for even if he is asleep, even if he or she is a drug addict, indeed high at the trial itself, it ain't no thing: counsel, under *Strickland's* tortured logic, is presumed effective. These are just a few of the many cases from across the United States that show the poverty of the Sixth Amendment. For more information you can read "Effective Assistance Isn't Much," an article by Robert Darlough in the January/February issue of the *American Lawyer*. Increasingly the amendments to the U.S. Constitution are merely filler for dusty history books, which have no application in real life—as the courts have shown repeatedly.

From death row, this is Mumia Abu-Jamal.

"**THAT'S WHAT CAPITAL** punishment really means. Those that ain't got the capital gets the punishment," is the old saying. Once again we see the inherent truths that lie in the proverbs of the poor. That old saying echoed when it was announced that the district attorney of Delaware County, Patrick Meehan, would not seek the death penalty in the case of John E. DuPont, the wealthy corporate heir charged with the shooting death of Olympic champion David Schultz. The Delaware County DA's office said, "No aggravated circumstances justifying the death sentence existed." Could it be that DuPont's personal wealth, estimated at over $400 million, was a factor? In one fell swoop, the state ensured that while millionaires may be murderers, they are not eligible for that preserve of the poor, America's death row.

As the case of O. J. Simpson showed us, the state is very selective in who it chooses to include in its macabre club of death. O. J., a bona fide celebrity, corporate pitchman, sports legend, and millionaire, was deemed, even though a suspect in a double murder, not fit for a death sentence. So whether or not one is of the opinion that Mr. Simpson was either innocent or guilty, the point remains that before the trial actually began, the DA of Los Angeles decided, No death penalty for O. J.—millionaires need not apply. As it was for Mr. Simpson, so it was for Mr. DuPont. Simpson's wealth compared to DuPont's makes him look like a pauper. As for DuPont, consider if you will the incredible spectacle of the DA, with all the identical facts, announcing he or she would not be seeking the death penalty if DuPont was the victim. I'm sure we can all agree that would be impossible.

Any poor man who slays a wealthy man will have the weight of the system fall on him like a ton of bricks. For a wealthy man, however, who finds himself charged with killing a poor man, the system becomes user-friendly. Why should this be so?

It's because the system serves the interests of the wealthy. It is their system. In essence, when a poor person comes before the court, he or she faces two things: the offense, and being poor. I am not suggesting that Mr. DuPont, or anyone else for that matter, should be sentenced to death, I am just noting how and why the death sentence is reserved for some and off limits to others. The death sentence remains a prerogative of the poor.

From death row, this is Mumia Abu-Jamal.

PHILADELPHIA, New York, New Orleans, Los Angeles. In city after city, we find case after case of not only police corruption but vicious police violence. Young people are beaten, women are assaulted, people who are taught to believe police are their friends find out they are often deadly enemies, armed with the power of the state.

In city after city, police corruption scandals blare across the front pages, telling us of cops who moonlight as drug dealers, sowing the seeds of social poison from their squad cars. The media react with manufactured outrage, and the cycles of corruption reoccur, again, again, and again.

The recent Mollen Commission* hearings held in New York City were but viler, more corrupt echoes of the Knapp Commission hearing into cop corruption a generation before. Cops caught stealing, thieving, and/or robbing excite the public mind, but what of cops who brutalize, beat, or kill?

How many cops, of the hundreds who beat, brutalize, or kill people all across the land, are ever prosecuted for their acts? How many are convicted? The numbers are minuscule.

---

*In July 1994, after an investigation that lasted almost two years, the Commission to Investigate Allegations of Police Corruption and the Anti-Corruption Procedures of the Police Department, also known as the Mollen Commission, issued its final report. The Mollen Commission had been formed in response to several widely publicized incidents of corruption involving New York City police officers. While the commission found that relatively few police officers have been found to engage in serious criminal activities, it also concluded that the Police Department's anticorruption systems had been allowed to deteriorate to the point where they "minimized, ignored and at times concealed corruption, rather than root it out."

The widely reported Rodney King beating case showed us how judges bend over backward to assure criminal cops that things will "be taken care of," and they won't be hurt badly if sentenced.

The white majority media treat cop stealings as worse offenses than cop killings and by so doing seek to minimize those acts in the public mind. Thus, it is the contention of many cops charged with such offenses that they "were only doing their job." Put quite another way, their "jobs" are to kill, to beat, to brutalize the poor and the powerless, to defend the interests of the rich.

That's what they are telling you!

When the human rights group Amnesty International recently released a report denouncing New York police brutality, that city's police hierarchy downplayed it, as if the Nobel Prize–winning group was "interfering."[*]

The status quo in America is white supremacy and oppression of peoples of color. And to protect that status quo is necessary to look the other way when cops beat, lie on the stand, brutalize the poor and the powerless, or even kill.

From death row, this is Mumia Abu-Jamal.

---

[*]Amnesty International news release, "Police Brutality Widespread Problem in New York City," AMR 51/50/96, June 27, 1996.

CAMPAIGN OF REPRESSION:
ATTACK ON THE LIFE OF THE MIND

THE MOST REPRESSIVE REGIME in America just got more repressive: The Pennsylvania Department of Corrections introduced administrative directives 801 and 802. These new regulations severely restrict information, communication, and visitation from very little to virtually nil. Generally, visits are pared down to one per month, with planned restrictions barring all but personal and legal mail, and a ban on all books, save a Bible or Qu'ran. It is a broad-based attack on the life of the mind. Newspapers are to be exchanged one for one, ostensibly to discourage hoarding but in reality to stem the flow of shared information between prisoners—a vital source of up-to-date information, especially in light of the fact that few have access to TV and radio.*

Provisions of the rules are so extreme that they can be interpreted to deny a man a piece of paper or an ink pen. Smokers are particularly hard hit: two packs a month are allowed. But most insidious are the provisions governing legal material. They suggest the other regulations are mere smokescreens designed to divert attention from the state's principal objective: the stripping of jailhouse lawyers. For the legal material sections of the Pennsylvania regulations govern all prisoners in the hole, whether for disciplinary or administrative reasons.

---

*Ironically the visiting room at SCI Greene had this mission statement prominently displayed: "We believe that every inmate should have an opportunity to be constructively engaged and involved in a program of self improvement. Authority exercised over inmates will be fair and professionally responsible. We recognize our responsibility to be open and to provide access to inmate families, religious groups, and community volunteers."

There is solid support from scholars, and statistical analysis, for the notion that jailhouse lawyers are the targets of the new rules. In 1991 one of the most exhaustive studies to date on the targets of the prison disciplinary system was released. That report, titled *The Myth of Humane Imprisonment*, found that there is a statistical hierarchy of who receives the harshest disciplinary sanctions from prison officials. Authored by criminologist Mark S. Hamm, Dr. Corey Weinstein, Therese Copez, and Frances Freidman, it presents tables reflecting the most frequently disciplined groups of prisoners. Here's an example:

Jailhouse lawyers constitute 60.8 percent of the sample; blacks, 48.5 percent. Prisoners with mental handicaps constitute 37.9 percent; gang members, 31 percent; political prisoners, 29.8 percent; Hispanics, 27 percent; homosexuals, 26.6 percent; whites, 22.2 percent; AIDS patients, 19.9 percent; prisoners with physical handicaps, 18.7 percent; and Asians, 5.1 percent.

In accounts supporting this statistical data, the authors wrote, "Respondents observed that guards and administrators had a standard practice of singling out jailhouse lawyers for discipline and retaliation for challenging the status quo." While the data supports the widely held notion that blacks are often targets of severe sanctions, that jailhouse lawyers are the *most* sanctioned is striking. For jailhouse lawyers, men and women self-trained in law and legal procedure, are among the most studious, in law at least, in the prison; and therein lies the rub.

The evidence suggests, and the new regulations clearly support, the notion that prison administrators *don't want* studious, well-read prisoners. Rather, they prefer inmates who are obedient, quiet, and dumb. Why else would a prison expressly forbid a person from expanding their learning through correspondence courses or educational programs? It would seem that any institution daring to use the term "corrections" would *require* all of its charges to participate in educational programs. For how else is one corrected? Yet disciplinary prisoners are forbidden from the one resource designed to moderate behavior and enhance self-esteem: education. For them, many of whom are illiterate, books are deemed contraband, and educational courses are proscribed.

In that regard, more than any other, lies the solution to the often bewildering conundrum mislabeled as "corrections." The state raises its narrow institutional concern, to control by keeping people stupid, over a concern that is intensely human: the right of all beings to grow in wisdom, insight, and knowledge, for their *own sakes* as well as their unique contribution to the fund of human knowledge. This intentional degradation of the soul by the state, which allows a being to degenerate, or vegetate, yet forbids one from mental expansion, is the most sure indictment available of a system that creates rather than corrects the most fundamental evil in existence, that of ignorance.

From death row, this is Mumia Abu-Jamal.

THANKS TO THE EFFORTS of premier filmmaker Spike Lee, the name Malcolm X is once again on millions of lips. Based largely on the *Autobiography of Malcolm X*, penned by the late Alex Haley, the film tells the epic tale of a man who was indeed larger than life.

This commentary is not, and cannot be, a film review, for I have never seen the film, for reasons that should be obvious. Rather, it is a musing on the life that gave both Haley and Spike grist for their mills.

There are few black men who lived a life as full of glory and tragedy as did Malcolm X; Martin Luther King Jr. was one; and to a lesser extent so was Marcus Garvey, as well as the late Black Panther cofounder Dr. Huey P. Newton. As were King and Newton, Malcolm X was assassinated, but perhaps there the similarity ends. For as America lionized, lauded, and elevated King (more for his nonviolent philosophy than for his person), it ignored and vilified Malcolm (as it did similarly with Dr. Newton, a Malcolmite, as were most Panthers), whose obituaries dwelt on the dark side, ignoring the brilliance of his life, a force that still smolders in black hearts thirty years after his assassination in New York City.

The system used the main nonviolent themes of Martin Luther King's life to present a strategy designed to protect its own interests—imagine the most violent nation on earth, the heir of Indian and African genocide, the *only* nation ever to drop an atomic bomb on a civilian population, the world's biggest arms dealer, the country that napalmed over ten million people in Vietnam to "save" it from communism, the world's biggest jailer, waving the corpse of King, calling for nonviolence!

The Black Panther Party considered itself the Sons of Malcolm (at least many male Panthers did) for the sons he never had (Malcolm and his wife,

Dr. Betty Shabazz, had a passel of stunning daughters), and inherited one of their central tenets, black self-defense, from his teachings.

While the eloquent, soaring oratory of Dr. King touched, moved, and motivated the southern black church, middle and upper classes, and white liberal predominantly Jewish intelligentsia, his message did not find root in the black working class and urban north, a fact noted by his brilliant, devoted aide-de-camp, the Reverend Ralph Abernathy, who noted in his autobiography how King, coming to Chicago Illinois, met glacial white hatred, black indifference, and near disaster.

Northern-bred blacks preferred a more defiant, confrontational, and militant message than turn the other cheek, and Malcolm X provided it in clear, uncompromising terms. And his message of black self-defense and African-American self determination struck both Muslim and non-Muslim alike as logical and reasonable, given the decidedly un-Christian behavior displayed by America to the black, brown, red, and yellow world.

The media, as Malcolm predicted, would attempt to homogenize, whiten, and distort his message. How many have read of him, in a recent newspaper, described as a "civil rights" leader—a term he loathed! Stories tell of his "softening" toward whites after his sojourn to Mecca, conveniently ignoring that Malcolm continued to revile white *Americans*, still in the grips of a racist *system* that crushes black life—*still!* Post-Mecca Malik found among white-skinned Arabs and European converts to Islam a oneness that he found lacking in Americans. So deeply entrenched was racism in American whites that Malcolm/Malik sensed the intrinsic difference in how the two peoples saw and described themselves. Arabs, calling themselves white, referred simply to skin tone; Americans meant something altogether different: "You know what he means when he says, 'I'm white,' he means he's *boss!*" Malcolm thundered.

Malcolm, and the man who returned from Mecca, Hajji Malik Shabazz, both were scourges of American racism who saw it as an evil against humanity and the God that formed them. He stood for—and died for—*human* rights of self-defense and a people's self-determination, not for "civil rights," which, as the Supreme Court has indeed shown, changes from day to day, case to case, administration to administration.

From death row, this is Mumia Abu-Jamal.

AS THE NIGHT SKY over Mogadishu explodes into blazing light, UN/U.S. armed forces clash with Somali irregulars in the Horn of Africa.

The East African nation, already ravaged by famine and the disintegration of the fallen Barre regime, is now the setting for war. So-called peacekeeping forces of the United Nations shoot live rounds into crowds of demonstrating Somalis, killing and wounding scores of them and further defaming the dead by calling them "shields" for Somali gunmen. Curiously, only the "shields"—Somalian women and children for the most part—are hit by gunfire, not gunmen. Curious too, how troops kill unarmed demonstrators, mostly women, as part of a "peacekeeping" mission.

The United States, although not yet involved in ground activity, has unleashed repeated air attacks on the capital city, making President Clinton's first use of arms as commander in chief (if one excludes the Waco massacre) in East Africa, against a small Somali militiaman commanding a minute squad of what appears to be armed (with small arms) children.

In a world where small wars and silent holocausts approach normalcy, where Serb/Muslim intergroup hatred has spawned concentration camps, mass rape, and "ethnic cleansing" of beleaguered Muslims, the United Nations can only drop leaflets and MRE food packages. But that is Europe—where we are told centuries of old hatreds make military intervention ill-advised. Where U.S. air forces dropped food relief to Bosnia-Herzegovina, they drop bombs in Mogadishu, East Africa. To "send a message" to a Somali general, his home, offices, and supporters were bombarded by U.S. air fire. Bosnian and Serb "cleansers," we can assume, do not need any "message."

In truth, however, every act, even nonaction, has a message.

The so-called international community, actually a minority of the world's people, have used force in an attempt to humble an African militia leader who has sought to control his own homeland. That same UN/U.S. force has refused to raise a finger where European militias have virtually razed cities and scattered countless numbers of Muslim families to "ethnically cleanse" Bosnia-Herzegovina.

To my mind, that's quite a message.

It is also illustrative of the way the UN has become the henchman for imperialist power. It doesn't matter if the generals are black, white, straight or gay, male or female: they serve the interests of the system.

Nor does it matter if the president is Democratic or Republican—he fights to preserve the system.

Is it coincidence that Clinton's first military strike—into the Horn of Africa—came days after his lowest poll readings? The American people, if they have shown anything in the last two centuries of existence, have shown a passion for war.

From death row, this is Mumia Abu-Jamal.

MANY AMERICANS have a skewed perception of Japan, as skewed, perhaps, as foreigners have of America, many of whom seem to expect cowboys and Indians. Of Japan, the image arises of the feudal Samurai, the ritual Hari-Kari, visions of what Westerners like to call "the inscrutable Orient." From such a martial, warlike history, one wonders what kind of justice system has evolved. Rates of homicide, rape, robbery, and theft are far, far lower than in other industrial societies such as the United States, England, and Germany.

Why are these rates so low in Japan?

If America's conventional wisdom holds true, Japan must be building plenty of prisons, levying increasingly harsh sentences, and subjecting prisoners to Draconian conditions—right? Wrong.

University of Washington law and Eastern Asian studies professor John O. Haley, author of *Mediation and Criminal Justice*, opines that the Japanese veer away from retribution and revenge and toward restoration and social reconciliation.

According to statistics published by the Supreme Court of Japan, the following median prison terms were returned for the following offenses:

1. HOMICIDE—FIVE TO SEVEN YEARS

2. ROBBERY TO THREE TO FIVE YEARS

3. ARSON—THREE TO FIVE YEARS

4. RAPE—TWO TO THREE YEARS

The median term for all criminal offenses combined was one to two years. Persons sentenced to prison rarely serve over one term in Japan. For example, in 1984, 64,990 persons were sentenced to prison. Of that total, 56 percent received suspended sentences, with less than 13 percent being subjected to prison terms exceeding one year. More surprisingly, 25 percent of those with suspended sentences were convicted of homicide or robbery, and of those convicted of arson or rape, 35 percent of the sentences are suspended. Only about 45 percent of all imprisoned persons serve full terms.

American critics view the Japanese penal practice with incredulity, if not outright amazement, and hasten to note the sharp distinctions in culture between the United States and Japan. Curiously, American industrialists and economists raise few "cultural" barriers when attempting to incorporate Japanese business and managerial wisdom to the U.S. workplace.

Seemingly, what works in a factory environment becomes unmanageable in the prison context.

But, truth be told, U.S. prisons are themselves in a state nearing physical, social, and ideological collapse, as over a million persons serve sentences, many set to expire, if at all, far into the next century. U.S. prisons, far from being a place of restoration, are social sinkholes of despair, of degradation, of spiritual death.

We could learn much from the Japanese—more than how to build a better mousetrap.

From death row, this is Mumia Abu-Jamal.

SINCE 1886 the mammoth monument has stood, its fabled torch and patinaed visage beckoning to the dregs of Europe, the starving many from Ireland blighted by the potato famine, the bearded and babushkaed Jews fleeing the pogroms of an Eastern European pale, the human excess of empires that now wane.

Upon a massive pedestal on which this statue stands, a tablet bears the chiseled words of the poet Emma Lazarus, saying:

> ...Give me your tired, your poor,
> Your huddled masses yearning to breathe free
> The wretched refuse of your teeming shore.
> Send these, the homeless, tempest-tost to me,
> I lift my lamp beside the Golden Door!

Lazarus gave voice to the massive Statue of Liberty, and carved human warmth into her stern copper face, through this Golden Doorway to America. How hollow these words sound, when measured against the slam of a door, shutting out Haitians fleeing repression in the bloody ghost towns of Port-au-Prince and Cité Soleil.

The United States–armed army of Haiti, seemingly but a uniformed division of the Ton-Ton Macoutes, has stained the Haitian dust crimson with the blood of its people, especially those who dared support the candidacy of the rebel priest Jean-Bertrand Aristide—the nation's first democratically elected president. Père Aristide, a favorite by an overwhelming majority of Haitians, found his candidacy and his presidency annulled by the army, acting as hit men for the elite class, and was considered by most observers lucky to have escaped alive. Meanwhile, thousands of other Haitians, numbered among Aristide's vast throng of supporters, have attempted to flee the flood of bloody repression, by dinghy, by makeshift craft, by stowaway, and by stealth—only to run into a United States wall of iron, denying entry.

The Bush administration, playing to his party's right wing, has gone one step further—Haitians cannot even set foot on United States soil. They are detained at Guantanamo military base, on Cuba's coast. That for some, return means clumsy attempts at torture, or a sudden death, merits little. The U.S. government has spoken, and its word is: "Haitians! Go back to your own country!"

Rarely has an entire people been so publicly maligned. Rarely has Emma Lazarus's poem seemed so misleading. Rarely has the racism underlying the decision been so naked.

Haiti—the legendary land of rebel general Toussaint L'Ouverture— gained its independence from France in 1804. After a period of United States intervention, the United States occupied the country from 1915 to 1934. Ever since, it has supported a series of satraps who've held state power to keep Haiti a sedate source of cheap labor for foreign capital investment. With multinationals fleeing the United States for a bigger profit margin abroad, with a deepening national depression, the government wants labor abroad compliant, and hopefully nonpolitical.

Haitians, radicalized by the astounding demonstrations of people's power that put Père Aristide into the office of president, are being told to go back—back to choking oppression and dead-end factory jobs, if any, for they were too "political," too "radical," too "lumpen," too black to pierce the veil of immigration.

Blacks here could only shake their heads at this dual moment of shame. Shame that stemmed from being both black and "American"; at an entity said to be "our" government.

From death row, this is Mumia Abu-Jamal.

IT'S BEEN A YEAR since the racist outrages of Hoyerswerda, the little East German town where rednecks and racists and skinheads torched refugee shelters while police stood by, and neighbors applauded.

A year later, and the whole of Germany, East and West, is gripped in a growing age of *Ausländerfeindlichkeit*: political exploitation of hostility against foreigners, called Ausländers in German. The images from the harbor town of Rostock, of crowds of neofascist youths torching the homes of Vietnamese families again, while cops stand by and neighbors clap approval, proves that Hoyerswerda was nothing but an ugly beginning to a national campaign of nakedly racist and antirefugee repression.

Politicians, eager to expand their constituencies, have almost totally refused to condemn the carnage, terrorism, and arson, opting instead to echo antirefugee concerns, thereby fueling a fireball of antiforeigner hatred. Their only concerns have been for Germany's image abroad, not the human concerns of safety, of personal integrity, of families terrorized by fires in the night. One district politician justified the problem by demeaning the refugees as too loud, too dirty, and too lazy. Others have campaigned for the repeal of section 16 of the German constitution, the guarantee-of-asylum clause.

In some respects, the burning of Rostock is a psychic descendant of Bitburg, where the U.S. commander in chief, then-president Reagan, saluted the Nazi/SS dead, and in so doing, gave imperial legitimacy to the neo-Nazi movement in Germany. His visit was a precursor to the celebrations of the Waffen-SS at the War Cemetery in Halbe, south of Berlin, in November

1991. The official government said they were going to prevent the gathering, but in the end did nothing, just as in Hoyerswerda, and in Rostock.

In Rostock, not only did the cops stand idly by while fascistic mobs firebombed a Vietnamese shelter, but firefighters did little better, unable to quell the flames of destruction. The state's inability, or unwillingness, to act, however, did not carry over to German antifascists, who days later, as they staged a counterdemo in Rostock, were met by 4,000 cops, who held up over 5,000 antifascist demonstrators for seven hours at police checkpoints on the highways. The delay, however, seemed to work in their favor, as over 20,000 people—from antifascist and autonomous groups, trade unionists, the Democratic Socialist Party, the Greens, immigrant groups, and other organizations—staged a demo on August 29 to denounce the Rostock outrages.

This, despite the slanted press coverage that painted the anti's as violent leftist mobs, the police intimidation and attempted obstruction, the political denunciations that fell only on those who dared stand against the terrorism, not the terrorists themselves.

As the "antifa" movement grows, so too does the reign of state-supported hatred that struck in the village of Kretzin, Brandenburg State, where another shelter was Molotoved and burned down.

In the streets and alleys of reunited Germany, the future of Europe and much of the world is being forged.

Time will tell whether it will be a future of promise, or of pogroms.

From death row, this is Mumia Abu-Jamal.

MUCH HAS BEEN SAID and written on NAFTA, the North American Free Trade Agreement. As the economy lurches into recession after recession, some are selling NAFTA as the be all, end all, the solution to the increasing cycles of bad economic times.

Economics, an intimidating, confounding science if ever there was one, does follow certain principles, among them that capital follows the profit margin, always. Always. The NAFTA backers claim the pact will provide many new jobs because of new business opportunities in Mexico and elsewhere. There may be jobs, but they will pay a bare pittance, and the businesses that remain behind will bludgeon their workers with the threat of relocation to the low-paying vistas south of the border. Indeed, it is already happening. Capital's trek to below the Rio Grande has created an ocean of *maquiladoras* hugging the U.S. border, where goods are produced by Mexican workers paid the barest peso, only to be shipped north for sale to Norteamericanos at regular prices, meaning ultimately a bigger margin of profit for the manufacturer, with less for laborers. NAFTA means an intensification of this trend. NAFTA means lower wages for workers. NAFTA is a political creation of U.S. and multinational capital, and thus designed to provide corporate interests with a larger pool for production, which Mexico obviously offers, with lower wages, ditto, and also with dramatically lessened environmental regulations.

Think of it this way: if you were a business producing widgets, and had an opportunity to produce them by nonunion, bargain basement, low-paid workers with no social security, no worker's comp, no OSHA (such as it is), and no EPA (Environmental Protection Agency) (such as it is), and still could sell your widgets at the same or even higher prices, would you do it? That's the question pondered by many a manager, board member, and director of U.S. business today; and in the harsh world of the economy, it is a force greater to capital than gravity itself.

NAFTA pulls the plug out of the tub, and quickens the economic whoosh down the drain for U.S. labor. To be sure, *maquiladoras* represent substantial investments and job opportunities for Mexican workers who are quite willing to work for meager, by U.S. standards, wages provided by U.S. business, but Mexico's gain will mean U.S. losses. Even given the far-fetched possibility that the U.S. Congress will reject NAFTA,* the inexorable southern flow will not end, for no Congress, nor any other purely political entity, can or will block the drive of capital for its highest return, a better "bottom line."

Consider any politician's stand on NAFTA, and you will know whether he supports the rights of those who labor, or those who boss and profit from labor.

From death row, this is Mumia Abu-Jamal.

---

*NAFTA was indeed ratified by Congress; and it went into effect on January 1, 1994.

IN THE LATEST ASSAULT against Peruvian civil society, President Fujimori has outlawed the country's Colegio de Abogados (the Peruvian equivalent of the Bar Association) in early December 1992, a slap at the Colegio's adoption of an eleven-point declaration condemning the Fujimori dictatorship's numerous violations of human rights. The Colegio, like most bar associations, is the main lawyers' organization, the one most lawyers must join in order to practice law. The banning of the Colegio was sparked by the group's condemnation of the "torture and humiliation" of Peruvian political prisoner Marta Huatay, and their opposition to state plans to reintroduce the death penalty (officially).

Marta Huatay, founding member of the Association of Democratic Lawyers of Lima, was charged with "terrorism" and summarily convicted by a military tribunal to life imprisonment. At the "trial," Huatay was unable to speak and seemed unaware of her surroundings. An examination by the International Red Cross revealed the presence of brain lesions and a fractured skull—telltale signs of government torture.

Peru's "courts" are administered by military officers who are "judges" in name only. There are three hooded soldiers, who are neither lawyers nor trained in the law, and just such a tribunal "tried" and sentenced Shining Path (Sendero Luminoso) founder Dr. Abimael Guzmán to life imprisonment in San Lorenzo Island military prison.

Most recently security police in Chiclayo, northern Peru, arrested and detained five defense lawyers for political prisoners and charged them with being "apologists for terrorism," a "crime" that can cost twelve years in prison.

The five—Miguel Olazabal Ancanino, Victor Siguenas Campos, Ruben Bustamente Banda, Ernesto Cuba Montes, and Gilver Alarcon Requejo—are also members of the Association of Democratic Lawyers of Peru, a special state target, as it is headed by Dr. Alfredo Crespo, Dr. Guzmán's lawyer.

The rampant government torture, intimidation of lawyers, banning of the Bar Association, and clandestine "trials" by hooded nonjudges are happening today in Peru, but you wouldn't know it from the silence of the U.S. news reporters and journalists. After portraying the election of President Alberto Fujimori as the best thing since sushi, the U.S. media has been remarkably silent on the remarkable events happening in Peru, many at the express direction of the U.S. military and intelligence services.

In London, an International Emergency Committee has been formed, to defend the life of Abimael Guzmán, and also to break the media blockade of the West on the torture, repression, and state terrorism of the Fujimori dictatorship. The committee, which issues periodic bulletins on the situation in Peru, can be reached at: International Emergency Committee to Defend the Life of Abimael Guzmán, BCM-IEC, 27 Old Gloucester St., London, WC1N 3XX, England. Fax/phone: (44) (71) 482-0853.

The latest bulletin includes a chilling quote from Peruvian dictator Fujimori made on December 8, 1992, during a speech to the military on an Armed Forces Day celebration, on the worsening health of Dr. Guzmán: "I will not assume under my government any 'personal' guarantees for the security of Mr. Abimael Guzmán in the treatment of his illness."

The implicit threat to Guzmán should be obvious.

Letters of protest are urged.

From death row, this is Mumia Abu-Jamal.

SOUTH AFRICA, the beautiful yet haunted land of racist repression most vile, has marched past its western neighbor, the United States, as its highest court, the eleven-member constitutional court, found the death penalty as applied in South Africa was unconstitutional. Court president, Arthur Chaskalson ruled there was no proof of the death penalty's deterrent value, and held it violated the interim constitution, which guarantees in section 9 the right to life. The ruling was unanimous.

The case stemmed from a challenge lodged by lawyers for two men sentenced to death after being convicted of murder, Themba Makwanyane and Mvuso Mchunu. Lawyers for the two men also argued that state executions violate the fundamental principle of equality, again because all people are supposed to be equal before the law, but in reality are not. A similar challenge, made in the infamous American case *McCleskey v. Kemp*,[*] raised similar issues of racial disparity, but what was found unconstitutional in South Africa was found perfectly fine in the United States.

South Africa continues to fascinate us in the United States, for it is in a sense a dark mirror through which we see ourselves as both lands are driven by racial conflict. Both nations are settler nations, created by European invasions of non-European territories. Both nations utilized the legal process to steal native lands, disinherit native peoples, and dislocate native populations. Indeed, the hated Bantustan system by which Africans were restricted to tribal homelands has its intellectual and legal genesis in the

---

[*]*McCleskey v. Kemp*, 481 U.S. 279 (1987).

American reservation system, where so-called Indians were sent—both native peoples corralled in their own national birthlands, to the poorest, most worthless bits of earth imaginable. For the better part of a century, weren't U.S. blacks relegated to ghettos because of restrictive covenants and housing laws?

After such a wretched history, only South Africa appears to be moving, incrementally, in the right direction, at least on this issue. South Africa, still one of the most violent nations on Earth, turned away from 350 years of capital punishment in one opinion issued by the constitutional court. Is the right to life more constitutional in South Africa than in the United States of America? It would seem so. Seen from this light, South Africa, once so roundly condemned by the world community, walks in step with the world majority who have damned the practice of capital punishment. Not so the U.S.A., where words on an age-stained document hold little meaning at all.

From death row, this is Mumia Abu-Jamal.

We believe these actions to have been taken in error.…
The actions taken can scarcely be reconciled with the principles
and purposes of the United Nations to which we have all subscribed.
And beyond this, we are forced to doubt if even resort to war will
for long serve the permanent interests of the attacking nations.…
There can be no peace—without law. And there can be no law—
if we were to invoke one code of international conduct for those
who oppose us and another for our friends.

—U.S. PRESIDENT DWIGHT DAVID EISENHOWER,
from a speech on the British-French invasion of Egypt
and Soviet invasion of Hungary, October 30, 1956

AS OF THIS WRITING, sabers are rattling in Washington. This time, a bare pittance of states have joined the fledgling number sworn to attack Iraq, a far cry from that of Iraq I—"Operation Desert Storm." As in the first engagement, this latest military option has less to do with "violating UN resolutions" than with securing future access to oceans of petroleum. What was somewhat obscured in the first wave of aerial assaults in 1991 has been clearly demonstrated in the second: that the UN is but a thin fig leaf for what are U.S. (and multinational corporate) interests.

Where was this high and mighty concern for the "sanctity" of neighbors and borders when the apartheid regime ruled in South Africa and raided, strafed, or bombed the frontline states of Angola and Mozambique? Where was the global umbrage about "weapons of mass destruction" when news emerged about the apartheid state in possession of nuclear arms? As an outlaw state South Africa tortured and killed thousands of her African "citizens," and shot down her own children in 1976 in Soweto. South Africa treated UN antiapartheid resolutions with a long train of contempt. It is interesting to note that her best friends in the international arena were the United States and Israel. During the long years of racist state terrorism, the United States never once hinted it was considering military action to liberate the oppressed black majority or to relieve the frontline neighboring states. Indeed it is remarkable that South Africa's beleaguered neighbors *did* receive military assistance—*not* from the U.S.A. but from the tiny island of Cuba, whose forces bested South Africa in battle in Angola's Cuito Carnivale.

What makes Iraq's neighbors so worthy of "help," and South Africa's so unworthy? In a word, oil. Iraq and her neighbors house over 65 percent of the world's oil reserves.

Once again, we are in the maw of war, where thousands (if not tens of thousands) face death—the deaths of Iraqi men, women, and children to protect the corporate interests of Western industry. Is there something obscene here? American politicians and their PR specialists in the media and the academy are revving up for death, and the voices of peace are silent. Americans talk of "collateral damage" on TV, as if they are talking about washing dishes, not the tortured, horrific death of babies.

The United States meanwhile, talks about upholding the dignity of the United Nations, while it refuses to pay millions of dollars in UN fees.

Once more, into the breach—for oil!

From death row, this is Mumia Abu-Jamal.

At a time like this, scorching irony, not convincing argument, is needed. O! Had I the ability, and could I reach the nation's ear, I would, today, pour out a stream of biting ridicule, blasting reproach, withering sarcasm, and stern rebuke. For it is not light that is needed, but fire; it is not the gentle shower, but thunder. We need the storm, the whirlwind, and the earthquake. The feeling of the nation must be quickened; the conscience of the nation must be roused; the propriety of the nation must be startled; the hypocrisy of the nation must be exposed: And its crimes against God and man must be proclaimed and denounced.

What, to the American slave, is your 4th of July? I answer: a day that reveals to him, more than all the other days in the year, the gross injustice and cruelty to which he is the constant victim. To him, your celebration is a sham; your boasted liberty, an unholy license; your national greatness, swelling vanity; your sounds of rejoicing are empty and heartless; your denunciations of tyrants, brassfronted impudence. To the slave your shouts of liberty and equality are hollow mockery; your prayers and hymns, your sermons and thanksgivings, with all your religious parade and solemnity, are, to him, mere bombast, fraud, deception, impiety and hypocrisy—a thin veil to cover up crimes which would disgrace a nation of savages. There is not a nation on the earth guilty of practices, more shocking and bloody, than are the people of these United States, at this very hour.

—FREDERICK DOUGLASS, JULY 5, 1852

July 4, 1993, saw African National Congress president Nelson Mandela in Philadelphia quoting this Honorable Frederick Douglass speech as he accepted the Liberty Medal, along with South African state president F. W. de Klerk. If the joint presence of Mandela and de Klerk were not enough to stir controversy, then the award presenters, Philadelphia mayor Ed Rendell and U.S. president Clinton, certainly stoked controversy among radicals. Hundreds of black Philadelphians, while certainly admirers of Mandela, took umbrage at de Klerk's presence.

Although the awarders are known as "We the People—Philadelphia," the actual everyday people of Philadelphia had little say in choosing the Liberty Medal awardees, and less say in rejecting the widely unpopular honoree de Klerk. The choice of Liberty Medalists was made not by the people but by corporate Philadelphia—big business.

Why? Why were the people, many of whom had worked for more than twenty years against apartheid and for Mandela's release, frozen out, their protests against de Klerk all but ignored? When the African majority takes power in South Africa, U.S. big business wants friends there. If one reads the names of corporate sponsors of the Liberty Medal, it sounds like roll call of the Chamber of Commerce: Unisys Corp., Pennsylvania Bell, and the like.

Mandela, who has not voted in a government election in seventy-four years,[*] and de Klerk, president by way of an election counting only minority, nonblack votes, have only the hope of liberty, no more.

The white minority in South Africa has done its level best to stifle African liberty for three hundred years.

The African majority, even after the awards, still isn't free.

From death row, this is Mumia Abu-Jamal.

---

[*] In 1994, after the first elections during which blacks could vote, Nelson Mandela was elected president of South Africa.

A DEATH ROW REMEMBRANCE OF THE ROSENBERGS
—NEVER AGAIN?

THE NAMES Julius and Ethel Rosenberg were known to most Black Panthers of the late 1960s and early '70s. And as lieutenant of information of the Black Panther Party's Philadelphia chapter in my teens, I made it my business to know.

We had heard about the notorious "Red scare" of the Smith Act, and the fate of the Rosenbergs, executed by the U.S. government on charges of being spies for the now-defunct Soviet Union. What we did not fully understand, however, was the nefarious lengths to which the state had gone to ensure not just their convictions, but their deaths. Even so, Black rebels who understood state repression firsthand still had no idea how cruelly elastic the "law" had been in bringing about Ethel and Julius's legalized murder.

Boston University historian Howard Zinn documents in his widely acclaimed *A People's History of the United States*,

> FBI documents subpoenaed in the 1970s showed that Judge Kaufman[*] had conferred with the prosecutors secretly about the sentences he would give in the [Rosenbergs'] case. Another document shows that after three years of appeal, a meeting took place between Attorney General Herbert Brownell and Chief Justice Fred Vinson of the Supreme Court, and the Chief Justice assured the Attorney General

---

[*]Trial Judge Irving Kaufman, later elevated to the U.S. Court of Appeals for the Second Circuit.

that if any Supreme Court Justice gave a stay of execution, he would immediately call a full court session and override it.*

That the highest magistrate of the United States could pull off such a dark maneuver shows both the limits of the "law" and how people could be demonized just for being "Communists" in the Cold War 1950s.

Fast forward to the 1980s, and the same demonization is afoot when the label "Black Panther" is affixed to any defendant. It is a mark that assures the state that the "law" can be safely twisted, flexed, and if need be discarded, when its application might help someone.

I know, for I am an ex-Panther, and I write from death's abode.

Judge and prosecutor met to discuss ways of assuring my quick dispatch with my "lawyer" present! One police officer, who wrote in his report that "the negro male made no comments" (in contrast to cops, who claimed a confession was given) was "unavailable" for trial. The prosecutor, after asking about Black Panther slogans uttered over a decade before the trial like "Power to the People," assured the jury that if death was the sentence, no worry, for there "would be appeal after appeal after appeal."†

I know the Rosenbergs in a way many will never know. I know the feeling of being pinpointed for one's political beliefs and associations. I know the profoundest loss that results from being separated from loved ones and sentenced to the gallows.

If the state has its way, I will join them in death. Your important assistance may thwart their aims.

From death row, this is Mumia Abu-Jamal.

---

*Howard Zinn, *A People's History of the United States* (New York: Harper Perennial, 1980), 426.
†See trial transcript for *Commonwealth v. Abu-Jamal.*

IN 1987 A TWENTY-EIGHT-YEAR-OLD West Virginia cemetery worker, Glen Dale Woodall, was convicted of the vicious, brutal kidnapping and rape of two women. His life almost ended when a judge sentenced him to two life terms, with an additional 325-year sentence for the crimes.

The evidence was convincing: the state's medical examiner testified that Woodall's semen was found in both victims. Medical examiners, like all expert witnesses, are accorded high respect in American courts, for they are thought to be totally impartial, allies only to science. In Woodall's case, the testimony of medical examiner Fred Zain was the key that locked him away in a dim prison cell for the rest of his natural life. There was only one problem: Zain, forensic expert for the West Virginia State Police for over a decade, was wrong.

After Woodall spent almost five years in prison, his lawyer, Lonnie Simmons, took a long shot by having remnants of the semen found in the victims tested by the new DNA method. The tests proved conclusively that Woodall's semen did not match the samples. Woodall, sentenced to two life terms plus 325 years, was innocent. The West Virginia Supreme Court ordered an examination of the forensic expert's testing in other cases and came up with the startling conclusion that Zain's work was systematically deficient, entering the following ruling: "Any testimony or documentary evidence offered by Zain, at any time, in any criminal Prosecution, should be deemed invalid, unreliable and inadmissable."

For thirteen years Zain had testified in hundreds of rape and murder trials in West Virginia, and later performed similarly in San Antonio, Texas, affecting, according to one attorney's estimate, more than forty-five hundred criminal cases in two states.

In 1990 a handyman, Jack Davis, was sentenced to life in prison for the 1989 murder and mutilation of a central Texas woman. Zain testified at Davis's trial that blood found under the victim's body placed the defendant at the scene. Davis's lawyer, Stanley Schneider, proved that in fact no test was done. Zain, according to forensic specialists in both states, wrote reports on tests that were never done, reported positive matches where negatives would have cleared suspects, and listed as "conclusive" test results that were inconclusive. His efforts to please cops and prosecutors sent thousands of possibly innocent men to serve centuries in prisons across two states, some on death row.

As of this writing, the ex–medical examiner hasn't been charged with a single offense in either state.* His lawyer, Larry Souza, laments that Zain's life has been "ruined. He can't find a job in his profession. He's been reduced to working as a common laborer. He has nowhere to go." I'm sure several thousand prisoners in West Virginia and Texas have some idea about where to send him.

From death row, this is Mumia Abu-Jamal.

*On November 5, 1999, the West Virginia Supreme Court reinstated charges against former serologist Fred Zain for defrauding the state and Kanawha County for providing fabricated evidence while he was in their employment. Newspapers noted the unanimous decision, but said nothing about the crimes of Zain, or about the many victims who remain to this day falsely incarcerated.

OVER 500 YEARS AFTER European conquest of the Americas, the native, indigenous peoples (that is, their few surviving descendants) still live on the margins of society—the poorest of the poor, the sickest of the sick, the most dispossessed people of so-called New World populations. Many of us forget that so-called Indians, not Africans, were the first slaves of the Americas, pressed into service by Admiral Cristobal Colon (known to the Americans as Christopher Columbus) and crew to dig for gold, and if they were felt to be unproductive, their hands were chopped off. This Columbian injustice was the opening that brought genocide to untold millions of natives, and transformed an ancient, "Indian" world into a "New" white one. Thus every country in this hemisphere—Canada, United States, Mexico—rests upon the shattered bones of native genocide, and may be seen as New Europe (Canada=New Britain and New France; United States=New England, New France; Mexico=New Spain) for the mass importation of Europeans, the decimation of natives, and the forced captivity and enslavement of Africans.

In the southernmost "kneecap" of Mexico, in the state of Chiapas, an indigenous revolutionary movement is growing, energized by the Mayan and "Indian" poor, who are injecting a remarkable vitality into the revolutionary tradition. In July–August 1996 the Zapatistas convened the First International Meeting for Humanity and against Neolibertarianism (called the Encuentro, or "the Encounter") in Chiapas. In their opening remarks one finds the emergence of something deeply moving in its vision and poignant in its poetic power. Please share it with us:

Let us introduce ourselves.

We are the Zapatista National Liberation Army. For ten years we lived in these mountains, preparing to fight a war. In these mountains we built an army. Below, in the cities and plantations, we did not exist. Our lives were worth less than those of machines or animals. We were like stones, like weeds in the road. We were silenced. We were faceless. We were nameless. We had no future. We did not exist. To the powers that be, known internationally by the term "Neoliberalism," we did not count, we did not produce, we did not buy, we did not sell. We were a cipher in the accounts of big capital. Then we went to the mountains [of southeastern Mexico] to find ourselves and see if we could ease the pain of being forgotten stones and weeds. Here, in the mountains of southeastern Mexico, our dead live on. Our dead, who live in the mountains, know may things. They speak to us of their death, and we hear them. Coffins speak and tell us another story that comes from yesterday and points toward tomorrow. The mountains spoke to us, the Macehualob, the common and ordinary people.

We are simple people, as the powerful tell us. Every day and the next night, the powerful want us to dance the X-tol [a "conquest dance" reenacting the struggle between the Christian and Moor, with the latter representing the conquered indigenous folk] and repeat their brutal conquest. The Kaz-Dzul [half-foreigner, or Mestizo, Ladino], the false man, rules our lands and has giant war machines, like the Boob [forest demon], half-puma and half-horse, that spread pain and death among us. The trickster government sends us the Aluxob [a small forest spirit, a trickster], the liars who fool our people and make them forgetful.

This is why we became soldiers. This is why we remain soldiers: Because we want no more death and trickery for our people, because we want no more forgetting. The mountains told us to take up arms so we would have a voice. It told us to cover our faces so we would have a face. It told us to forget our names so we could be named. It told us to protect our past so we would have a future.

This is who we are. The Zapatista National Liberation Army. The voice that arms itself to be heard, the face that hides itself to be seen, the name that hides itself to be named, the red star that calls out to humanity around the world to be heard, to be seen, to be named. The tomorrow that is harvested in the past.[*]

Named after the "Indian" Revolutionary Emiliano Zapata (1879–1919), whose forces fought against the Spanish dictator Porfirio Diaz under the slogan, "Libertad Y Tierra" (Liberty and Land), the Zapatistas draw their strength, their imagery, and their vision from the most oppressed segments of Mexican life, the indigenous, the conquered ones who have sustained themselves in the face of over 500 years of conquest.

That they exist is something of a miracle, and they bring something to life's table that is wonderful.

From death row, this is Mumia Abu-Jamal.

---

*Opening remarks at the First Intercontinental Meeting For Humanity and Against Neoliberalism, the Indigenous Clandestine Revolutionary Committee—General Command of the Zapatista National Liberation Army. Reprinted from "Dark Night" field notes, no. 8, p. 34. For reprints of Zapatista documents, write to P.O. Box 3629, Chicago, IL 60690-3629.

Brothers and Sisters, Why?
How many more?
Until when?

—SUBCOMANDANTE MARCOS,
ZAPATISTA ARMY, DECEMBER 1997

The brutal, premeditated massacre of at least forty-five indigenous poor men, women, and children several days before Christmas 1997 by armed paramilitaries of the ruling Institutional Revolutionary Party (PRI) of Mexico sent shock waves through the international community.

In a slaughter of the innocent that took over four hours, the so-called PRIistas revealed their malevolent intent, to attack and disable the indigenous (Indian) support network for the Zapatista army. Thus, the ruthless killing of forty-five civilians had a clear political objective, one verbalized by the "Red Mask" paramilitaries as, "We are going to put an end to the Zapatista seed" (*Nuevo Amanecer Press*, December 26, 1997). Seen in this light, the forty-five men, women, and children of San Pedro de Chenalhó were but a means to a dastardly end.

How, one wonders, can such a thing happen? Until we address this question, how can we begin to answer those posed above? For over fifty years, especially after the Nazi period in Europe, psychologists have studied this destructive phenomenon. The famous Milgram Ssudies (1963) taught us the limits of "destructive obedience," where so-called normal people shocked innocent others up to 450 volts, up to levels reading "DANGER: SEVERE SHOCK," only because authority figures told them to do so, with 65 percent obeying to the end (other Milgram studies found over 90 percent compliance).

Scholars H. C. Kelman and V. L. Hamilton have advanced the notion of "sanctioned massacres," no stranger to American or world history: "Within

American history, My Lai had its precursors in the Philippine war around the turn of the century... and in the massacres of American Indians... one recalls the Nazi's 'final solution' for European Jews, the massacres and deportations of Armenians by Turks, the liquidation of the Kulaks and the great purges in the Soviet Union, and more recently the massacre in Indonesia and Bangladesh, in Biafra and Burundi, in South Africa and Mozambique, in Cambodia and Afghanistan, in Syria and Lebanon."* In many of those cases, we find the "sanctioning" of heinous massacres by authorization, routinization and dehumanization.

Authorization is when persons in power order or allow atrocities to occur in furtherance of political ends. Routinization is the internal process by which those authorized make it "okay" to do what is an obvious evil, like slaughtering babies. Dehumanization is the social and ideological process by which a people are projected, perceived, and then treated as somehow less than human. In each of the historical instances noted above, we have seen these diabolical features at work.

It happened in America, where the Declaration of Independence describes "merciless Indian savages"; and where children learned the phrase "The only good Indian is a dead Indian" at an early age. Such a mindset made Wounded Knee an historic inevitability. These same features were found in the Chiapas area, where minions of the state attacked the most powerless and the most maligned segment of Mexican society: Indians, the indigenous peoples. For centuries they, as well as Africans, have been subjected to dehumanization. In Chiapas they were seem not as full human beings, with inherent rights, but as tools used in the "dirty war" of the government against the Zapatistas.

"How many more?" Marcos asked.

"Until when?" he wonders.

The true shame is that we cannot say.

From death row, this is Mumia Abu-Jamal.

---

*Neil J. Kressel, ed., *Political Psychology: Classic and Contemporary Readings* (New York: Paragon House, 1993), 223.

CONVERSATION BETWEEN MUMIA AND NOELLE HANRAHAN MINUTES AFTER THE 1995 DEATH WARRANT WAS READ TO MUMIA IN HIS CELL

MUMIA ABU-JAMAL: This is just a fight from another front, you know. Don't panic folks.

NOELLE HANRAHAN: My God, the guy signed a warrant for political reasons! He knew you were filing an appeal the next day.

MAJ: They just allowed me to sign my Petition for Post Conviction Release (PCRA). And it was no secret that we were going to file Monday. Every lawyer in Philadelphia knew we were filing. To sign a death warrant Friday was clearly politically motivated!

NH: It was printed in the *Harrisburg Patriot News*.

MAJ: Judge Sabo, you know, ups the ante. The fact is that we are dealing with a certifiable maniac, someone who is called a "prosecutor in robes" by ex- prosecutors. It is very clear the Department of Corrections and the General Assembly and the politicians have been angling to sign more death warrants, sign more death warrants, sign more death warrants. What they have said publicly is the reason they are doing this is not to kill people, but to force inmates to file papers and force this process along. To force inmates to file their appeals.

NH: What's the advantage for Ridge to sign the warrant today? What does he get out of this?

MAJ: He says, "I've done it!" He has heeded the call of the people who have been calling for my blood since he became governor.

NH: The recusal motion is a very powerful document. *(referring to the motion to recuse Judge Albert Sabo)*

MAJ: It causes me to cringe. What you have in the recusal motion are very clearly documented cases of a jurist who doesn't know whether he wants to be a prosecutor or a thirteenth juror! You have a list of five or six of the most distinguished lawyers in Philadelphia, in contemporary history, who are excellent defense lawyers, but more importantly, were themselves prosecutors. They say, in sworn papers, that Sabo is a "prosecutor in robes." They say, in sworn papers, that when they came into the courtroom they had to restrain the judge from leaning over too far to help the prosecutor. They say that no defendant can get a fair trial or a fair hearing in front of him. It's not what Jamal says. It's not what Jamal's lawyers say. It's not what Jamal's supporters say. It's what fifteen years' history on the bench have shown and revealed is a biased jurist—someone who doesn't know the meaning of the word *impartiality*.

NH: The recusal is a great document. We were really glad to see it.

MAJ: Very good. Well, I think that anyone outside the sworn, paid membership of the FOP, if they look at the record of this [Judge Sabo's] handling of cases.... I mean I just found out this morning from my Phase II mate next door that another guy on death row just filed a petition, PCRA, in front of Sabo and had it thrown out.

NH: Mumia, is Sabo hearing his PCRAs?

MAJ: To my knowledge, yes. The power that they accord a judge is extraordinary. Judge Albert Sabo is hearing PCRAs. Ernie Porter was in front of him—the guy I was talking about. He was on trial before him. Sentenced before him. Files a PCRA a few weeks ago, a few days ago, and has it denied by Sabo. I mean anybody who's watched the O. J. trial and so forth, or any trial in California, knows that any defendant has an automatic right of recusal in front of any judge. If he gets in front of any judge he has an automatic right to say no. Not this guy. Such a right does not exist in Philadelphia. They are not rules that govern the conduct of the Court of Common Pleas of the First Judicial District in Philadelphia or any district. The fact is that a recusal motion, no matter how damning, has to go before that judge and he has the word. He decides. So that's where we're going. The exhibits and the documents in the PCRA really tell the story. The statements made by the lawyers and supporting other peoples' recusal motions are extraordinary. I mean they're extraordinary. I mean, Norris Gelman, Richard Sprague. Those are some of the lawyers that are named. They are excellent defense lawyers. But they were also good prosecutors. And for them to come forward and say what they say should mean something. Well, the point I'm making is, the papers that were filed in that Melman case were filed in front of His Honor Judge Sabo as part of a petition for recusation and recusal and he refused them. [Laugh.] You know.

NH: How quickly do you think Sabo could move? Within days?

MAJ: Well, it's hard to say. I mean, he could deny it in a day if he wishes. And he may. Who knows.

NH: You said all your materials are in the hands of the state.

MAJ: I have nothing but a handful of materials right now with me. When they came and told me that I was going to Phase II about 8:45 this morning I was in the law library. I wasn't in my cell. All of my legal mail, my trial transcripts, personal mail, you know, everything, is in my cell. I had nothing. And I had to leave what I had in the law library and proceed to Phase II. There they strip-searched me, changed my clothes, and then took some photographs for the department's records.

NH: So, Mumia, you're saying that they signed your death warrant yesterday and then they effectively took away all your opportunities to work on your appeal?!

MAJ: Absolutely. I mean, well, let me read to you what it says here. They have to by law give the person on Phase II a photocopy of the actual death warrant that comes from the governor's office. It reads on this last page, and I quote, "Given under my hand and Great Seal of the state and city of Harrisburg, this first day of June in the year of Our Lord one thousand nine hundred and ninety-five, and of the Commonwealth in two hundred and nineteenth, by the governor Thomas J. Ridge, with his signature and attested by the Secretary of the Commonwealth." So you know, we're learning from the Patriot that they knew days ahead they were going to sign the warrant, that they signed it a day ahead. They served it about 8:45 this morning while I was outside my cell doing legal work, you know. Working. I was working on one of the civil cases that the capital case prisoners are filing against the Department of Corrections precisely for access to their legal material. They have a situation right now where I cannot go now—I cannot go back into the law library, and no one in Phase II can go into that law library, even though, according to the administrative directive that provides legal access for all capital cases, a memo of June 2, 1989, signed by the commissioner of corrections, all capital cases, whether on Phase I or Phase II, must have direct access to the law library. I cannot go back into that law library as long as I have an active death warrant over me. This is the practice that the Department of Corrections has concerning and governing people on death row.

NH: My God! You know—that's worse than "Kafka"!

MAJ: Well, check this out. A few days ago I got a, well, it might have been Monday last, a guard came by and says, "Jamal, you have law library." I said, "Okay." He said, "You have signed up for Atkins?" This is, you know, one of the brothers on Phase II. I said, "Okay, good. I'll be able to see him, talk to him, and help him, you know, put his paperwork together." I came into the law library that morning, and there were four men in there, and not one of them was on Phase II, and I said, "What's going on? What's happening? Where's so-and-so?" And everybody said, well apparently we're here for them. I found out after I got to the law library that I was a proxy for the man that was on Phase II because he couldn't come to the law library. Now he was allowed to send me a note. He wanted me to write up a motion for him. I did the best I could, based on a very unclear handwritten note of what he wanted done. I can't read a law book for another man. I can't reason for another man. I mean, I'm not really a lawyer, you'all. But here's a man, the other man, who had a death date within thirty days or thirty-five days. He could not walk into the law library in a cage—where there are two cages—read a book or write a brief in his own hand. You know. That's the Commonwealth of Pennsylvania.

NH: It's just like the high-tech version of taking away people's pencils, you know.

MAJ: Well, I don't have a pencil. I don't have a pencil. I have to stop a guard if I want a pencil. And if he, you know, wants to give me a pencil, he gives me a pencil. I write what I need and I must give it back to him as soon as I finish writing. Well, I haven't been able to stop a guard yet. That's the reality of Phase II right now.

But you know, when you look at the conditions that the Commonwealth has people on Phase II under, I mean, it goes beyond bizarre, it goes beyond Kafka, you know. I mean it is illegal for me now in Phase II to go into a law library that's about a hundred feet away and read a book.

NH: Right, and you can't when you have an execution warrant signed.

MAJ: When you don't have one, you can get in there maybe every three or four days, [laughter], you know. What the Commonwealth has really designed at bottom is a system where everyone is under the most pressure that the government can bear on any human, and is denied most access to legal material. The persons who need legal research and material most are able to get access to it least. And that's the reality. And if that doesn't show a biased system, what does?

NH: Hey, what are they doing, building something in there?

MAJ: They're probably building new Phase IIs. This block has I think about eight Phase IIs, and I'm sure there are more to come.

NH: Who can visit you in Phase II?

MAJ: Only personal family and lawyers, right. Anybody else needs a court order. Incidentally, I'm glad we talked because last night or yesterday I was in the law library and a guy comes up and says, "I want to see you in the Counselor's Office." I'm like—Oh wow, I've never seen this before. This is new, you know, I'm being counseled. All right. So I go to the Counselor's Office. I get handcuffed and I go there and the guy says, "Look, I got a direct order from the Security Captain that you must remove everyone from your visiting list who has a prison record." Ahhh, you know, I haven't done anything and, because I was contemplating some legal action against these people.... Here I am in a noncontact visiting situation. I could be visited by Satan, and he couldn't do anything. You know what I'm saying?

NH: Yes.

MAJ: I think it was a premeditated planned attempt to block and bar my support from members of the MOVE organization. As everybody knows, many MOVE people have been in prison and in jail. I am prohibited from having anyone who has been in jail visit me. But now, because I am on Phase II, I am prevented from having anybody visiting me, except people who have a court order.

NH: Mumia, talk for just a brief second about who they have prevented from seeing you. Also, put it in the context of where Waynesburg is.

MAJ: Waynesburg is at the farthest southwest corner of the state. It is as far as one can go in the state of Pennsylvania and still be in the state of Pennsylvania. We are bordering Ohio to the west, and West Virginia to the South and, ah, about I guess about fifty miles away from Pittsburg. It is, well, conservative would be an understatement, a nicety. For the last few months now, what we have found out is that no reporter, agency, newspaper, broadcast employees can come and interview me. I have been under what is an investigation status, said to have been around as to whether I had been operating a business connected with the writing and publishing of *Live from Death Row*.

NH: So you are saying that, and if you could repeat this for me, that the *Wall Street Journal, People* magazine, *20/20*, the *Washington Post*, the *New York Times* have all been denied access?

MAJ: I am saying that every news agency on the planet earth from the *Welcomemat* in Philadelphia, *People, 20/20, NBC Evening News*, the *Wall Street Journal*, the *Washington Post*, ah, the *Philadelphia*-whatever, whatever news agency you can name, has been denied access to this institution based upon a continuing investigation into whether I have been conducting a business in the writing of *Live from Death Row*.

NH: What have they done about your paralegals?

MAJ: They have denied all paralegals based upon the fact that they have said that they have not graduated from recognized and certified legal teaching institutions and don't have degrees in paralegal science. They have used that as a pretext to further isolate and restrict people. Understand that this is the most isolated prison in the Commonwealth. People have told me, and I don't remember, but I don't remember seeing it though, that when they drive by if they don't look to the left quickly when they are driving down Roy Furman Highway, they will miss a small sign that announces the existence of this place. If they don't look above the hills and see the razor and concertina wire, then they will not know that the prison sits on the hill to the left. This place is for all intents and purposes buried in the boondocks of Pennsylvania, as far as possible from most of the people's [homes] who are situated here. Of course, most of the people on death row are from Philadelphia County—if you drew a line diagonally from Waynesburg to Philadelphia it would be literally be slicing the state in a parallel line from one corner to the next.

NH: So they have attacked your paralegals, who are your lawyers' agents, your lawyers are forced to come hundreds, hundreds, and hundreds, of miles. They have shut down all journalists' access to you, and now they are attacking your visiting list in various ways.

MAJ: Yeah. So the goal is obviously isolation, restriction. Not only that. What we have been finding out is that what I said months ago is absolutely true. They have rifled through legal mail from my paid criminal capital case lawyer and from my legal staff. They have read my legal mail before I have read it. And not only that, they have sent it throughout the Commonwealth.

NH: How do you know that?

MAJ: We know that for a fact. It will come out more on Monday.

NH: So literally you are having guards there opening and copying your legal mail, which is completely unconstitutional.

MAJ: Absolutely.

NH: And sending it around to what you presume are the prosecutors.

MAJ: Well, maybe the FOP wants a file, what can I tell you.

NH: Talk just a second about my denial for taking an unauthorized picture.

MAJ: Well, it seems to me that for you to be excluded took them watching you through a telescope. You reportedly took a photograph of SCI Greene from a certain distance, and you credited yourself as photographer, and this was published in the *Jamal Journal.* Several weeks ago I received from the warden a notice that was copied and sent to all staff members throughout the department. It said that one Noelle Hanrahan would not be allowed in until further notice for violating the security of SCI G, by taking a photograph, a photograph that appears to have been taken off of the grounds of State Correctional Institute at Greene, and it was published in the *Jamal Journal.*

NH: When people see the photo, they see it is pretty muddy and it is really only of the concertina razor wire. It just seems like [the prison authorities] don't want any representation of the prison anywhere at all.

MAJ: No.

NH: Then certainly it is also another attack on your visiting list.

MAJ: Absolutely. I mean from day one we knew, if you look at *Attack on the Life of the Mind,* which was written years ago, the central theme in *Attack on the Life of the Mind* is isolation of one man from another. Isolation of prisoners for bullshit reasons, you know, that is essentially the guiding theme of this jail. To isolate people further, and further, and further away from those they love, from those they need. And to thereby make it easy [to kill people], and for some people, like Keith Zettlemoyer, to make them have a desire to leave this life. I am told I am out of time. Give my love to everyone.

NH: Stay strong, Mumia.

MAJ: I have no choice. Tell them that this is just one other front to fight from.

NH: Alright.

MAJ: Thank you all. You're doing a hell of a job. On a MOVE.

NH: You, too.

MAJ: Love.

NOTES ON THE COMPOSITION AND RECORDING OF THE TEXTS

"From an Echo in Darkness, a Step into Light," first section, was written on September 20, 1992, and recorded on April 15, 1994, at Huntingdon State Prison, Huntingdon, Pennsylvania, and has never been aired. The recording of this essay remains censored and locked in NPR's vault. A version of this section was included in *Live from Death Row* with the same title.

"From an Echo in Darkness, a Step into Light," second section, was written on September 6, 1992, and recorded on April 15, 1994, at Huntingdon State Prison, Huntingdon, Pennsylvania, as "Requiem for Norman," and has never been aired. The recording of this essay remains censored and locked in NPR's vault. It is previously unpublished.

"From an Echo in Darkness, a Step into Light," third section, was written in fall 1990, and was recorded on April 15, 1994, at Huntingdon State Prison, Huntingdon, Pennsylvania, as "Yard In," and has never been aired. The recording of this essay remains censored and locked in NPR's vault. Portions of this section were published in the *Yale Law Journal* in January 1991, and in *Live from Death Row.*

"From an Echo in Darkness, a Step into Light," fourth section, was written on June 17, 1989, and recorded on April 15, 1994, at Huntingdon State Prison, Huntingdon, Pennsylvania, as "'On Tilt' by State Design,"and has never been aired. The recording of this essay remains censored and locked in NPR's vault. Portions of this section were published in the *Yale Law Journal* in January 1991, and in *Live from Death Row.*

"From an Echo in Darkness, a Step into Light," fifth section, was written in fall 1990, and was recorded on April 15, 1994, at Huntingdon State Prison, Huntingdon, Pennsylvania, as "Control," and has never been aired. The recording of this essay remains censored and locked in NPR's vault. Portions of this section were published in the *Yale Law Journal* in January 1991, and in *Live from Death Row.*

"From an Echo in Darkness, a Step into Light," sixth section, was written on March 30, 1994, and recorded on April 15, 1994, at Hundingdon State Prison, Huntingdon, Pennsylvania, as "Already Out of the Game," and has never been aired. The recording of this essay remains censored and locked in NPR's vault. It is previously unpublished.

"From an Echo in Darkness, a Step into Light," seventh section, was written on March 31, 1994, and was recorded on April 15, 1994, at Huntingdon State Prison, Huntingdon, Pennsylvania, as "Acting Like Life's a Ballgame." It was included in *Live from Death Row*. It is included on the compact disc, *All Things Censored*, as read by William Kunstler, recorded on May 21, 1995, for broadcast on *Democracy Now!* The recording of this essay remains censored and locked in NPR's vault.

"From an Echo in Darkness, a Step into Light," eighth section, date of composition unknown, was recorded on April 15, 1994, at Hundingdon State Prison, Huntingdon, Pennsylvania, as "Pennsylvania Takes a Giant Step—Backward," and has never been aired. The recording of this essay remains censored and locked in NPR's vault. It is previously unpublished.

"The Sense of Censory," written on March 4, 1997, was recorded in August 1998 by Martin Espada for broadcast on Pacifica Radio's *Democracy Now!* It is previously unpublished.

"Another Write-Up… for Rapping!" was written on August 14, 1999. It has not yet been recorded and is not previously published.

"A Bright, Shining Hell," date of composition unknown, was recorded by Mumia on October 31, 1996, on death row at State Correctional Institute at Greene, in Waynesburg, Pennsylvania. It was included on the 1997 CD released as *Mumia Abu-Jamal Spoken Word, with Music by Man Is the Bastard*.

"No Law, No Rights" was written on February 14, 1993, and recorded by Mumia on October 31, 1996, on death row at State Correctional Institute at Greene, in Waynesburg, Pennsylvania. It was included in *Live from Death Row* and on the 1999 CD release *All Things Censored*.

"A Letter from Prison," written in March 1998, was recorded by Ossie Davis in April 1998 for broadcast on Pacifica Radio's *Democracy Now!* It is previously unpublished.

"The Visit" was written on November 1, 1994, and recorded by Judi Bari on June 25, 1995 for broadcast on Pacifica Radio's *Democracy Now!* It appeared in *Live from Death Row*.

"Black August," written in August 1993, was recorded on August 16, 1993, by Mumia on death row at Huntingdon State Prison, Huntingdon, Pennsylvania. It was included on the 1997 CD released as *Mumia Abu-Jamal Spoken Word, with Music by Man Is the Bastard*.

"A Single Spark Can Start a Prairie Fire," written on October 25, 1989, was recorded by Mumia on October 15, 1992, on death row at Huntingdon State Prison, Huntingdon, Pennsylvania. It is previously unpublished.

"Meeting with a Killer," was written on July 18, 1995, and was recorded by Peter Coyote in June 1998 for broadcast on Pacifica Radio's *Democracy Now!* A version of it appears in *Death Blossoms*.

"Manny's Attempted Murder," written in April 1989, was recorded on July 15, 1992, on death row at Huntingdon State Prison, Huntingdon, Pennsylvania. It was included in *Live from Death Row*.

"Days of Pain, Night of Death," written in November 1989, was recorded on May 21, 1995. A version of it appears in *Live from Death Row* by Ramona Africa for broadcast on Pacifica Radio's *Democracy Now!*

"An Uncivil Action" was written by Mumia in September and October 1999. It is previously unpublished.

PART II: PERSPECTIVES

"Mother Loss and Father Hunger," first section, was written on July 1, 1995, and was recorded on August 16, 1993, by Mumia at Huntingdon State Prison, Huntingdon, Pennsylvania, as "Mother Loss." A version of it was previously published under that title in *Death Blossoms*.

"Mother Loss and Father Hunger," second section, was written on May 13, 1996, and recorded by Mumia on October 31, 1996, at State Correctional Institute at Greene, in Waynesburg, Pennsylvania, as "Father Hunger." A version of it was previously published in *Death Blossoms*.

"Musings on 'Mo' and Marshall," written on January 25, 1993, was recorded by Mumia on August 16, 1993, on Death Row at Huntingdon State Prison, Huntingdon, Pennsylvania. It is previously unpublished.

"Philly Daze," written in part in 1994 and updated fall of 1996, was recorded by Terry Bisson on May 21, 1995, for broadcast on Pacifica Radio's *Democracy Now!* A version of it was published in *Live from Death Row*.

"Essays from an Outcast from the Fourth Estate" was written on October 13, 1999. It is previously unpublished.

"Deadly Drug Raid," written April 6, 1994, was originally intended for National Public Radio, but was censored before the recording session. It has not been recorded or previously published.

"First Amendment Rites," first section, was written on June 4, 1995. It has not yet been recorded or previously published.

"First Amendment Rites," second section, written on June 10, 1995, was originally titled "First Amendment Rites." It has not yet been recorded or previously published.

"A Rap Thing," written on December 17, 1995, was recorded on October 31, 1996, on death row at SCI Greene, Waynesburg, Pennsylvania. It was included on the 1999 CD release *All Things Censored.*

PEN Award acceptance speech was written and recorded by Mumia in June 1999 via phone from death row at SCI Greene, Waynesburg, Pennsylvania.

"Legalized Crime," date of composition unknown, was recorded by Mumia on October 31, 1996, on death row at SCI Greene, Waynesburg, Pennsylvania. It was included on the 1997 CD released as *Mumia Abu-Jamal Spoken Word, with Music by Man Is the Bastard.*

"Absence of Power," written in April 1993, was recorded by Mumia on August 16, 1993, on death row at Huntingdon State Prison, Huntingdon, Pennsylvania. It is previously unpublished.

"A Crisis in Black Leadership," written on June 11, 1989, was recorded by Mumia on October 15, 1992, on death row at Huntingdon State Prison, Huntingdon, Pennsylvania. It is previously unpublished.

"Liberty Denied in Its Cradle," written on June 16, 1989, was recorded by Mumia on July 15, 1992 on death row at Huntingdon State Prison, Huntingdon, Pennsylvania. It is previously unpublished.

"Slavery Daze II," written in July 1989, was recorded on July 15, 1992, on death row at Huntingdon State Prison, Huntingdon, Pennsylvania. It was included in *Live from Death Row.*

"Memories of Huey," written on August 27, 1989, was recorded on July 15, 1992, on death row at Huntingdon State Prison, Huntingdon, Pennsylvania. It is previously unpublished.

"To War! For Empire!" written on February 1, 1991, was recorded on July 15, 1992 on death row at Huntingdon State Prison, Huntingdon, Pennsylvania. It is previously unpublished.

"Capture Him, Beat Him, and Treat Him Like Dirt," written on July 12, 1991, was recorded on July 15, 1992, on death row at Huntingdon State Prison, Huntingdon, Pennsylvania. It is previously unpublished.

"The Lost Generation?" written in June 1992, was recorded on July 15, 1992 on death row at Huntingdon State Prison, Huntingdon, Pennsylvania. It is previously unpublished.

"May 13 Remembered," section one, written in 1993, was recorded on August 16, 1993, on death row at Huntingdon State Prison, Huntingdon, Pennsylvania. It was included on the 1997 CD released as *Mumia Abu-Jamal Spoken Word, with Music by Man Is the Bastard.*

"May 13 Remembered," section two, was written in 1993, and was recorded by

Mumia on August 16, 1993, Huntingdon State Prison, Huntingdon, Pennsylvania. It is previously unpublished.

"And They Call MOVE 'Terrorists!'" written on November 21, 1989, was recorded by Mumia on July 15, 1992, on death row at Huntingdon State Prison, Huntingdon, Pennsylvania. It is previously unpublished.

"Justice Denied," section one, written on January 31, 1992, was recorded by Mumia on July 15, 1992, on death row at Huntingdon State Prison, Huntingdon, Pennsylvania. It is previously unpublished.

"Justice Denied," section two, written on April 1, 1992, was recorded by Mumia on July 15, 1992, as "The Ramona Africa Suit," on death row at Huntingdon State Prison, Huntingdon, Pennsylvania. It is previously unpublished.

"Justice for Geronimo Stolen by Star Chamber," written on July 24, 1989, was recorded by Mumia on August 16, 1993, on death row at Huntingdon State Prison, Huntingdon, Pennsylvania. It is previously unpublished.

"Eddie Hatcher Fights for His Life!" written on June 10, 1991, was recorded by Mumia on August 16, 1993, on death row at Huntingdon State Prison, Huntingdon, Pennsylvania. It is previously unpublished.

"Seeds of Wisdom," date of composition unknown, was recorded on August 16, 1993, on death row at Huntingdon State Prison, Huntingdon, Pennsylvania, by Mumia. It is previously unpublished.

"Sweet Roxanne," date of composition unknown, was recorded by Mumia on October 31, 1996, at SCI Greene in Waynesburg, Pennsylvania. It is previously unpublished.

"A House is Not a Home," written in April 1992, was recorded by Mumia on August 16, 1993, and April 15, 1994, on death row at Huntingdon State Prison, Huntingdon, Pennsylvania. It previously appeared in *Live from Death Row*.

"Prisons vs. Preschools," written on July 26, 1992, was recorded by Mumia on October 15, 1992, on death row at Huntingdon State Prison, Huntingdon, Pennsylvania. It is previously unpublished.

"Raised Hope, Fallen Disappointment," written on November 8, 1992, was recorded by Mumia on August 16, 1993, on death row at Huntingdon State Prison, Huntingdon, Pennsylvania. It is previously unpublished.

"With Malice toward Many," written on November 29, 1992, was recorded by Mumia on August 16, 1993, on death row at Huntingdon State Prison, Huntingdon, Pennsylvania. It is previously unpublished.

"Legalized Cop Violence," written on February 10, 1999, was recorded by Bear Lincoln in April 1999 for broadcast on Pacifica Radio's *Democracy Now!* It appears in *Live from Death Row*.

"Men of Cloth," written in August 1996, was recorded by Mumia in June 1999 via phone from death row at SCI Greene in Waynesburg, Pennsylvania. It previously appeared in *Death Blossoms*.

"A Drug That Ain't a Drug," written on March 9, 1996, was recorded by Mumia on October 31, 1996, on death row at the State Correctional Institution at Greene in Waynesburg, Pennsylvania. It is previously unpublished.

"How Now Mad Cow?" written on April 9, 1999, was recorded by Mumia on October 31, 1996, on death row at the State Correctional Institution at Greene in Waynesburg, Pennsylvania. It is previously unpublished.

PART III: ESSAYS ON JUSTICE

"De Profundis," date of composition unknown, was recorded by Mumia on October 31, 1996, at the State Correctional Institute at Greene in Waynesburg, Pennsylvania. It is previously unpublished.

"Five Hundred Years: Celebrations or Demonstrations?" written on New Year's Eve, December 31, 1991, was recorded on July 15, 1992, on death row at Huntingdon State Prison, Huntingdon, Pennsylvania. It is previously unpublished.

"The Illusion of 'Democracy,'" written on June 12, 1992, was recorded on July 15, 1992, on death row at Huntingdon State Prison, Huntingdon, Pennsylvania. It is previously unpublished.

"A Nation in Chains," written on June 13, 1992, was recorded on July 15, 1992, on death row at Huntingdon State Prison, Huntingdon, Pennsylvania. It is previously unpublished.

"Live from Death Row," written in April 1989 and updated December 1994, was recorded on July 15, 1992, on death row at Huntingdon State Prison, Huntingdon, Pennsylvania. It was published in *Live from Death Row*.

"War on the Poor," written on March 24, 1994, was recorded on April 15, 1994, on death row at Huntingdon State Prison. It was included on the 1999 CD release *All Things Censored*.

"Why a War on the Poor?," written on February 18, 1998, was recorded by Ruby Dee in April 1998 for broadcast on Pacifica Radio's *Democracy Now!* It is previously unpublished.

"The Death Game," first section, was written in April 1994 for National Public Radio, but censored by NPR before recording session. Originally titled "Jury of Peers?," a version of it was published in *Live from Death Row*.

"The Death Game," second section, was written in 1994 for National Public Radio, but censored before recording session. Originally titled "Blackmun Bows Out of the Death Game," a version of it, recorded on April 15, 1994, was published in *Live from Death Row.* It was included on the 1999 CD release *All Things Censored.*

"Black March to Death Row," written in 1991, was recorded by Mumia on August 16, 1993, at Huntingdon State Prison, Huntingdon, Pennsylvania. It was included in *Live from Death Row.*

"On Death Row, Fade to Black," written in April 1990, was recorded by Mumia on October 15, 1992, on death row at Huntingdon State Prison, Huntingdon, Pennsylvania. It was included in *Live from Death Row.*

"Fred Hampton Remembered," written on September 11, 1990, was recorded by Mumia on October 15, 1992, on death row at Huntingdon State Prison, Huntingdon, Pennsylvania. It is previously unpublished.

"'Law' that Switches from Case to Case," written on January 20, 1992, was recorded by Mumia on October 15, 1992, on death row at Huntingdon State Prison, Huntingdon, Pennsylvania. It is previously unpublished.

"Two Blacks, Two Georgians," written on October 16, 1992, was recorded by Mumia on October 15, 1992, on death row at Huntingdon State Prison, Huntingdon, Pennsylvania. It is previously unpublished.

"Cancellation of the Constitution," written on May 17, 1994, has not yet been recorded or previously published.

"L.A. Outlaw," written in April 1993, was recorded by Mumia on August 16, 1993, on death row at Huntingdon State Prison, Huntingdon, Pennsylvania. It is previously unpublished.

"Media Is the Mirage," date of composition unknown, was recorded on October 31, 1996, at SCI Greene in Waynesburg, Pennsylvania. It was included on the 1999 CD release *All Things Censored.*

"True African-American History," date of composition unknown, was recorded by Mumia on August 16, 1993, on death row at Huntingdon State Prison, Huntingdon, Pennsylvania. It was included on the 1999 CD release *All Things Censored.*

"When Ineffective Means Effective," date of composition unknown, was recorded on August 16, 1993, on death row at Huntingdon State Prison, Huntingdon, Pennsylvania. It was included on the 1999 CD release *All Things Censored.*

"Death: The Poor's Prerogative?" date of composition unknown, was recorded on October 31, 1996, on death row in Waynesburg, Pennsylvania. It was included on the 1999 CD release *All Things Censored.*

"Campaign of Repression: Attack on the Life of the Mind," date of composition unknown, was recorded by Mumia on August 16, 1993, on death row at Huntingdon State Prison, Huntingdon, Pennsylvania. It is previously unpublished.

"Musings on Malcolm," written in December 1992, was recorded by Mumia on

August 16, 1993, on death row at Huntingdon State Prison, Huntingdon, Pennsylvania. It was included in *Live from Death Row*.

"In Defense of Empire," written on June 13, 1993, was recorded by Mumia on August 16, 1993, on death row at Huntingdon State Prison, Huntingdon, Pennsylvania. It is previously unpublished.

"Build a Better Mousetrap," written in 1991, was recorded by Mumia on August 16, 1993, on death row at Huntingdon State Prison, Huntingdon, Pennsylvania. It is previously unpublished.

"Haitians Need Not Apply," written on April 9, 1999, was recorded by Mumia on October 15, 1992, on death row at Huntingdon State Prison, Huntingdon, Pennsylvania. It is previously unpublished.

"Rostock, Germany, and Anti-Immigrant Violence," date of composition unknown, was recorded by Mumia on October 15, 1992, on death row at Huntingdon State Prison, Huntingdon, Pennsylvania. It is previously unpublished.

"NAFTA: A Pact Made in Hell" was written in October 1992, and was recorded by Mumia on August 16, 1993, on death row at Huntingdon State Prison, Huntingdon, Pennsylvania. It was included on the 1999 CD release *All Things Censored*.

"Fujimori Bans the Bar in Peru," written in January 1993, was recorded by Mumia on August 16, 1993, on death row at Huntingdon State Prison, Huntingdon, Pennsylvania. It is previously unpublished.

"South Africa," written on June 9, 1995, was recorded by Mumia on October 31, 1996, on death row at the State Correctional Institute at Greene, in Waynesburg, Pennsylvania. It was included on the 1999 CD release *All Things Censored*.

"Warlust—Again! (Iraq II)," written on February 17, 1998, was recorded by Adrienne Rich in December 1998 for broadcast on Pacifica Radio's *Democracy Now!* It is previously unpublished.

"What, to a Prisoner, Is the Fourth of July?" written in July 1993, was recorded by Bernadette Devlin McAliskey in May 1998 for broadcast on Pacifica Radio's *Democracy Now!* It appears in *Live from Death Row*.

"A Death Row Remembrance of the Rosenbergs—Never Again?" written in 1993, was recorded by Martin Sobell in March of 1999 for broadcast on Pacifica Radio's *Democracy Now!* It is previously unpublished.

"Expert Witness from Hell," date of composition unknown, was recorded by Juan Gonzalez on May 21, 1995, for broadcast on Pacifica Radio's *Democracy Now!* It appears in *Live from Death Row*.

"Zapatista Dreams" was written on May 19, 1997. It has not yet been recorded or previously published.

"What Made the Acteal Massacre Possible?" was written on January 10, 1998. It has not yet been recorded or previously published.

"Conversation between Mumia and Noelle Minutes after the 1995 Death Warrant Was Read to Mumia in His Cell" took place on June 2, 1995, at 11:00 A.M., by phone, between Mumia Abu-Jamal in his Phase II strip cell, just after he was told of his death warrant, and Noelle, in Hyattsville, Maryland. It aired that day on Pacifica Radio's *National News*.

C. Clark Kissinger

THE CASE OF MUMIA ABU-JAMAL has become a showdown on the death penalty in the United States. His threatened execution has been condemned by political and cultural figures throughout the world, and the international movement to grant him a new and fair trial is raising questions about the arbitrariness of the death penalty in the minds of millions. Mumia Abu-Jamal is the only political prisoner in the United States facing execution.

As a radio journalist in Philadelphia, Jamal became known as "the voice of the voiceless" during the years of the infamous mayor Frank Rizzo. He had attended Goddard College, was a recipient of the Major Armstrong Award for radio journalism, and was named one of Philadelphia's "people to watch" in 1981 by *Philadelphia* magazine. He was president of the Association of Black Journalists in Philadelphia, and he had no prior criminal record.

Jamal was shot by a police officer when he intervened in a street incident involving Jamal's brother, another man, and the officer. He survived the shooting, and was charged with the murder of the officer who was killed in the incident. No one else was charged with the shooting, and the trial at which Jamal was condemned has been termed a travesty of justice by every impartial observer.

The targeting of Jamal was overtly political. The FBI began amassing a 600-page file on him when he was a fifteen-year-old high school activist. He subsequently worked on the national staff of the *Black Panther* newspaper. Later as a radio journalist he regularly exposed incidents of police brutality. In the sentencing phase of his trial, the prosecutor used political quotes from an interview with Jamal from ten years earlier as an argument to the jury for his execution.

2000 is a critical year for Jamal's case. He has filed his application for a federal writ of habeas corpus, but under the onerous provisions of the Effective Death Penalty Act of 1996, federal courts are now required to give a presumption of correctness to state court findings of fact. This throws Jamal's appeal back into the era of "state's rights," as if the civil rights movement never happened. The public must demand a full federal evidentiary hearing on this case.

Jamal's case is where we must draw the line on "no questions asked" executions used to suppress dissent. It is critical that people and organizations of conscience take up this case, as its outcome will affect the lives of thousands for years to come.

JAMAL'S TRIAL

Mumia was brought to trial in June 1982 and sentenced to death on July 3, 1982. The judge, Albert Sabo, had sentenced more people to death than any other sitting judge in the United States. In an unrelated case, six Philadelphia lawyers, some former prosecutors, offered to testify that no accused could receive a fair trial in his court.

The jury was empaneled only after eleven qualified African Americans were removed by peremptory challenges from the prosecution, an illegal practice that was recently revealed as having been taught to Philadelphia prosecutors in a special training videotape.

The defense attorney testified that he didn't interview a single witness in preparation for the 1982 trial, and he informed the court in advance that he was not prepared. Jamal was also denied the right to act as his own attorney. When Jamal protested, he was removed from the courtroom for much of his trial, with no provisions to allow him to follow the proceedings.

The defense investigator quit before the trial began because the meager court-allocated funds were exhausted. Neither a ballistics expert nor a pathologist were hired because of insufficient funds.

The use of statements made years earlier by Jamal as a member of the Black Panther Party, as an argument for imposing the death penalty, is a practice that was later condemned as unconstitutional by the U.S. Supreme Court in another case.

Philadelphia has been so notorious for racial bias in the application of the death penalty that it is the subject of a recent academic study on the issue.

The prosecution claimed that Jamal loudly confessed at the hospital where he was taken after being shot by the slain officer and beaten by police. But the jury never heard from police officer Gary Wakshul, who was guarding Jamal at the hospital and who wrote in his report, "The Negro male made no comments."* When Wakshul was called as a defense witness, the prosecution contended that he was on vacation and unavailable. The judge refused a continuance so he could be brought in, when in fact he was home and available.

Today we know that none of the police officers or hospital guards who now claim to have heard this "confession" reported it to investigators until two months after it allegedly occurred, and after Jamal had filed police brutality charges.† The attending physician also denies that Jamal said anything.

The prosecution claimed that ballistics evidence proved that Jamal was the shooter. But the jury never saw the written findings of the medical examiner, which contradicted other prosecution testimony by writing "shot w/ 44 cal" in his report (Jamal's gun was .38 caliber). Jamal's court-appointed attorney said he didn't see that portion of the report, so he never raised it to the jury.

Today we know that the police never tested Jamal's gun to see if it had been recently fired, never tested Jamal's hands to see if he had fired a gun, have no proof that Jamal's gun was the fatal weapon, and have lost a bullet fragment removed by the medical examiner. Jamal was carrying a legally purchased gun on his job as a late-night cabdriver because he had been robbed several times.

The prosecution claimed that eyewitnesses identified Jamal as the shooter. But the jury never heard from a key eyewitness, William Singletary, who saw the whole incident and has testified that Jamal was not the shooter. Singletary, a local businessman, was intimidated by police when he reported this, and he subsequently fled the city.‡

---

*Hearing transcript, August 1, 1995, 38.
†Hearing transcript, August 1, 1995, 78–79.
‡William Singletary's testimony began on August 11, 1995, at page 204 of the transcript. He describes how police tore up his written statement and forced him to sign a different statement, which they dictated.

Today we know why the key witnesses Veronica Jones, Cynthia White, and Robert Chobert testified as they did in 1982. Jones, who now testifies in support of Jamal, was threatened with the loss of her children if she did not support the police story.* Chobert, a white cab driver, first told the arriving police that the shooter ran away.† White backed the whole police story, but none of the other witnesses can remember seeing her at the immediate scene.‡ Both Chobert and White received very special treatment, including exemptions from criminal prosecutions.§ By contrast, when Veronica Jones testified in Jamal's support, she was arrested in the courtroom on an old out-of-state warrant.

JAMAL'S POLITICAL HISTORY

Mumia Abu-Jamal was born on April 24, 1954. At the age of fourteen, Jamal was beaten and arrested for protesting at a rally for segregationist presidential candidate George Wallace. At the age of fifteen he took part in the campaign to change the name of his high school to Malcolm X High School. That same year the Federal Bureau of Investigation began keeping a file on him. In 1969 he was a cofounder and minister of information of the Philadelphia chapter of the Black Panther Party, and later worked in Oakland, California, on the staff of the party's newspaper. In 1970 he was featured in a front-page article in the *Philadelphia Inquirer*. The FBI added his name to the National Security Index and the ADEX index of those persons to be rounded up and interned in a national emergency.

After attending Goddard College, Jamal became an active critic of the Philadelphia police department as a radio news reporter. In addition to local FM stations, Jamal was broadcast on the National Black Network, the

---

*Hearing transcript, October 1, 1996, 20.
†Trial transcript, June 1, 1982, 70.
‡White was a prostitute with thirty-eight arrests and had two pending cases.
§For example, when Cynthia White was arrested in 1987 (five years after the trial) on armed robbery charges, Philadelphia homicide detective Douglas Culbreth appeared in court and asked that White be released without posting bail because she was "a Commonwealth witness in a very high profile case." White subsequently failed to show up for her court date and has since disappeared. See hearing transcript, June 30, 1997, 99–100.

Mutual Black Network, National Public Radio, and the Radio Information Center for the Blind. He interviewed such public figures as Julius Erving, Bob Marley, Alex Haley, and Puerto Rican independence fighters.

Jamal's style of journalism allowed the voices of ordinary people to be broadcast, including members of the MOVE organization, which angered public officials. In 1978 Jamal reported on the siege of the headquarters of MOVE, where scenes of police beating MOVE members were telecast. On August 8, Jamal attended an angry press conference in city hall. In response to a question asked by Jamal, Mayor Frank Rizzo responded, "They believe what you write, what you say. And it's got to stop. And one day, and I hope it's in my career, you're going to have to be held responsible and accountable for what you do."

During the summer 1981, Jamal covered the federal trial of John Africa, founder of the MOVE organization. John Africa was charged with a number of conspiracy and weapons charges, typical of those brought against black dissidents during this period. He successfully defended himself and was acquitted on all charges. Jamal was deeply impressed by John Africa during this trial and drew closer to the MOVE organization.

After Jamal's shooting and arrest in December of 1981, the *Philadelphia Inquirer* headlined: "The Suspect—Jamal: An Eloquent Activist Not Afraid to Raise His Voice." The story described him as a "gadfly among journalists and easily recognizable because of his dreadlock hairstyle, revolutionary politics and deep baritone voice."

Since his conviction and death sentence in 1982, Jamal has been held twenty-two hours a day in a solitary cell. He is denied contact visits with his family, and he has grandchildren he has never been allowed to touch. Journalists are no longer allowed to record or photograph him. The last entry in the sections of his FBI file that have been released shows the federal government monitoring his prison visitors as late as 1991.

CENSORSHIP OF JAMAL'S WRITINGS

In 1994 National Public Radio hired Jamal to do a series of commentaries on prison life. NPR was immediately warned by the Fraternal Order of Police, the *New York Times*, and Senate majority leader Robert Dole about allowing "a convicted cop killer" on the air. NPR canceled the series on the day it was to begin.

In 1995 Jamal's book *Live from Death Row* was published by Addison-Wesley. The Fraternal Order of Police attempted to have the book banned, and members of the state legislature called for seizing any proceeds from the book. (When Sgt. Stacy Koons, in prison for beating Rodney King, published *his* book, the FOP did not complain.) Jamal was denied visitors and phone calls as punishment for writing *Live from Death Row*. This sort of practice by other countries is usually condemned by the United States as a human rights violation.

The federal district court in Pittsburgh ruled that Pennsylvania had illegally singled out Jamal, when they barred the press from interviewing him in retaliation for his book. Shortly after this 1996 ruling, the prison system instituted a new rule banning the media from recording or photographing *any* prisoner in the state system.

In 1997 Pacifica Radio's program *Democracy Now!* broadcast a series of Jamal's recordings. These were to be carried in Philadelphia on WRTI, the radio station of Temple University. The FOP again protested. WRTI canceled the show the day it was to air.

In January 1999 Rage against the Machine and three other bands rented the Continental Arena in East Rutherford, New Jersey, to hold a benefit concert for Jamal. Governor Christine Whitman expressed public regrets that the program could not be legally banned, and called on people to boycott the performance. (The concert was a sellout success anyway.) Since then the FOP has called for a boycott of any performers or businesses that express support for a new trial for Jamal. As Jamal has commented, "They don't just want my death, they want my silence."

APPELLATE HISTORY

Jamal was sentenced to death on July 3, 1982. On March 6, 1989, his conviction and sentence were upheld by the Pennsylvania Supreme Court. Oddly, only four of the seven justices participated in the decision. The chief justice, who was the only black justice on the court, recused himself without giving an explanation.

On October 1, 1990, Jamal's petition for a writ of certiorari was denied by the U.S. Supreme Court. In petitioning for a rehearing, Jamal cited the fact that the Supreme Court had accepted a similar case from Delaware, where political association had been used as an argument for imposing the death penalty (*Dawson v. Delaware*, 1992). In the Dawson case, prosecutors used Dawson's membership in a white supremacist prison gang as an argument for imposing the death sentence, and had even cited the Jamal case in Pennsylvania as precedent. Inexplicably, the Court refused to hear Jamal's claim, while reversing the death sentence of Dawson.

In 1992 Leonard Weinglass became Jamal's lead attorney and began preparing a motion for a new trial under Pennsylvania's Post Conviction Relief Act. This petition was filed on June 5, 1995. Weinglass notified the governor's office of the impending filing. The governor then rushed to sign a death warrant at the end of the last working day before the filing. (Only after these events did the defense learn that prison officials had opened and illegally copied Jamal's privileged legal mail, and sent copies to the governor's office.) The trial judge then refused to grant a stay of execution, claiming that Jamal's attorneys had "waited years" until a warrant was signed before filing. While the hearing on the petition was taking place in July and August of 1995, Jamal came within ten days of execution. A stay was finally granted only as the result of an unprecedented international outcry.

Under Pennsylvania law, the trial judge hears all postconviction motions. Thus it fell to Judge Albert Sabo, the same judge who had conducted the original trial, to rule on whether the original trial was fair. Sabo was able to preside, even though he was well past the constitutionally mandated retirement age. He was permitted to remain on the bench to rule on the Jamal appeal because the chief justice of the state Supreme Court allowed him to stay on under emergency provisions of the state constitution.

Not surprisingly, in the course of the hearings Sabo quashed defense subpoenas, denied discovery motions, threatened witnesses, and even had one of Jamal's attorneys taken out in handcuffs. After the 1995 hearing, followed by two remand hearings in 1996 and 1997, Sabo ruled that the original trial had been flawless and denied the petition for a new trial.

This denial was appealed to the Pennsylvania Supreme Court, and on October 29, 1998, that court unanimously upheld Sabo's ruling. In fact, the Pennsylvania Supreme Court was unable to find any errors in the seventeen years of trial, direct appeal, and collateral appeals. A motion for a rehearing was denied on November 25, 1998. Court papers revealed that five of seven justices had been endorsed for election to the court by the Fraternal Order of Police.

Then Jamal's attorneys petitioned the U.S. Supreme Court for a writ of certiorari on the denial of Mumia's Sixth Amendment rights (denial of *pro se* status, denial of attorney of choice, and removal from the courtroom with no provision for being informed of developments while on trial for his life). On October 4, 1999, the Supreme Court denied cert, and on October 13 Governor Tom Ridge signed a new death warrant for Jamal. The warrant set an execution date of December 2, 1999, the 140th anniversary of the execution of John Brown.

On October 15, 1999, Jamal's lawyers filed for a writ of habeas corpus in the Federal District Court for eastern Pennsylvania. The case was assigned to Judge William H. Yohn, who stayed the December 2 execution. A major issue before Yohn is whether to grant an evidentiary hearing to allow presentation of the evidence that was denied by the Pennsylvania courts, or whether the whole federal process will be based on the court record developed by Judge Sabo.

ISSUES CONCENTRATED IN THE CASE

Mumia Abu-Jamal is both the exception and the rule. As "the exception," he was singled out by authorities because of his political journalism. His brother was not charged with the shooting and was released with a suspended sentence for a misdemeanor. It is unheard of for two black men to be involved in an altercation that results in the death of a white police officer, and then one of them to just be released. But it was Jamal that the police wanted, and his political statements were used as an argument for imposing the death sentence.

Since Jamal's conviction, the government has tried in every way to censor his voice. The Fraternal Order of Police has managed a national campaign calling for his execution, using right-wing talk shows and a full-page ad in the *New York Times*. The widow of the slain police officer has been showcased in Washington, on stage with President Bill Clinton and Attorney General Janet Reno.

As an example of "the rule," Jamal has faced what most young men of color face in the criminal justice system every day. If the new Effective Death Penalty Act had been in force at the time of his arrest, Jamal would be dead today. Nobody without financial means can assemble the case needed to overturn a murder conviction in the 12 months allotted by the new law for all federal habeas appeals.

The manner in which Black jurors were purged from Jamal's jury pool is in violation of international law as established by the International Convention on the Elimination of All Forms of Racial Discrimination, to which the United States is a signatory. During the period 1983–1993, one study found that blacks were 5.2 times more likely to be challenged than whites in the jury selection process in Philadelphia. In Jamal's jury selection process, Blacks were 16.2 times more likely to be challenged. The result of such disparities is that over 60 percent of all prisoners on death row in Pennsylvania are African Americans, in a state that is only 10 percent Black.

Jamal's case has come to symbolize the societywide criminalization of black males and the bipartisan program for quicker executions with fewer appeals. If he is executed, he will be the first black revolutionary to be legally executed in the United Sates since the days of slavery.

WHO IS CALLING FOR JUSTICE FOR JAMAL

Numerous statements and full-page ads have appeared on the case of Mumia Abu-Jamal. Among those who have questioned his conviction or publicly opposed his execution are:

African National Congress
Amnesty International
Maya Angelou
Ed Asner
Julian Bond
Reverend Dr. Joan Campbell
Rep. John Conyers, Jr.

Angela Davis
Ossie Davis
Rep. Ron Dellums
Jacques Derrida
E. L. Doctorow
The European Parliament
Rep. Chaka Fatah

Mike Farrell
Henry Louis Gates
Stephen Jay Gould
Bishop Thomas Gumbleton
State Rep. Vincent Hughes
Int'l. Parliament of Writers
Rev. Jesse Jackson
Coretta Scott King
Barbara Kingsolver
Jonathan Kozol
Rep. Cynthia McKinney
Danielle Mitterrand
Toni Morrison
National Black Police
    Association

National Coalition to Abolish the
    Death Penalty
National Lawyers Guild
Helen Prejean, C.S.J.
Rep. Charles Rangel
Salman Rushdie
Susan Sarandon
Rev. Al Sharpton
Gloria Steinem
Wole Soyinka
Archbishop Desmond Tutu
Alice Walker
John Edgar Wideman
Elie Wiesel
Howard Zinn

CONTACT INFORMATION

Mumia Abu-Jamal, #AM 8335
SCI Greene, 175 Progress Drive, Waynesburg, PA 15370-8090

International Concerned Family & Friends of Mumia Abu-Jamal
P.O. Box 19709
Philadelphia, PA 19143

SOURCES OF MORE INFORMATION

Race for Justice by Leonard Weinglass (Common Courage Press, 1995).
    Complete text of Jamal's motion for a new trial, together with exhibits
    and supporting documents.
Resource Book on the Case of Mumia Abu-Jamal (Refuse & Resist! 1998).
    Collection of articles on the case, including an analysis of Pennsylvania
    Supreme Court decision denying Jamal a new trial.
"Racial Discrimination and the Death Penalty in the Post-Furman Era: An
    Empirical and Legal Overview, with Recent Findings from Philadelphia"

by David C. Baldus et al. (*Cornell Law Review* 83: 1638)

Legal Lynching by Rev. Jesse Jackson (Marlowe & Company, 1996). This book against the death penalty uses Jamal's case as one example.

Live from Death Row by Mumia Abu-Jamal (Addison-Wesley, 1995)

Death Blossoms by Mumia Abu-Jamal (Plough Publishing, 1997)

All Things Censored (CD by the Prison Radio Project, 1998). Recordings of Jamal reading his columns made before Pennsylvania banned all recording of Jamal.

Mumia Abu-Jamal: A Case for Reasonable Doubt? (Documentary video, HBO.)

25 Years on the MOVE (MOVE, 1996). History with photographs of MOVE organization and the government's war on them. Includes section on Jamal.

"Guilty *and* Framed" by Stuart Taylor Jr. (*American Lawyer,* December 1995). Concludes that Jamal probably fired one shot, but he was framed in a totally unfair trial.

Jamal's weekly columns are available on www.mumia.org, and information about his case and the international movement in his support are available on www.calyx.com/~refuse and www.peoplescampaign.org.

C. CLARK KISSINGER is a journalist and activist whose experience stretches back to the early 1960s. He is a member of Refuse & Resist! and has written extensively on the case of Mumia Abu-Jamal.

MUMIA ABU-JAMAL was born April 24, 1954, in Philadelphia. At the time of his arrest there on December 9, 1981, on charges of the murder of a police officer, he was a leading broadcast journalist and president of the Philadelphia chapter of the Association of Black Journalists. Widely acclaimed for his award-winning work with NPR, the Mutual Black Network, the National Black Network, WUHY (now WHYY), and other stations, he was known in the city as Philly's "voice of the voiceless."

At the age of fourteen, Jamal was beaten and arrested for protesting at a presidential rally for George Wallace. In the fall of 1968 he became a founding member and lieutenant minister of information of the Philadelphia chapter of the Black Panther Party. During the summer of 1970, he worked for the party newspaper in Oakland, California, returning to Philadelphia shortly before the city police raided all three offices of the Panther Party there.

Throughout the following decade, Jamal's hard-hitting criticism of the Philadelphia Police Department and the Rizzo administration marked him as a journalist "to watch." His unyielding rejection of Mayor Rizzo's version of the city's 1978 siege of the MOVE organization, in the Powelton Village neighborhood of West Philadelphia, in particular incensed the establishment, and eventually his advocacy cost him his broadcast job. In order to support his growing family, Jamal began to work night shifts as a cabdriver.

In the early morning hours of December 9, 1981, Jamal was critically shot and beaten by police and charged with the murder of Officer Daniel Faulkner. Put on trial before Philadelphia's notorious "hanging judge," Albert Sabo, he was convicted and sentenced to death on July 3, 1982.

Jamal's appeal to the Pennsylvania Supreme Court was denied in March 1989, and the U.S. Supreme Court refused review of his case. Pennsylvania governor Tom Ridge signed Jamal's death warrant, scheduling his execution for December 2, 1999. The death warrant was stayed on October 26, pending a federal hearing. Although Jamal's petition was denied by Judge Sabo, new evidence of prosecutorial misconduct and of the defendant's innocence has been presented to the appeals court. His appeals process continues as of this date.

Despite eighteen years on death row, Jamal continues to speak out. His commentaries on racism, politics, and the American judicial system have been printed in hundreds of newspapers throughout the United States and Europe. He has also been published in the *Yale Law Journal* and the *Nation*.

In 1994, a series of commentaries scheduled for broadcast on NPR's *All Things Considered*, which described life behind bars, caused such controversy that the broadcast was abruptly canceled, sparking intense debates about censorship and the death penalty. A year later, despite considerable pressure to stifle their publication, Addison Wesley released the commentaries in print under the title *Live from Death Row*. The book has since been translated into French, German, Dutch, Spanish, Portuguese, and Italian; an interactive CD-ROM version is also available.

While in prison Mumia has received his GED (July 1992); a BA from Goddard College, January 1996; an honorary doctorate of Law from the New College of California, May 1996; a Blackstone School of Law paralegal degree; an Emerson College of Canada herbalism degree; and has completed course work and thesis for an M.A. with a major in humanities history and a minor in African-American Literature at California State University, Dominuez Hills, California, Fall 1999.

Mumia resides on death row at the State Correctional Institute at Greene a supermaximum security "control unit" in Waynesburg, Pennsylvania.

Mumia Abu-Jamal
AM 8335
SCI Greene
175 Progress Drive
Waynesburg, PA 15370

NOELLE HANRAHAN is an investigative journalist and the director of Prison Radio, a project of the Redwood Justice Fund. Since 1992 she has been producing Mumia Abu-Jamal's radio commentaries. In 1994 she recorded and placed the commentaries of Mumia Abu-Jamal with National Public Radio's premier newsmagazine *All Things Considered*. The essays were censored at the behest of Senator Bob Dole and the Fraternal Order of Police. These unique and rare recorded essays remain locked in NPR's vaults.

Hanrahan initiated the books *Live From Death Row* by Mumia Abu-Jamal (Addison Wesley/Avon) and *Race for Justice* by Leonard Weinglass (Common Courage Press). She has produced Jamal's radio essays on two compact discs: *Mumia Abu-Jamal Spoken Word*, with music by Man is the Bastard, and *All Things Censored Vol. 1*, both on Alternative Tentacles Records. She is the winner of two National Federation of Community Radio Broadcasters Golden Reel Awards, one for local radio news coverage for her story "The Death Penalty and the Execution of Robert Alton Harris" (1993), and the other, in the National Radio Documentary category, for the radio adaptation of the film *Mumia Abu-Jamal: A Case for Reasonable Doubt* (1998).

She is a graduate of Stanford University, where she designed her own major in Gender, Race, and Class Studies, and received the Lloyd W. Dinkelspiel Award for outstanding service to undergraduate education.

Hanrahan is currently working on the Redwood Summer Justice Project's civil rights lawsuit resulting from FBI and Oakland Police Department misconduct surrounding the May 1990 car-bomb assassination attempt against Earth First! leaders Judi Bari and Darryl Cherney. She lives in northern California with her three-year-old daughter, Miranda.

ALICE WALKER was born in Eatonton, Georgia, and now lives in Northern California. Her novel *The Color Purple* won an American Book Award and the Pulitzer Prize.

CD CREDITS

Producer: Noelle Hanrahan/Prison Radio/Redwood Justice Fund
Audio Engineer: David Kaplowitz, Noelle Hanrahan
Field & Production Engineers: Mike Alcalay, Blangton, Ray Grott, Janice Leber &
    David Rubin/ Chopped Liver Productions, Walter Turner, Noelle Hanrahan
Design: David Kaplowitz